There are no grown-ups. Everyone else is winging it too.

Does it ever feel like everyone – except you – is a
bona fide adult? Do you wonder how real grown-ups
got to be so mysteriously capable and wise?

When she turns forty, Pamela Druckerman wonders
whether her mind will ever catch up with her face.
Waiters start calling her 'Madame', and she detects
a disturbing new message in mens' gazes: I would
sleep with her, but only if doing so required
no effort whatsoever.

What is modern midlife, and what do we
know once we reach it? What makes someone a
'grown-up' anyway? And why didn't anyone warn
us that we'd get cellulite on our arms? With frank
personal stories and witty maxims, Druckerman
hilariously navigates the unexplored zone between
young and not-so-young. *There Are No Grown-Ups*
is a midlife coming-of-age story, a quest for wisdom,
self-knowledge and the right pair of pants. It's a
seriously funny book for readers of all ages
about – finally – becoming yourself.

Also by Pamela Druckerman

French Children Don't Throw Food
French Parents Don't Give In

and published by Black Swan

THERE ARE NO GROWN-UPS

A Midlife Coming-of-Age Story

PAMELA DRUCKERMAN

BLACK SWAN

TRANSWORLD PUBLISHERS
61–63 Uxbridge Road, London W5 5SA
www.penguin.co.uk

Transworld is part of the Penguin Random House group of companies
whose addresses can be found at global.penguinrandomhouse.com

First published in Great Britain in 2018 by Doubleday
an imprint of Transworld Publishers
Black Swan edition published 2019

Portions of this book first appeared in *The New York Times* under the titles
'What You Learn in Your 40s', 'How to Find Your Place in the World
After Graduation', 'How to Talk to Children About Terrorism' and
'In Paris, a Night Disrupted by Terror', and in *Marie Claire* under
the title 'How I Planned a Ménage à Trois'.

A CIP catalogue record for this book
is available from the British Library.

ISBNs
9781784160449
9781784164553

For Simon, Leila, Joey and Leo

contents

Forty is a fearsome age.
It's the age when we become who we are.

CHARLES PÉGUY

THERE ARE NO GROWN-UPS

bonjour, madame

IF YOU WANT TO KNOW how old you look, just walk into a French café. It's like a public referendum on your face.

When I moved to Paris in my early thirties, waiters called me "mademoiselle." It was *"Bonjour, mademoiselle"* when I walked into a café and *"Voilà, mademoiselle"* as they set down a coffee in front of me. I sat in many different cafés in those early years—I didn't have an office, so I spent my days writing in them—and everywhere I was "mademoiselle." (The word technically means "unmarried woman," but it's come to signify "young lady.")

Around the time I turn forty, however, there's a collective code switch. Waiters start calling me "madame," though with exaggerated formality or a jokey wink. It's as if "madame" is a game we're playing. They still sprinkle in the occasional "mademoiselle."

Soon even these jocular "mademoiselles" cease, and my "madames" are no longer tentative or ironic. It's as if the waiters of Paris (they're mostly men) have decided en masse that I've exited the liminal zone between young and middle-aged.

On one hand, I'm intrigued by this transition. Do the waiters gather after work for Sancerre and a slideshow to decide which female customers to downgrade? (Irritatingly, men are "monsieur" forever.)

I'm aware of the conventions of aging, of course. I've watched as small crinkles and creases appeared on the faces of my peers. Already, in my forties, I can see the outline of what some people I know will look like at seventy.

I just didn't expect "madame" to happen to me, or at least not without my consent. Though I'd never been beautiful, in my twenties I'd discovered my superpower: I looked young. I still had the skin of a teenager. People honestly couldn't tell whether I was sixteen or twenty-six. I was once standing alone on a New York subway platform when an older man stopped and said, sweetly, "You've still got your baby face."

I knew what he meant, and I was determined to preserve this small advantage. Long before any of my peers fretted about wrinkles, I used sunblock and eye cream each morning, and rubbed on more potions before bed. I didn't waste a smile on something that wasn't truly funny.

All this effort paid off. Into my thirties, strangers still routinely assumed I was a college student, and bartenders asked to see my identification. My compliment age—the age people say you look, to which you must add six or seven years—hovered safely around twenty-six.

In my forties, I expect to finally reap the average-looking girl's revenge. I've entered the stage of life where you don't need to be beautiful; simply by being well preserved and not obese, I would now pass for pretty.

For a while, this strategy seems to work. Fields of micro-wrinkles appear on the faces of women who'd always been far better-looking than me. If I haven't seen someone in a few years, I brace myself before meeting her, lest I accidentally gawk at how much she's changed. (The French call this tendency to look the same for a long stretch, then to suddenly look much older, a *coup de vieux*, an "age blow.")

I regard the graying roots and creased foreheads of many of my peers with sad detachment. I am proof of the adage that everyone eventually gets the face she deserves. And what I deserve is, obviously, a permanently youthful glow.

But in the course of what seems like a few months, something changes in me, too.

Strangers no longer gush about how young I look, or seem shocked when I reveal that I have three children. People I haven't seen in a while clock *my* face for a few extra beats. When I arrive to meet a younger friend at a café, he stares right past me at first; he doesn't realize that the middle-aged lady standing in front of him is me.

Not everyone my age is distressed by these changes, but many seem to be suffering from a kind of midlife shock. One friend says that when she walks into a party, there's no longer a Cinderella moment when everyone turns to look at her. I've noticed that men only appraise me on the streets of Paris now if I'm in full hair and makeup. And even then, I detect a disturbing new message in their gazes: I would sleep with her, but only if doing so required *no effort whatsoever.*

Soon the "madames" are coming at me like a hailstorm. It's *"Bonjour, madame"* when I walk into a café, *"Merci, madame"* when I pay my bill, and *"Au revoir, madame"* as I leave. Sometimes several waiters shout this at once.

The worst part is that they're not trying to insult me. Here in France, where I've lived for a dozen years as an expatriate, "madame" is a routine form of politeness. I call other women "madame" all the time, and teach my kids to say it to the elderly Portuguese lady who looks after our building.

In other words, I'm now considered to be so safely into madame territory, people assume the title can't possibly wound me. I realize that something has permanently shifted when I walk past a woman who's begging for money on a sidewalk near my house.

"Bonjour, mademoiselle," she calls out to the young woman in a miniskirt a few steps ahead of me.

"Bonjour, madame," she says when I pass in front of her a second later.

This has all happened too quickly for me to digest. I still have most of the clothes that I wore as a mademoiselle. There are mademoiselle-era cans of food in my pantry. Even the math seems fuzzy: How is it that, in the course of a few years, everyone else has become a decade younger than me?

What are the forties? It's been my custom not to grasp a decade's main point until it's over, and I've squandered it. I spent my twenties scrambling in vain to find a husband, when I should have been building my career as a journalist and visiting dangerous places before I had kids. As a result, in my early thirties I was promptly fired from my job at a newspaper. That freed me up to spend the rest of my thirties ruminating on grievances and lost time.

This time, I'm determined to figure out the decade while I'm still in it. But while each new birthday brings some vertigo—you're always the oldest you've ever been—the modern forties are especially disorienting. They're a decade without a narrative. They're not just a new number; they feel like a new atmospheric zone. When I tell a forty-two-year-old entrepreneur that I'm researching the forties, his eyes widen. He's successful and articulate, but his age leaves him speechless.

"Please," he says, "tell me what they are."

Obviously, the forties depend on the beholder, and on your family, your health, your finances and your country. I'm experiencing them as a privileged, white American woman—not exactly a beleaguered group. I'm told that when a woman turns forty in Rwanda, she's henceforth addressed as "grandma."

With their signature blend of precision and pessimism, the French have carved up midlife into the "crisis of the forties," the "crisis of the fifties" and the "noonday demon," described by one writer as "when a man in his fifties falls in love with the babysitter." And yet, they have an optimistic story about how to age, in which a person strives to become free. (The French are flawed, but I've learned from some of their better ideas.)

Wherever you are, forty looks old from below. I hear Americans in their twenties describe the forties as a mythic, far-off decade of too-late, when they'll regret things that they haven't done. When I tell one of my sons that I'm writing a book about the forties, he says that he'd like to write a short one about being nine. "It'll say, 'I'm nine years old. I'm so lucky. I'm still young.'"

And yet for many senior citizens I meet, the forties are the decade that they would most like to time travel back to. "How could I possibly have thought of myself as old at forty?" asks Stanley Brandes, an anthropologist who wrote a book about turning forty in 1985. "I sort of look back and think: God, how lucky I was. I see it as the beginning of life, not the beginning of the end."

Forty isn't even technically middle-aged anymore. Someone who's now forty has a 50 percent chance of living to age ninety-five, says economist Andrew Scott, coauthor of *The 100-Year Life*.

But the number forty still has gravitas and symbolic resonance. Jesus fasted for forty days. Mohammed was forty when the archangel Gabriel appeared to him. In the Biblical flood, it rained for forty days and forty nights. The Israelites wandered the desert for forty years. Brandes writes that in some languages, "forty" means "a lot."

And there is still something undeniably transitional about age forty. You've only ever known yourself as a certified young person, and now you've left one stage of life, but you haven't quite entered the next. The Frenchman Victor Hugo supposedly called forty the "old age of youth." While studying my face in a well-lit elevator, my daughter described this crossroads more bluntly: "Mommy, you're not old, but you're definitely not young."

I'm starting to see that as a madame—even a newly minted one—I am subject to new rules. When I act adorably naive now, people aren't charmed anymore, they're baffled. Cluelessness no longer goes with my face. I'm expected to wait in the correct line at airports, and to show up on time for my appointments.

To be honest, I feel myself becoming a bit more madame on the inside, too. Names and facts don't just pop into my mind anymore; I sometimes have to draw them up, like raising water from a well. And I can no longer wing it through a day on coffee and seven hours' sleep.

Similar complaints trickle in from my peers. At dinner with friends my age, I notice that each of us has a sport that our doctor forbids us to play. There's nervous laughter when someone points out that, under American law, we're now old enough to claim age discrimination.

New brain research documents the downsides of the forties: on average we're more easily distracted than younger people, we digest information more slowly and we're worse at remembering specific facts. (The ability to remember names peaks, on average, in your early twenties.)

And yet, science also shows the many upsides of the forties. What we lack in processing power we make up for in maturity, insight and experience. We're better than younger people at grasping the essence of situations, and at controlling our emotions, resolving conflicts and understanding other people. We're more skilled at managing money and at explaining why things happen. We're more considerate than younger people. And, crucially for our happiness, we're less neurotic.

Indeed, modern neuroscience and psychology confirm what Aristotle said some two thousand years ago, when he described men in their "primes" as having "neither that excess of confidence which amounts to rashness, nor too much timidity, but the right amount of each. They neither trust everybody nor distrust everybody, but judge people correctly."

I agree. We've actually managed to learn and grow a bit. After a lifetime of feeling like misfits, we realize that more about us is universal than not. (My unscientific assessment is that we're 95 percent cohort, 5 percent unique.) And like us, most people focus on themselves. The seminal journey of the forties is from "everyone hates me" to "they don't really care."

In another ten years, our fortysomething revelations will no doubt seem naive. ("Ants can see molecules!" a man told me in college.) And even now, the decade can seem like contradictory ideas that we're supposed to hold in our minds at once: We can finally decode interpersonal dynamics, but we can't remember a two-digit number. We're at—or approaching—our lifetime peak in earnings, but Botox now seems like a reasonable idea. We're reaching the height of our careers, but we can now see how they will probably end.

If the modern forties are confusing, it's also because we've reached an age that's strangely lacking in milestones. Childhood and adolescence are nothing but milestones: You grow taller, advance to new grades, get your period, your driver's license and your diploma. Then in your twenties and thirties you romance potential partners, find jobs and learn to support yourself. There may be promotions, babies and weddings. The pings of adrenaline from all these carry you forward and reassure you that you're building an adult life.

In the forties, you might still acquire degrees, jobs, homes and spouses, but these elicit less wonder now. The mentors, elders and parents who used to rejoice in your achievements are preoccupied with their own declines. If you have kids, you're supposed to marvel at *their* milestones. A journalist I know lamented that he'll never again be a prodigy at anything. (Someone younger than both of us had just been nominated to the US Supreme Court.)

"Even five years ago, people I met would be like, 'Wow *you're* the boss?'" says the forty-four-year-old head of a TV production company. Now they're matter-of-fact about his title. "I've aged out of wunder-kind," he says.

What have we aged into? We're still capable of action, change and 10K races. But there's a new immediacy to the forties—and an awareness of death—that didn't exist before. Our possibilities feel more finite. All choices now seem to exclude others. And there's a now-or-never-mood. If we were planning to do something "one day"—to finally change careers, read Dostoyevsky or learn how to cook leeks—we should probably get moving on it.

This new time line prompts a reckoning—sometimes a painful one—between our aspirational and actual lives. False things we've been saying for years start to sound hollow. It's pointless to keep pretending to be what we're not. At forty, we're no longer preparing for an imagined future life, or collecting notches on our résumés. Our real lives are, indis-putably, happening right now. We've arrived at what the German phi-losopher Immanuel Kant called the *Ding an sich*—the thing itself.

Indeed, the strangest part of the forties is that we're now the ones writing books and attending parent-teacher conferences. People our age have titles like "chief technology officer" and "managing editor." We're the ones who cook the turkey on Thanksgiving. These days, when I think, "Someone should really do something about that," I re-alize with alarm that the "someone" is me.

It's not an easy transition. I'd always been reassured by the idea that there are grown-ups in the world. I imagined them out there curing cancer and issuing subpoenas. Grown-ups fly airplanes, get aerosol into bottles and make sure that television signals are magically transmitted. They know whether a novel is worth reading, and which news belongs on the front page. In an emergency, I've always trusted that grown-ups—mysterious, capable and wise—would appear to rescue me.

Though I don't believe in conspiracy theories, I can see why people are drawn to them. It's tempting to think that a cabal of grown-ups secretly controls everything. I understand the appeal of religion, too: God is the ultimate grown-up.

I'm not thrilled about looking older. But I realize what unsettles me most about becoming "madame" is the implication that I'm now a grown-up myself. I feel like I've been promoted beyond my competence.

What is a grown-up anyway? Do they really exist? If so, what exactly do they know? And how can I make the leap to become one of them? Will my mind ever catch up with my face?

You know you're in your *early* forties when . . .

- Your age feels like a secret.
- You become impatient while scrolling down to your year of birth.
- You're surprised when a saleslady steers you to the "antiaging" cream.
- You're surprised to learn that a friend has a child in college.
- People are surprised when you reveal that you have three kids.

1

how to find
your calling

WHEN I WAS GROWING UP, my family didn't do bad news. My maternal grandmother responded to everything from family squabbles to the Israeli-Palestinian conflict by declaring cheerfully, "I'm sure they'll work it out!"

There are worse things for a child to endure than relentless optimism. My plight wasn't even unique: lots of middle-class Americans grow up in sunny, nonintrospective homes. But I suspect that mine was more relentlessly positive than most. In order to avoid unpleasant subjects, we didn't go into much detail about anything, including our own ancestry. I was nearly a teenager when I discovered that two of my grandparents and all of my great-grandparents came to America as immigrants, mostly from Russia. Since no one had said otherwise, I'd assumed that we'd been Americans forever.

Even our immigration story was vague. My grandmother said her parents came from a place called "Minski Giberniya." But she didn't know exactly where this was, and when she once searched the Ellis Island records, there was no trace of either of them. And after her family settled in South Carolina, they instantly went native. My grandmother became a Southern belle and a sorority sister who lived by the local maxim: If you don't have something nice to say, don't say anything.

No one in my family ever mentioned that we had close relatives who stayed behind in "Minski Giberniya." When I eventually questioned my grandmother about this, she acknowledged that her mother used to send care packages of dried beans and clothing to siblings and cousins who'd remained in Russia. But after World War II, she didn't send them packages anymore.

"We lost touch," my grandmother said.

This is how my family explained the fate of relatives who were probably rounded up and murdered in the Holocaust: we lost touch.

This extreme positivity seemed to run in my maternal line, with each generation shielding the next from bad news. I first noticed it at my father's fortieth birthday party, when I was six. We were celebrating at home in Miami, the city where I grew up. Guests were having drinks on the patio, around our swimming pool. I was in the house when I heard a splash and saw a commotion.

"What happened?" I asked my mother.

"Nothing happened," she assured me.

For the record, my mother was loving, warm and well intentioned. She was trying to protect me. But I suspect I'd be a different person today—perhaps working in a different profession—had she simply said, "Larry Goodman got drunk and fell in the pool." Then we could have agreed that bad things sometimes happen, and that I was a reliable witness of them.

Instead, I came to feel that bad things occur in a fuzzy far-off dimension, always patio-distance away. If you don't examine them too closely, it's as if they never happened.

This view of life was easy to sustain in Miami. The city is perpetually sunny, and was literally invented out of air, since it only started to boom once air-conditioning became widely available in the 1950s and

'60s. Years later, when my future in-laws visited one of Miami's oldest homes—now part of a historic state park—they pointed out that it was roughly the same age as their house in London.

People are often surprised to hear that I spent my childhood in Miami. They think it's a city of grandparents. But that's mostly Miami Beach, a slender island off the city's eastern coast. There's a whole other hot, unglamorous inland area where most inhabitants live.

My parents bought their first home on land that had previously been a mango grove. The mango trees were still there, and the fruits would splatter on our cars, ruining the paint. Like the other homes in the neighborhood, ours was concrete, air-conditioned and built to keep out the salamanders, the burglars and the weather. Occasionally, a black ringneck snake would slither inside through the vents. We almost never saw the beach.

Practically everyone in Miami was displaced. Our Cuban neighbors were certain that they would soon be returning to Havana. Most of my parents' friends had Brooklyn or tristate accents. We pretended that South Florida had the same seasons as New York, though in department-store photographs of me with Santa Claus, I'm tanned and wearing shorts.

Miami's lack of context and aura of wishful thinking suited us perfectly. When my mother had to disclose any unpleasant news—say, that someone we knew had cancer—she'd sandwich it between reports of dinner plans and cheerleading practice. The bad news would flash by so quickly, I'd doubt whether I'd really heard it.

It was the 1980s and the peak of the American divorce boom, so I'd often learn that grown-ups I knew were splitting up, but never the reasons why. My parents didn't say much about people they knew, or describe relationships between our family members. I once noticed them whispering about an alcoholic aunt, but when I asked for details, they went silent. (I learned years later that the aunt would launch into anti-Semitic rants after her first Bloody Mary.)

Such facts weren't considered child friendly. In fact, almost nothing was. We described world events, new outfits and summer vacations with vague catchphrases like "It's terrible," "That looks adorable" and "We had the best time." People we approved of were "fabulous" (one of my mother's friends liked to call pretty women "delicious"); those we didn't like were "annoying." Someone who spoke about any one subject for too long was "boring" or "not regular." (I would later realize that these "boring" people were the semi-intellectuals in our midst.)

My parents weren't my only source of information, of course. I knew about AIDS, political prisoners and the fact that Colombian drug cartels murdered people in Miami. I read books in which characters had backstories, contradictory qualities and inner lives. But as an obedient oldest child, I also believed that what happened at home was real life. And in our house, we didn't gather facts into patterns, analyze our own experiences or speculate about other people. Nor did we discuss our own history, ethnicity or social class. Pointing out complicated truths just made everyone uncomfortable. It was like saying that Larry Goodman fell in the pool.

As I grew older, I came to assume that a separate grown-up conversation about life went on when I wasn't there, or that all this small talk was a prelude to the day when we would finally sit down and discuss everything. I was relieved when, on successive trips to the supermarket, my mother brought home volumes of a down-market encyclopedia. Finally, there were some facts in the house. (We had to wait for certain popular volumes, like "S," to be restocked.)

The irony is that my childhood was a cover-up without a crime. I'm pretty sure that Larry Goodman climbed, unharmed, out of our swimming pool. He probably didn't even have a drinking problem. For the most part, behind the smoke screen of pleasantries and good news, nothing terrible was happening.

My parents did have one dark secret: we weren't rich. Unlike many of their friends, they worried constantly about money. By any reasonable standard, we weren't poor, either. But it felt like we were, because we were clinging to the bottom of the upper middle class.

Money mattered tremendously in Miami. Regardless of your social skills, or even your criminal record, being wealthy gave you status and mystique. (Florida has always attracted people with "an inordinate desire to get rich quickly with a minimum of physical effort," the economist John Kenneth Galbraith said.)

And in the 1980s, Miami was on its way to becoming one of America's most unequal cities. Friends of my parents sold their starter homes near us and built larger ones closer to the bay, with wet bars and tennis courts. Soon they were dressing up for charitable galas, driving Mercedes and summering in Colorado to escape Miami's heat.

My family was left behind in the mango grove, and we were perplexed. Where did all this money originate? How exactly did someone come to own a bank, as several of my friends' parents did?

My father was old-world. He was born in Brooklyn just before World War II, to working-class immigrant parents who lived next door to relatives with names like Gussie, Bessie and Yetta. His own father, Harry, had dropped out of school at age twelve to deliver newspapers— first from a horse-drawn wagon and later from a truck, and usually with a cigarette in his mouth. One day, when my father was a teenager, he turned up at the truck after school to help out. He found his father in the back, hunched over stacks of newspapers, dead of a heart attack.

My father did a couple years of college, then got a series of jobs in TV production. When my mother met him in New York City, on a blind date, she saw a handsome, appropriately aged man who wore a suit to work, and who—unlike a recent succession of boyfriends she'd had—was actually nice.

That was all true. But what she didn't see, in her optimism, were the vast differences between them. My mother's branch of the family had bounced cheerfully out of the shtetl and into the sunshine. Her American-born parents were established, canny and successful.

My father was patriotic, nostalgic, dreamy and loyal. Though dazzled by my mother's social skills and fancier family, he would always long for the old neighborhood.

They moved to Miami, where my mother had grown up. There weren't many TV jobs in town, so my father opened a small advertising agency, and made commercials for flea markets and local horse-racing tracks.

"Nice" melted in the sun and became depression. He was good at the creative part. But to get more business, he had to sell himself to potential clients. And to be good at sales, either you have to see into people's minds to know what they want or you must be so magnetic that they want whatever you're selling.

My father had neither quality. He enjoyed going to bed early, and making puns and canned remarks. (A favorite of his, to this day, is "Even a stopped clock is right twice a day.") Countless fights erupted between my parents either because my father drove too slowly, or because he'd fallen asleep at a dinner party again. "I was just resting my eyes," he would say.

He was also, perpetually, down to his last advertising account. And he blamed himself for this. We'd have a kind of absurdist daily dialogue, in which I'd ask him how his day had gone, and he'd reply, shamefully, that he'd been "busy." Even then I realized he wasn't, and that my parents' arguments weren't really about his slow driving; it was that he wasn't in the fast lane of life.

My mother was his opposite: outgoing, charismatic, confident and able to sell anything. Popular and pretty, she'd been voted best dressed in high school, then earned a degree in retail at Ohio State. She was interested in whatever was new: the newest clothing styles, the latest restaurants. She turned our living room into a gallery and hosted shows for up-and-coming artists. She and a partner opened a successful women's clothing boutique that served as a kind of clubhouse, where women came to talk as much as to buy. Miami's climate is technically "tropical monsoon." But since it was always freezing inside from the air-conditioning, her customers stocked up on cashmere sweaters.

I grew up in my mother's world. When I wasn't at her boutique, I was tagging along with her in department stores to see what the competition was carrying. Age eight, while other kids were breaking bones on the sports field, I got a shopping injury: my brother and I were horsing around in the ladies' sportswear section of Burdine's, when a cart holding the cash register fell over and fractured my wrist.

Shopping was one topic we discussed in depth. It was even a source of wisdom. "If you don't love it, don't get it," my grandmother would say. Our retail equivalent of a Buddhist koan was "Why, once you bring an outfit home, doesn't it ever again look as good as it did in the shop?"

When it was time to choose a theme for my bat mitzvah party, I eschewed the standard ones of the era—tennis, space travel, Hawaiian luau—and picked "shopping" instead. It was the only topic that I knew intimately. My mother and I made place cards shaped like credit cards, and hired a party planner to make centerpieces out of bags from Bloomingdale's and Neiman Marcus. The planner looked surprised when we described the shopping theme, but no one in my family thought this was an odd way to mark my passage into adulthood.

They did mention that we couldn't afford the party. In a rare disclosure of bad news, my mother called me into her bedroom one day and said we might need to cancel it, for lack of funds. (We downsized to a cheaper venue instead.)

Our lifestyle was made possible by my mother's father, who paid for most of the party and for the new roof on our house. Though my grandfather, like my father, was the son of poor immigrants, he had the ability to connect with people, make deals and make money.

My grandfather paid for the private schools where I mingled with the offspring of Miami's superrich. Some of my classmates lived in waterfront mansions on Miami Beach that they rented out as movie and TV sets. Some got Porsches when they turned sixteen. When my mother arrived at school once to pick me up in her Toyota, a boy sneered, "Is that your maid's car?"

I never questioned this cosmology. I figured that an optimal outcome for me would be to marry a plastic surgeon. (Another of my grandmother's maxims was "It's as easy to fall in love with a rich man as a poor one.")

Though I didn't realize it at the time, my life changed when I discovered *The Official Preppy Handbook*—a satirical guide to the habits of old-money East Coast WASPs. It described a world in which people owned Irish setters, went skiing in Gstaad and wore duck-motif belts. ("The less an object has to do with ducks, the more it cries out for duck adornment.")

Before reading the book, I'd barely clocked the fact that there were Americans who were neither Latino nor Jewish nor black. And I was unfamiliar with the WASP aesthetic: Who knew it was good to have used furniture?

I knew that I wasn't preppy. I didn't know anyone nicknamed Skip or Bink (though I had a Cuban friend we called "Juanky"). I could sail a bit, but my house wasn't scattered with cigarette boxes that my father had won at regattas.

But the book confirmed my suspicion that there really was a lot my family wasn't saying. Daily life—even mine—could be decoded and mined for meaning. Your clothes, your carpeting, the words you used and the objects scattered around your house all amounted to a kind of tribal map.

We never discussed what our tribe was, and our religious observance was bare-bones. (At my shopping-themed bat mitzvah, we served shrimp cocktail.) But when I walked into a restaurant with my parents,

I could spot which women my mother would know, even if I'd never seen them before. They had the same faces, clothes and hairstyles that we did. Most of their parents or grandparents had come to America from the same general European vicinity as ours, at roughly the same time. It was as if entire Belorussian villages had been transported to South Florida, and their descendants were now having dinner in the same Italian restaurants.

I didn't quite know it then, but I craved a *Preppy Handbook* equivalent of my own life, which would explain *our* ritual objects, outfits and customs. I wanted to know the invisible meaning of everything—from what we wore, to why we all had quasi–New York accents, to exactly where we all came from. But how could I do an anthropology of my own life? I wasn't even a reliable witness of who had fallen in the pool.

As I got older, I came to trust my own judgment more. At an airport about to fly home from a high school trip—financed by my grandfather—I ran into an older cousin's husband in the departure lounge. Only he wasn't with my cousin and their two sons; he was with a pretty blond lady and a similarly blond toddler. When he saw me, he looked panicked.

"Cousin Neil has another family," I told my mother, when I got back to Miami.

"Impossible," she said. (With no push from me, my cousin and her husband soon divorced.)

Once I'd had this taste of truth spotting, I wanted more. I began to read my mother's Cold War spy novels, and to dream of having a piercing intellect that I would use to crack codes and solve crimes.

Never mind that I couldn't even follow the plots of spy *movies*, and that I was unable to memorize a phone number or keep a secret. I imagined a future in which I remembered license plates as they flashed past me and I unraveled the motives of foreign agents. Surely the CIA would spot my talents and recruit me.

When I went away to college, I would have been a natural as an English major (the real takeaway from all those spy novels was that I liked to read). But literature seemed like too soft a subject. I majored in philosophy to hone my analytical skills. I stuck with this, despite having no talent for it and not enjoying my classes. When I asked a professor for a letter of recommendation, she wrote: *Pamela will probably be good at something, but it's not philosophy.*

I got some perspective on Miami when I studied in Mexico for a semester. As part of a program called "La Realidad," I lived with a family of seven in their cinder-block house off a dirt road. The one tap in the house had only cold water, so I bathed with heated water in a bucket. When they served an exotic mamey fruit after dinner one night, I devoured it. I looked up to find seven despondent faces; the one fruit was supposed to be dessert for all of us.

"We're not poor!" I told my father, excitedly, when I got back to Miami. By Mexican standards, our midmarket Toyota was a luxury object. But he wasn't comforted by my new perspective. He didn't want to debunk Miami's games. He just wanted to stop losing at them. One day, sitting in the Toyota in our driveway, beneath the mango trees, he made a confession.

"I don't know how to make money," he told me.

I had no idea, either. After college, I briefly worked for an Israeli internet start-up whose entire business model, as I understood it, was to post information about Jewish holidays. To my credit, I did wonder why it had so many employees, most of them young men. What I didn't notice was that, behind a closed door twenty feet from where I sat, a team of programmers ran its real business: online pornography. (A former coworker revealed this to me years after we'd both left.)

I entered adulthood still lacking laser-sharp powers of perception. I wanted to have a brain like a knife, but mine was more like a spoon. I could dig into things, but it took me some time. Though I wasn't stupid, I was far from cunning. My insights sometimes came years after the fact. When something bad or even surprising happened, my first impulse was to ignore it.

So I decided to become a journalist. Some people become reporters because they're keen observers, or because they want to expose wrong-doing. I had a different reason: I wanted to finally figure out what was going on.

You know you're in your forties when . . .

- You're matter-of-fact about chin hair.

- You've discovered cellulite on your arms.

- Everyone you meet looks a little bit familiar.

- You sometimes wake up hungover even when you've had nothing to drink.

- Having older friends no longer makes you feel young.

how to choose
a partner

I EVENTUALLY MADE AN IMPORTANT life decision: if I can't be a grown-up, I'll sleep with one.

Symmetrical Hollywood film stars didn't make my heart beat faster. I liked my men shlumpy and brilliant. In high school, I'd taped a head shot of Barney Frank—the brainy, liberal congressman from Massachusetts—to my bedroom wall. (Since it was a celebrity crush, it seemed irrelevant that he was gay.)

In real life, I dated men who were, if not wiser than me, then at least quite a bit older. I was especially drawn to foreigners who read newspapers in exotic languages. I embarked on a romantic world tour, dating a German-speaking genius in New York who was unable to make eye contact and a Hungarian psychiatrist who—when dumping me—explained that I simply wasn't emotionally wounded enough for him.

My pool of eligible foreigners expanded when I was hired by a newspaper to cover Latin America. During a stint in Brazil, I made a tear through the Jewish men of São Paulo, ending up with a DJ who lived with his mother and—judging by the dirty looks she gave me at breakfast—had recently had a fling with his live-in maid.

I was easily dazzled by worldliness. A Russian suitor of mine spoke four languages fluently; it took me nearly a year to realize that he didn't have a sense of humor in any of them.

I knew it was a bad sign when a Mexican banker brought nothing to read on our beach holiday except a bond-trading manual. But I only ended things after I gave him a leather-bound journal for his birthday and he asked what he was supposed to do with an empty book.

When I finally went American and dated a lawyer's son from the Chicago suburbs, he decided that I wasn't exotic enough for *him*. "Sometimes I think you're just a Jewish girl from Miami," he confessed. I feared the same thing.

The putative goal of this world tour was marriage, but few people I knew actually wed. Those who did married badly. One man married a lesbian who left him almost immediately for her pretty Pilates coach. My friend Elaine was briefly married to a grumpy poet whom her friends called, from the outset, "Elaine's first husband." Another friend was so panicked about possibly ending up childless that she wed the younger man whom she'd long referred to as "the one before the one."

I'd always envisioned a romantic chronology that resembled my mother's: I'd have a few boyfriends, and then get married at twenty-seven. No one warned me that members of my generation might spend fifteen or even twenty years hopping between relationships. When age twenty-seven came and went, I interpreted this not as a demographic shift but a personal failure.

Hardly anyone I knew was coping well with the new pace of courtship. For a few months, I attended a weekly group therapy session in New York that consisted of stressed-out singletons griping about their love lives. At an after-work fiction-writing class, practically every student's short story concerned twentysomethings on a date. "On to the next couple," the teacher would say.

My own romantic life felt like a procession of sitcom episodes. There was the improv instructor who split every bill down to the penny, and the first-time novelist who broke up with me after I didn't show enough enthusiasm for his book. Once, while waiting in a restaurant for my blind date to arrive, I gave my phone number to a man at the next table who was waiting for his date, too.

In the midst of all this, my parents flew to New York to break the news that they were divorcing. "What took you so long?" my brother and I replied, almost simultaneously.

I knew what an incompatible couple looked like, and I had no trouble replicating this. On an airplane, I met a handsome mergers-and-acquisitions specialist whose hands felt like sandpaper, and who kept nothing but bottled water in his refrigerator. It was clear we weren't in love. In a moment of postcoital angst, I asked him why we were doing this. He gestured toward our naked bodies and said, "Because we'll never look this good again."

I'm not sure how I got any work done. I was flying around Latin America covering elections and financial crises. Meanwhile, I was in an almost perpetual state of romantic anguish, as I tried to extract myself from poorly chosen couplings, or as others extracted themselves from me.

But dating also had an addictive thrill. Each new person contained the possibility of both heartbreak and homeownership. And practically everyone I knew was ping-ponging between suitors, too: When one person had a terrible flaw—say, they were jealous—we'd find someone else who was the opposite in that one area and wasn't jealous at all. But the new person would have a whole new flaw, so we'd ping to someone else with some new problem.

It was rare to get any concrete guidance on how to choose a partner. I ignored the aunt who warned me that a man "won't buy the cow if he can get the milk for free." (She was on her third husband at the time, and had given away a lot of milk.) My mother and I didn't analyze my boyfriends, but she sent regular care packages of clothes from her store. I was relieved when someone told me that everyone has thirty potential soulmates in the world. Though when I repeated this to a single colleague, he said, "Yes, and I'm trying to sleep with all of them."

Once, when I was wrestling with whether to break up with a Lebanese filmmaker, I asked an Indian journalist for advice. "There's only one question: Do you believe in the man?" he said. (This sounds more profound in a Hindi accent.) In other words, if the filmmaker lost everything—his job, his status and all of his money—would I still have faith in him?

The answer was no. If the world rejected him, I'd agree with the world. Although the men I dated were mostly older (my sweet spot, for a decade, was thirty-four-year-olds), none of them had that magical grown-up essence I was seeking.

Then a romantic miracle happened. While I was covering Argentina's debt crisis, a mutual friend introduced me to Simon at a bar. Simon was a British journalist who lived in Paris, and who was in Buenos Aires for a few days to write an article about soccer.

Within minutes of our meeting, Simon told me his theory that there are three kinds of people: strivers, slackers and fantasists. Strivers actually work. Slackers don't even pretend to work. And fantasists dream of greatness but don't really do anything. On the spot, he diagnosed me, correctly, as a striver with fantasist tendencies.

It helped that he was handsome and had a winning London accent. And there was the great relief that he was a bookish writer, too. (In later years he will be overjoyed with the leather-bound journals that I give him for many birthdays.) But the clincher was that, already in his early thirties, Simon had developed a plausible—or at least amusing—theory of humanity. He was the living equivalent of the *Preppy Handbook*; someone who constantly classified everything.

I soon learned why. His parents were anthropologists who raised him in six different countries. Everywhere they lived, they analyzed the natives and themselves. Before meeting his father, an esteemed professor, I asked Simon for advice. "It will be fine," he said. "Just don't use the word 'culture.'"

Simon's family was different from mine. Their house contained several thousand books, including many written by family members, friends and colleagues. They discussed their own history, going back many generations.

They knew world history, too, and brought it up often. When Simon's father was shocked by a question I asked him, he replied, "But it was in the *third century*," certain that this would clarify the answer.

Facts orbited constantly around Simon's childhood home, and every subject was open to discussion. Dinners with his family included long analyses of the news, everyone's current work, and the foibles of various relatives. There were elaborate conversations about social class, including their own.

Bad news was mentioned often. People spoke even if they didn't have anything nice to say. While I'd been tagging along after my mother in ladies' sportswear, Simon had been learning how to name what was happening in front of him.

All this early training had turned him into a kind of human decoder. He could spot someone's motivations, and explicate their good and bad qualities, as clearly as I could detect the brand of shoes and handbag they were wearing.

Being with Simon was like having a personal Rosetta Stone who could translate every perplexing interaction. When we emerged from a dinner, I'd ask for his take on what everyone present had been signaling and saying. He had plausible answers to all my vexing questions: Why were the neighbors so mean to us? Why was the US still fighting in Iraq? I wanted to know what he thought about everything.

One day, at a hotel, we caught sight of ourselves in a mirror. There was light streaming in from a window. In the foreground, some left-over room service sat like still life on a table. "We look like we're in a Vermeer painting," he said. I'd spent fifteen years waiting for a man to say something like that to me. I imagined it's what Barney Frank would have said.

I didn't need to see all possible men. Finally, my answer to "Do you believe in the man?" was yes.

It took me awhile to understand why Simon liked me back. He'd been ping-ponging between paramours, too. And I got lucky. He'd discovered that a previous girlfriend, who was getting her doctorate in English literature, didn't know who Joseph Stalin was. ("Mao either," he adds, when I remind him of this years later.)

I wasn't perfect, but I knew the name of every major twentieth-century dictator. When I was sacked from my newspaper, amid mass layoffs, I moved to Paris and became a freelance journalist. Soon afterward, Simon proposed.

He and I were lying in bed one night when I turned to him with a confession.

"I'm with you because you're a grown-up," I said, afraid this will shock him.

"I know," he replied. Then he turned around and fell asleep.

You know you're in your forties when . . .

- Your crush on Jesse Eisenberg feels inappropriate.

- You're aware of mansplaining while it's happening.

- Any man without a paunch seems skinny.

- You drink coffee *before* going out to dinner.

- You've outgrown "adult acne."

how to turn forty

SIMON AND I MARRIED in our midthirties, so we're in a hurry to procreate. Within a few years, we have a daughter and then twin boys. (We're the DITT generation: double income, toddler twins.)

I've acquired some trappings of adulthood. I'm now a married homeowner who does laundry for a family of five. I have my own in-house wise man, and I'm a de facto authority figure to my kids. I've found my family. But I still don't feel like a grown-up, in part because I haven't found my tribe.

Just as I had trouble screening romantic partners, I've had trouble screening friends. Since childhood, I've regularly found myself as the sidekick of beautiful, self-obsessed women. One of them arrived at my wedding wearing a white dress.

Simon is astonished by some friends of mine who pass through Paris. A New Yorker stays in our basement for several weeks, only coming upstairs to criticize my posture, disparage my writing and boast about his wealth. As a parting gift, he presents us with several wooden clothespins.

A high school classmate insists on staying with us weeks after the twins are born. He barely acknowledges the babies, except to complain about the "incessant noise." Another man, whom I'd met while traveling, arrives for the weekend with his new girlfriend. He immediately borrows our washing machine, hangs up their wet clothes around the apartment, then announces that they'll return in a few days, when the clothes are dry. (I'm noticing that my friendships have a laundry theme.)

Simon doesn't get it. I'm clean, friendly and reasonably nice. Why would I invite these people into our lives? Of everyone I could choose to befriend, why them? Must friendships cause such pain? Unlike me, Simon has many thoughtful, devoted, long-term friends. They comprised most of our wedding guests. And none of the women wore white.

I'm drawn to larger-than-life people who require lots of attention. The upside of narcissists is that they don't seem to suffer from self-doubt. They're fake grown-ups; they have little wisdom but lots of certainty. And they instinctively spot my own cocktail of awe, insecurity and tolerance for bad behavior.

When I point out to Simon that his friends aren't as unpredictably thrilling as mine are, he says it's important to surround yourself with people who are kind, funny, trustworthy and smart. He urges me to study people before I befriend them, and to back off if they're missing any of these qualities. ("Ponder for a long time whether you shall admit a given person to your friendship," the Roman philosopher Seneca said two thousand years ago.)

But I'm not focused on analyzing other people; I'm worried about myself. Others seem three-dimensional and solid to me, with enduring qualities like insight and wit. I worry that, beneath my good-natured topsoil, I might not have any fixed qualities at all. I'm surprised when facial-recognition software can identify pictures of me.

Perhaps because of this, I don't trust my friendships to last. It's as if I'm onstage playing the role of affable individual, and I've appointed my new friend as audience and chief critic. This means I can bomb at any moment. What if my next line of dialogue doesn't hold her attention? Have I banked enough amusing remarks to relax into my natural state and be boring for a bit? The other person might like me for now, but what if she changes her mind?

I start off warmly with new friends and genuinely like them. But staying in character is exhausting. To hide my inner flimsiness, I grow increasingly secretive and distant. Soon I won't reveal trivial details about my life, like the subject of an article I'm writing, or the date that I'm leaving on vacation.

The only friends who aren't bothered by this are the ones who are very focused on themselves. They don't care, or even notice, that I don't reveal much about myself. When I read online that one symptom of narcissism is the feeling that your life is a cover for your emptiness, I worry that I might be one, too.

"You're self-absorbed, but you're not a narcissist," Simon reassures me.

As we all approach the forties, I notice that some of my more self-obsessed friends are getting worse. Qualities that were adorable at twenty, and worrisome at thirty, now seem dangerous at forty. Youthful quirks are hardening into adult pathologies.

My circumstances have changed, too. It's one thing to expose myself to difficult people. It's quite another to expose my marriage and my children to them. I don't even need to break up with most of my "friends." As soon as I stop letting them monologue about their lives or camp out in my basement, they stop calling.

Once I've cleared out the narcissists, there are very few people left. And I'm okay with that. The mere fact that I like someone now feels like proof that there's something dangerously wrong with them.

I replace my dysfunctional friendships with people who are more than acquaintances but less than close friends. Most are expatriates, too, and happy to mix with almost anyone who speaks English and can pay their share of the dinner check. I can satisfy my need to occasionally socialize without putting myself at anyone's mercy.

But as my fortieth birthday approaches, this starts to seem pathetic. Surely being a grown-up isn't about having cordial relations with nice people who barely know me. And my kids are getting older and starting to notice more. How can I model what healthy relationships look like if I have so few of them?

To turn things around, I decide to celebrate my fortieth birthday with a party. However, I don't invite any of the middle-class professionals and stay-at-home moms I've been socializing with. Instead, I invite the people I'd like to befriend, and who I suspect are part of my real tribe: a handful of writers and intellectuals whom I know a little bit. My carefully curated guest list has a half-dozen people and their partners, including an Ivy League professor, a documentary filmmaker, a celebrated South African journalist and a woman whose boyfriend writes for the *New Yorker*. Some of them I've only met once.

Since my birthday falls on a Sunday, I decide to hold an afternoon "open house" in my apartment between four and six. It's a small commitment, and there isn't much else happening on a wintry Sunday afternoon, so everyone accepts.

I spend the day arranging flowers, Italian cheeses and hors d'oeuvres on my kitchen counter, and setting out a dozen glass flutes for champagne. I dress my kids in their most adorably Parisian outfits, and warn them not to touch the food. Minutes before four o'clock, I put on some calm-but-complicated jazz: the sound track for my new life.

Then I wait for my forties to begin. For the first hour of the party, no one comes. My children sit quietly at first, then beg to be allowed to eat something or to go outside. Soon they're watching me with what seems like pity: Why doesn't Mommy have any friends at her birthday party? My amused husband reads a book on the couch.

At five o'clock, the filmmaker texts to say that he and his wife can't make it after all. I put away two empty flutes. At five fifteen, the South

African journalist arrives with his boyfriend. They chat politely with me and Simon, while glancing around at our near-empty apartment. They barely know me; are they meant to be the only guests?

Around five thirty, four or five others show up and situate themselves in small clusters around my kitchen island. I flit anxiously between them, trying to conjure a salonlike atmosphere. But it is not a dazzling Parisian salon. It's a sparse, awkward, excessively catered gathering of people who aren't sure why they've come. They all leave by six fifteen, having failed to finish even the first bottle of champagne. No one except my children eats anything.

My failed fortieth makes a few things very clear: I am too old to have an aspirational birthday party. And though it's been less than a day, I'm already doing the forties all wrong.

You know you're in your forties when . . .

- There is no longer any trace of you in your childhood bedroom.

- You have full-on adult memories of things that happened a long time ago.

- You see a sepia photograph of a weathered Native American woman sitting beside a wooden loom, and you realize that she's probably your age.

- You leave the house without makeup, and people keep asking whether you're tired.

- You're not considering Botox, but you are considering bangs.

4

how to raise
children

I COMPENSATE FOR MY OWN family's smoke screen of good news by talking to my kids about practically everything. We dissect the characters of everyone we know, including all their friends.

I may have overdone it. When I'm walking my daughter (we call her "Bean" because a nurse put a beanie on her head when she was born) to school one morning, I mention that when I was growing up, we almost never analyzed other people. She finds this inconceivable.

"That's been my entire childhood," she says.

Looking back now, it seems like raising very young kids was largely a test of physical endurance. (I wrote a book about how to make this test somewhat easier to endure.) As they get older, it becomes a test of judgment, and a measure of your own grown-up-ness. I often feel like the ruler of a tiny country who's constantly called upon to make laws and adjudicate disputes. You have to be wise—or at least fair—to have any credibility with your subjects.

That's especially true with twins. When my older son has a

nightmare and cries out at three a.m., I rush into his room. Was he dreaming of monsters? Terrorists?

Nope. In the dream "You gave Leo Smarties, but you didn't give any to me," he says. (I've realized that, though the boys were born minutes apart, they still think of themselves as the middle and youngest children, so I think of them that way, too.)

During waking hours, I'm often torn between playing the reassuring authority figure who can handle anything and taking a more naturalistic we're-all-exploring-life-together approach. Should I act "parental" or act like myself? If I seem too flawed, will my kids feel safe?

Organizationally, I'm practically infallible. Studies show that people in their forties are at a lifetime peak in "conscientiousness." Parenting sometimes seems to require little else, as I label their windbreakers, sign their permission slips and enforce their tooth-brushing regimens. I'm an organizational Olympian.

My kids are not. It's as if the physical world is outside their control. During preschool, my younger son once came home with a purple stain on the rear of his pants. He said it was pie. (Technically, he said it was *tarte*.)

"How did you get pie on your tush?" I asked, genuinely baffled.

"It wasn't my fault. It fell on the chair and then I sat on the chair," he explained.

"Do you go to the Three Stooges school?" I asked.

It's been years since I lost anything. But even now that my kids are older, they can't keep track of a sweatshirt. My older son often dashes around our apartment saying, "I've lost my marbles!" (He means this literally; marbles are all the rage at his school.) I supply each child with a laundry bag when we travel, but they repack their smelly clothes mixed up with their clean ones.

I'm less competent when they pepper me with factual, moral and quasi-philosophical questions: Guess who's my third-favorite soccer player? Why didn't we give that homeless person money? How many countries have I vomited in? Why did Hitler dislike Jews?

Spiritual conversations are especially daunting.

"If there was a God, he would make it sunny every day. It's not sunny today, so there is no God," my older son explains during an overcast picnic.

"That's what's known as 'the weather proof,'" I reply.

I can fake my way through some questions, but as a foreigner, I don't always have the option of coming across as a capable adult. Even after a dozen years in France, daily life can be baffling. My kids—who were born here and attend French schools—quickly realize that I don't know third-grade French grammar, and that I can't do long division the "French" way. They insist on spell-checking every note I send to their teachers or to parents of their friends. When I get creative in the wording of the boys' birthday party invitation, my younger son draws the line diplomatically: "Mommy, I promise you, nobody says that."

My children do see advantages in having foreign parents. When they use bad words in French, I usually don't even notice. I only figured out one word was unacceptable when a French boy slept over and exclaimed, "Your mother lets you say that?"

I try to coax the kids into my American realm, where I have impeccable spelling and grammar. Simon and I only speak to them in English, and we seed their bookshelves with English-language stories. But this doesn't transform them into cultural Americans. They speak in French-influenced syntax ("Is it wet, the grass?") and there are words they've only seen in books and don't know how to pronounce. On Armistice Day, Bean tells me that her class saw a World War I "plake" (she means a plaque). Once when she's upset, she says that she's "de-VAST-ed."

"You're DEV-astated," I clarify.

I'm constantly translating from their English into mine.

"What's a 'pee-oh-ner'?" Bean asks me while I'm cooking dinner one night.

"A what?"

"A 'pee-oh-ner.' Like in Laura Ingalls Wilder times."

"Spell it?"

"P-I-O-N-E-E-R."

I do manage to transmit American humor, or at least the vaudeville variety. My kids like the joke about how many Jewish mothers it takes to change a lightbulb. ("None, I'm fine, I'll just sit here in the dark.") They also enjoy the one about the son who comes downstairs wearing one of the two sweaters his mother has just given him. My younger son delivers the punch line in a Franco-Yiddish accent: "Vat, you didn't like the other one?"

To my delight, they pick up some American expressions, but I have no control over which ones. Being French, my sons are delighted by "Who cut the cheese?" Bean, who watches lots of American television, is especially fond of "Shut up!" when it means, "Keep giving me those compliments!"

"My blood is boiling," I tell her once when I'm angry.

"I hope that's an expression," she replies.

Unlike me, they only use Celsius. When I accidentally tell them the temperature in Fahrenheit on a warm day, they're terrified. "We can't go outside, we'll burn!" one of the boys exclaims.

The holy grail of my Americanization project is sending them to sleepaway camp in the United States. After three weeks in cabins with kids from the Boston suburbs, the acculturation will be done for me. They'll form an emotional bond with my country and learn American slang.

I send away for catalogs and show the kids a promotional film in which children their age sing songs around campfires and wax about all their new friends. I get goose bumps watching campers splash around in tree-lined lakes, just as I used to do, while uplifting background music plays.

But my children are horrified. Having been raised in France, they don't believe that anyone would be that cheerful voluntarily. Bean thinks it looks like a hostage video.

"They definitely made those children say that. Can't you tell?" she asks.

It's not just the "camp spirit" that bothers her. It's getting up to a bugle and being forced to sing in unison. "Mommy, I'm not going to have your American childhood," she says. "I don't want to wake up at seven a.m. and make bracelets. I just don't. Accept it."

You know you're a fortysomething parent when . . .

- You've decided that swimming counts as a shower.
- You find it tedious to tell your third child how babies are made.
- You struggle to explain what life was like before YouTube and cell phones.
- You carefully restrict your children's screen time, but check your phone every fifteen minutes.
- You can't believe it takes so many years of school to learn everything.
- You are sometimes tempted to let your kids skip class so you can stay in bed.

5

how to hear

WHEN WE VISIT SIMON'S FAMILY in London over the Christmas holidays, I keep asking people to repeat themselves. This happens most often when I'm speaking to Simon. The last few words of his sentences sometimes seem to disintegrate.

I blame Simon for this on two counts: he has a British accent, and he mumbles. Both intensify when he's with his family. I've zoned out anyway, since we spend most of Christmas playing a British edition of Trivial Pursuit that requires an encyclopedic knowledge of Welsh road signs and 1970s English soccer.

Of course, I also have a catastrophic second suspicion about why I can't hear: I'm going deaf. I don't mention anything to Simon, but as soon as we're back in Paris I arrange to visit an ear doctor who works out of a local hospital. (Contrary to American beliefs about "socialized medicine," most doctors here are in private practice and I can see whichever one I want.)

The ear doctor is an amiable Frenchman in his sixties who listens attentively while I describe my husband's problem. (I've looked up the

French verb "to mumble"; it's *marmonner*.) He hears me out, then puts me in a booth with headphones on. Whenever I hear a beep, I raise my hand in the manner of French schoolchildren, with one finger pointing toward the sky. Then I repeat a series of faintly uttered French words: *jardin, esprit, fréquence.*

When I emerge from the booth, the doctor is grinning at me.

"How old are your ears?" he asks.

We go over to his desk, and he takes out a chart showing the normal progression of hearing over a lifetime. The line slopes gently downward. At twenty years old, "your hearing is perfect," he says. By my age, the lowest and highest tones are harder to hear. "You can't blame your husband for this," he says. I'm within the normal range.

I'm relieved, but surprised. I'd always assumed that a person's hearing is more or less the same until he enters his seventies or eighties, at which point everyone starts shouting at him through an ear trumpet. I had been somewhat prepared to cope with an aging face and mind in my forties. I hadn't counted on my ears entering midlife, too.

Nor does this bode well for my marriage. The tones I've lost seem to be precisely the ones that my husband speaks in. And apparently, the physical declines of midlife are just beginning. Anthropologist Richard Shweder writes that when he injured his lower back playing squash, and couldn't stand up straight, his squash partner declared, "Welcome to middle age!"

A girlfriend who just turned forty tells me over lunch that she has developed a "ptosis," a slight droop in one of her eyelids. Her doctor said the precise cause is "age."

A man in his midforties who never had any trouble sleeping says that he now wakes up several times each night to urinate. His doctor explained that his newly enlarged prostate is pressing on his bladder, and suggested that he exercise, drink tomato juice and try several different pills. When none of these help, the doctor says he'll just have to live with the wake-ups. (In the modern forties, just as our children start sleeping through the night, we stop.)

Most people in their forties are healthy, of course. Plenty of us run marathons, play tennis and shoot hoops. The odd fortysomethings still play professional hockey or golf, pitch baseballs, swim competitively and dance in ballet companies. But we've gotten at least slightly worse at practically every sport, thanks to longer reaction times, lower lung capacity and less muscle mass. Doctors have started mentioning words like "arthritis." If we could ever run like a gazelle, that ability evaporates by our forties. "Now it's impossible to go that fast, no matter how hard I try," says a fit forty-two-year-old who's been a recreational runner for decades.

At least there's good news about fertility. Doctors used to cite sobering statistics, including one claiming that women who don't have children by their late thirties have a 30 percent chance of remaining childless forever. It turns out that those figures were based in part on seventeenth- and eighteenth-century French birth records, and other historical data, that predate antibiotics, ultrasound and modern statistical methods.

Since 1990, the rate of babies born to American women ages forty to forty-four has nearly doubled. This is partly thanks to technology. A forty-nine-year-old I know just gave birth to a baby girl who came from a donated sperm and egg. A woman I met on a playground had twins from her husband's defrosted sperm after he'd been dead for several years.

Of course, child-rearing can be more exhausting in the forties, and it brings other challenges. A forty-two-year-old new mother tells me that she needs reading glasses to clip her baby's fingernails. By the time your child learns to walk, it can feel as if, in a blink, you've gone from fecund young mother to madame.

And small bodily changes are starting to accumulate. My yellowing front tooth resists all dental interventions. I used to only wear glasses outdoors; now I need them to navigate my apartment. I panic when a BB-sized bump appears on the floor of my mouth. After sending me for a scan, a doctor says it's a harmless bone growth that's not uncommon in "people my age."

"When will it go away?" I ask.

"It won't," he says. "And you'll probably get one on the other side, too."

Once again, my mind hasn't caught up with my chronological age. When the ear doctor shows me the hearing-loss chart, I tell him that I had planned to skip all these little breakdowns that come as you get older. I wanted to be the exception.

"I know, in your head you're still twenty years old."

"No, in my head I'm about thirty-seven," I say.

"I'm sixty-nine. But in my head I'm twenty," he says, smiling again.

"Twenty? I wouldn't want to be twenty," I say, suddenly wondering how many wives he's had.

"You're right, thirty. But in fact, I'm sixty-nine. And this doesn't end well."

"It's hard to believe that two-hundred-fifty-year-old people aren't discovered every now and then," I tell him.

"I will be one of them!" he replies, then he adds: *"L'amour n'existe pas"*—love doesn't exist.

"L'amour?" I ask, confused.

"La mort!"—death!—he clarifies. I'd misheard him. "Of course love exists. *Death* doesn't exist. Or at least our own death doesn't. We have proof of other people's death, but not of our own."

When I get home, I don't mention any of this to Simon—not my ears, not love, not death. It's odd to age alongside your partner, and sometimes it's best to pretend that you're not. There are probably things he's not telling me, either. I keep after him to enunciate, though I think he knows that our misunderstandings aren't entirely his fault. We've struck an unspoken agreement: He'll pretend I still have the same ears as when he married me. And I'll pretend that I've heard every word.

You know you have a fortysomething body when . . .

- You select restaurants because they're quiet.

- Sleep no longer means just flopping into bed. You have elaborate rituals involving medication, eyeshades, earplugs and a particular type and quantity of pillows.

- When reading a document online, you increase its magnification to at least 200 percent.

- You've bought a scale with a bigger digital display so you won't have to weigh yourself wearing glasses.

- You have gained and lost the same ten pounds so many times you feel a certain affection for them.

how to have sex

"DO YOU HAVE A LOVER?" Charlie asks, as we cross the Place de la République.

Charlie is a friend from high school who's visiting Paris with his wife and son. We're on a walk, alone, near my house. He's just like he was when I first met him: handsome, whip smart and magnetic. I was madly in love with him at fifteen, but so were a lot of people. He married Lauren, his college girlfriend, who now has a big job in medical research. Charlie works part-time and looks after their son.

His question takes me by surprise. We've never discussed this topic before, and it's outside my skill set. Simon and I don't swing or have an open marriage. Our main objective is to be asleep by eleven p.m.

"No, I don't have a lover," I reply, trying not to seem flustered. "Do you?"

"Yes, Lauren and I both do," he says, grinning at me.

"How often do you see your . . . special friend?"

"About once every three weeks," he says. "For a while Lauren had a lover and I didn't. And it was awful. And I just had to think, 'I will find someone and this will get better.' And it did."

He says it's exciting to see that your partner is attractive to other people. And there's the energizing swoon of having a crush. "You don't have to go all the way with someone. Sometimes it's just the electric charge of their hand touching yours." Meanwhile, back at home, "Your relationship stays dynamic. I don't want to be stuck in a rut."

Charlie seems to relish my shock at hearing all this. He's always been the guy with the tantalizing new idea. When we were fifteen, I felt similarly blown away when he introduced me to reggae music. I wonder whether he's bringing up the topic because he wants to cheat on his lover with me. All these years later, there's still the same fizzy energy between us. Talking to him brings back a part of myself that I'd forgotten existed. He's a madeleine of my teenage mind.

I tell him about my one puny extramarital adventure: Years ago, I kissed a man I met at a friend's wedding. I was drunk and happy, and we were all on a farm. It didn't go any further than that, and afterward, I felt that I'd transgressed. Monogamy is a strange idea, but I've always assumed that it is nevertheless an important one.

Charlie isn't impressed. "Flirting, and making out with people at weddings, that ought to be just permitted," he says. At a rural wedding he went to with his wife, they swapped with another couple and had sex side by side in a cabin. "What I really want now is for us to share a lover," he says.

He makes all this seem so normal, I suddenly feel like the only idiot who doesn't have an open marriage. I'm at 1.0 for infidelity; he's at 8.0.

Charlie urges me to "take a lover," and he warns me that one won't be enough. "The important thing is to do it at least three or four times. Because the first couple of times you're so self-conscious, you can't really relax and enjoy it." Then he encourages me to do it soon. At my age, he says, "You're still cute, but you're not sure how much longer it's going to last."

A re these my last viable years, before I fall into the sexual abyss?
I'm getting that message from others, too. "Do you feel like you have five years left before no one wants to sleep with you anymore?" a writer in his late thirties asks me. A Canadian friend who's about my age tells me that, as he rounded a corner recently, he came face-to-face with a "fifty-year-old woman" who suddenly grabbed his crotch and kissed him on the lips. To emphasize how unwelcome the encounter was, my friend keeps repeating, "She was fifty!" There's practically no group of people you're allowed to mock on television anymore. The exception is older women: you can say how repulsive it would be to see them naked.

There are exceptions. A friend who's a social activist tells me, encouragingly, about an "incredibly hot" sixty-year-old woman whom he met at a wedding.

"She was a Bond girl," he explains.

"You mean she looked like she could have been a Bond girl?" I ask.

"No," he says, "she was literally in a James Bond movie when she was younger."

American women in their forties still have sex on a fairly regular basis. But according to national statistics, a third of women in their fifties haven't had sex in the past year. And nearly half of women in their sixties haven't. The seventies are practically celibate. The findings for British women are similarly grim. Men claim to fare much better at all ages.

I usually avoid even saying the word "menopause," out of an unscientific fear that, by uttering the word, I'll trigger it. (After all, just looking at a baby can trigger the release of breast milk.) But I summon the courage to do a Google search, and learn that menopause typically begins around age fifty-one, bringing symptoms like vaginal dryness, loss of breast fullness and my personal favorite, "vaginal atrophy," in which the birth canal loses elasticity. All this happens just as sexual activity really starts to drop off. Though the symptoms and the sexlessness all sound very unpleasant, I have to admit that there's an evolutionary logic: What good is a sex drive if you can no longer reproduce? Perhaps Charlie was right to warn me that I'm approaching my sexual sell-by date.

And yet, France has a slightly different sexual narrative for women. Over the years, I'd been surprised by the French couples in their sixties perusing lingerie racks together, and the plum movie roles for women *d'un certain âge*. My Australian neighbor marvels that, every week after her Pilates class, a fit woman in her seventies changes into lacy ensembles.

These norms aren't confined to a few well-maintained ladies in Paris. National sex statistics tell a similar story. Among French women in their fifties, just 15 percent haven't had sex in the last year (compared to 33 percent in America). Among those in their sixties, just 27 percent haven't (versus 50 percent in the US).

In France, too, women have less sex, on average, as they get older. But it's a gentle decline, not an abyss. Most French women remain sexually active well into their sixties, and possibly beyond.

To be sure, youthful beauty is celebrated here. There are taut twenty-two-year-olds in many advertisements. A Parisian professor in her sixties warns me, over *soupe à l'oignon*, that after age fifty "women in France are decapitated." The difference is that people who aren't young and gorgeous generally expect to have sex, too. It's just something that most healthy adults do on a regular basis throughout their lives.

When I arrive at the fiftieth birthday party of a Parisian friend—a scientist and mother of three—several dozen people are in her living room drinking red wine, eating Moroccan food, flirting and dancing to the Village People. (My generation's nostalgia music is similar in America and France.)

"Not bad for fifty!" I remark to one of her friends. When he looks confused, I realize that I've misread the dance party. It's not a performance of youth. It's a straightforward, exuberant celebration.

Nor are such moments meant to be a last hurrah. The fifties and beyond can be sexy decades here. Through a colleague, I meet Hélène, a married sixty-eight-year-old French journalist and grandmother. Hélène isn't a Bond girl, but she's fit and well put together in a sweater, knee-high boots and a leather pencil skirt. She emits an attractive, kinetic energy, and she knows it.

"There are thirty-year-old women who don't radiate, and there are older people who radiate. I'm an older one who radiates," she tells me, smiling warmly. "I love life very much, very much. Enormously. So I think it's that that comes through. A little light in the eyes, a desire to wake up in the morning."

She says radiating like this is an active choice. Early on in her life, "I decided one thing: that I will be *belle dans mon âge*—beautiful within my age. I'm not going to resort to artifice or face-lifts and all that. No face-lift. But I'll be elegant, and wear makeup, and please myself." She repeats this last part for emphasis: *"I will please myself."*

Hélène pleases herself by having brief, secret affairs. She says her fifties were a sexual heyday. "I've done things that were totally crazy. I mean, meeting a man on the street, who I like, and going to a hotel with him. I did that. I'm still capable of doing that."

Hélène is very discreet about these affairs. Her husband is "someone for whom I have a lot of respect, whom I love. I don't want him to know about my naughtiness." One of her lovers liked her to wear garter belts. So after an assignation with him, she would stop at her parking garage and change back into regular stockings in her car.

She smiles at the memory of her most recent adventure, two years ago. In her mind, she's swooning. "It was with a very handsome man, younger than me. We met, we liked each other, I went to a hotel with him. The relationship lasted two months, I think. And then I ended it."

Hélène is a well-off Parisian with a country house and a university degree. She can afford hotel rooms. But she's following a cultural script that other older French women describe, too.

Indeed, the same professor who told me that French women are "decapitated" at fifty also says that, over the years, she's had a series of brief, discreet affairs.

She, too, is married and a grandmother. She's very committed to both roles. However, "there's a time for work, there's a time for your family and then there is time for yourself," she explains. With a lover, "You will feel loved and appreciated as yourself, not as the 'wife of,' or the 'mother of,' the professional. You will be loved as yourself, just you, disconnected, just you, the inner core."

Being mindful of what's happening is part of the pleasure. (Another part, I suspect, is shocking an American writer with your stories.)

In the French telling, these private experiences also pay dividends in the rest of your life. The professor says that "in your work, you will do it better because you feel so good. You will reverberate when you talk to your children and your husband, because you will feel so good."

She adds that she doesn't want to be remembered as a dutiful mother and wife. "Come on, how boring. No! It's very, very important that when you die in the end, you will think, 'I had a great time in my life. I had all these moments that were stolen, that were just for myself.'"

Which version of sexuality is the real one, the Anglo-Saxon declinist narrative or the French idea that we can stay sexy—and sexually active—much longer? I decide to study the research. Sitting in a café in my neighborhood—where all the servers call me "madame"—I read an Australian academic paper titled "Sex and the menopausal woman: A critical review and analysis." (I do my best to keep the title hidden.)

The paper makes a strong case for the French approach, explaining that women's sex drives don't inevitably decline with age, and that "some women report improved sexual desire and functioning at midlife and beyond." Yes, falling estrogen levels can cause problems like vaginal dryness and the infamous "atrophy." But these are symptoms of sexual functioning, not of sexual desire. They mean that a woman now needs lubricant for intercourse in the same way that, if her eyesight declined, she would need glasses. No one would argue that she'd lost the desire to see.

I soon realize that this isn't just the view of a few Australian feminists. A paper led by a researcher from America's National Institutes of Health concludes that "menopausal status, at least in the early stages, is only minimally associated with sexual practices and functioning."

Some women do lose their sex drives in midlife. But cultural narratives play an important role, too. Another paper, in the *Journal of Aging Studies*, notes that "ageism and sexism, which together promote a view of older women as undesirable or inappropriate sexual partners (even among women themselves), lie at the heart of these patterns."

In other words, if the people around you insist that you're no longer sexy after a certain age, or that you're going to fall into a sexual abyss in your fifties, this is more likely to actually happen. Or as the writer Susan Sontag put it, "Growing older is mainly an ordeal of the imagination."

I forgive my friend Charlie for absorbing some of America's cultural norms. I think he was mostly trying to flirt with me and have fun. And I realize that—in the absence of much professional status—he has invested in building his sexual status. He's highly skilled at making women swoon.

"He's a courtesan," says Simon, who meets and likes him. "In Holland he'd be considered completely normal."

Anyway, Charlie's view of my sex appeal hasn't changed much so far. As we walk across northern Paris, I wonder if he's going to suggest that we pop into one of the many small hotels we pass. I'm not sure what I'll say if he does. But he doesn't. He wants an open marriage, but not an open marriage with me. In fact, I realize that our dynamic hasn't changed at all in thirty years. I still adore him, and he still adores making me swoon. There's still understanding, affection and frisson between us. And that's still the end of it. It will probably be like that thirty years from now, too, when we're hobbling across some other city together, discussing another big idea that I'm late to. I also realize that I'm okay with that. When I was younger, I needed my relationships to be resolved and defined. Now I see that some people occupy an in-between place, and my world is richer for it. I'm lucky to have Charlie in my life exactly as he is.

You know you have a fortysomething sex life when . . .

- You no longer care (or remember) how many people you've slept with.

- You realize that you shouldn't marry the person with whom you had the best sex of your life.

- The thought of any adult you know having sex, even your own parents and grandparents, no longer makes you squeamish.

- You have a back catalog of fantasies that you can call up at will.

- You sometimes fantasize about your own partner.

- You can't imagine exposing your naked body to anyone else.

7

how to plan a ménage à trois

I SAID I'VE ONLY HAD one extramarital adventure. That was true. But I had a marital one, too. It began on the eve of my husband's fortieth birthday, when I would soon turn forty myself.

The question on his birthday is always, what do you get for the man who has nothing? Simon isn't a shopper. Standing in front of his closet, he once declared that he has enough pants to last the rest of his life. When I inquired about his plans for a drawer containing dozens of stray socks, he said, "My heirs will sort it out."

For his fortieth birthday, I decide to buy him a vintage watch. It will declare to the world that—despite his tattered sweaters—he's an employed adult.

It's an expensive, nonreturnable gift, so I mention my plan to him one night before bed. (This is the main time that we talk.) He balks, and says that what he really wants for his birthday isn't a good, it's a service: a threesome with me and another woman.

I'm not exactly shocked by this request. He'd floated the idea of a threesome before (though never as a gift). And although I'd never done it, going to bed with two women is a standard-issue male fantasy, and the plot of most heterosexual pornography.

Simon's request is spontaneous, but serious. And just as spontaneously, I say yes. As a journalist, I have trouble resisting a deadline. (He'll turn forty in about six weeks.) I also like the idea of a gesture to show that I'm not slipping quietly into middle age. Plus, I'm pretty sure that Simon would lose the watch, or submerge it in the bathtub. (His exact words are "I'd lose it, *and* break it.")

And frankly, I'm procrastinating. I need a distraction from the parenting book that I've been struggling to finish but can't figure out how to write.

We agree on the threesome in principle. But the idea is so exotic that for a few weeks it just sits there. Occasionally, I mention the name of a female friend.

"Would she be acceptable?" I ask Simon.

"Absolutely," he says each time. It turns out that practically every woman we know—all of my female friends and the wives of practically all of his male friends—would potentially make the cut, including the pregnant ones. Simon doesn't want to spoil his chances by being picky.

That hardly matters, because at first I'm too embarrassed to raise the topic with anyone we know. And though I'm a novice, I'm pretty sure that recruiting a friend would be a mistake. There's the enormous potential for awkwardness on the day itself, and long afterward. And I don't want someone creating a wedge in our cozy twosome. I'm envisioning this as a one-off.

Anyway, I wouldn't know which girlfriend to ask. Straight women don't often discuss their same-sex fantasies with each other. I'm not sure who'd be tempted by the idea and who'd be appalled.

Finally, over brunch, we summon the courage to discuss our plans with friends of Simon's who are visiting from London. One of them, a single British banker who's nearing forty herself, grimaces and then goes silent.

"You look horrified," I say.

"Yes, I mean, I just think it's extraordinary!" she says, blushing.

Soon after the brunch, I get an email from an editor I know at a women's magazine in New York. She's short on first-person essays and wonders whether I have any ideas.

As a freelancer, I'm not used to being asked to write anything. I quickly send her three story ideas: one on making friends in Paris, another on the travails of renovating my kitchen and a third on planning a threesome for my husband's birthday. I honestly don't realize that there's an obvious front-runner.

She replies almost immediately, and wants to know details about the threesome, including whether I've already found the other woman. Soon I have a contract obliging me to deliver a 2,800-word essay titled "Fortieth Birthday Threesome." She says I can opt not to publish it under my real name.

To be fair, I was planning to have the threesome anyway. But after I sign the document, I realize that I'm now more or less contractually obliged to go through with it. I'll be paid by the word, and a sexless version, in which I back down, would probably get less space.

More critical than whether I might have sex for money is whether I'll have sex at all. I've realized that women aren't falling over themselves to sleep with a soon-to-be middle-aged married couple. Simon and I rule out advertising online, since that seems like an open call for venereal disease.

We decide that the ideal third party would be a sexy acquaintance. She'd be vetted (everyone knows acquaintances don't have herpes) but easy enough to avoid afterward. A candidate soon emerges. She's an American friend of a friend whom I've met a few times at dinner parties. By chance she's seated behind us at a concert, with a man who appears to be her date. For the first time, I notice that she's quite attractive. She's tall and thin, with a little ballerina's waist. And I'm pretty sure she's sassy.

"How about her?" I whisper to my husband, as the music starts.

"Yes!" he says, too loudly.

After the concert, the four of us chat. I make firm eye contact with the woman, work out that her name is Emma and pretend to be fascinated by her views on the performance. When I suggest that she and I have lunch, she seems flattered. A few days later, I get gussied up to meet her for Thai food. I'm pleased to see, when I arrive, that she has dressed up, too. Does she realize that she's on a date?

I'm usually so concerned about what other people think of me that my lunch companion could be bleeding to death and I wouldn't notice. But the threesome planning has made me more attentive. Over soup, I listen carefully to Emma and quickly understand something that would have once taken me years to realize: under a pond of sassiness is a lagoon of insecurity. The common theme of her stories is that she clings to boyfriends who mistreat her. I'd mistaken tall for self-possessed.

She's probably too emotionally fragile for a threesome, but I broach the topic anyway, to get some practice. I do this under the guise of exchanging girly confidences, saying, "You won't believe what my husband wants for his birthday." I explain that I've agreed to this in principle, but that I haven't yet found the third party.

I think she understands that I'm propositioning her. But instead of taking the bait, she morphs into the Cassandra of threesomes. She describes the ex-boyfriend who pressured her to go to bed with him and his other lover, and the couple who swapped partners for the night, then never swapped back. She warns me that I'll be scarred by images of my husband doing unspeakable things to another woman. "And what if it's someone who's incredibly hot? How could you possibly handle that?"

Not only is Emma out of the running, She talks of future lunch dates at other Asian restaurants. To my horror, she seems to want to become my friend. I'm suddenly sympathetic to those male "friends" of mine who disappeared the moment I got engaged. Why stick around?

That night I tell Simon about my "date," which cost me fifty euros and consumed half of my workday.

"Thanks for taking care of that," he says, without looking up from his computer. It's exactly what he says when I've waited at home all morning for the plumber to arrive, or I've replaced the rechargeable batteries in our phones. Planning the threesome has become another one of my administrative tasks.

Nevertheless, my new man's-eye view of the world is thrilling. I now notice women everywhere: browsing in bookstores, in line at the supermarket. I even scan my book group—middle-aged expatriates who like to read about the Holocaust—for candidates.

Though I've only managed one failed seduction, my posture toward the world has changed. Instead of sitting pretty and hoping that others notice me, I feel like someone who decides what she wants and goes after it. I'm less interested in what others think of me and more focused on what I want from them. I can suddenly envision myself walking into a room and demanding a promotion. (That's easy for me to say, since I'm freelance. "I want a promotion!" I'd say. "But you don't work here," they'd reply.)

It's also energizing to put this once-furtive fantasy on the table. Threesomes suddenly seem to be everywhere, although the message about them is paradoxical: every straight man supposedly wants to have one, but no one seems to have had a good one. A friend tells me that he bedded two women on the night of September 11, 2001, as they all watched the news on television together. But like many threesome stories, his is a cautionary tale: one of the women developed a serious, unreciprocated crush on him. "Inside every threesome is a twosome and a onesome," a character on a TV show warns. When I discuss the planning with my therapist, a Briton who works in Paris, he warns me that introducing a third party could damage my marriage.

I'm undeterred but still no closer to finding the other woman. When the magazine editor emails asking for an update, I explain that Simon and I have extended the deadline a few weeks past his actual birthday.

I decide to look at some websites. Perhaps not everyone on them has gonorrhea? I quickly see that we have competition. At least a dozen couples—all of them claiming to be gorgeous and under thirty—are seeking women for a threesome, too.

Since I can't compete on looks or age, I decide to distinguish myself by sounding desperate. My post reads: "I'd like to give my partner his best birthday present ever: an experience with me and another woman. Will you help me?" Fifteen minutes later, I get a reply that's literate and nice.

"Hi, I also have a boyfriend with the same fantasy (not very original, I know, but boys will be boys!!). Maybe we could end up doing a deal (though not necessarily). If we like each other, I'd be happy to help out. What kind of scenario did you have in mind?"

She signs it "N."

It's probably imprudent to pledge loyalty to an anonymous woman who scans "no-strings" websites, but I decide on the spot that I won't respond to anyone else. I like her sisterly tone and her perfect spelling. I'm not sure about the exchange deal, but that doesn't seem to be mission-critical for her. (Though when I read her message to Simon that night, he immediately says, "I'll swap you.")

We exchange several more emails. I call myself "P." "N," a Briton living in Paris, claims to be a straight, divorced, disease-free mom in her late forties. She's relieved to hear that I have kids, too. She says that she responded to my ad out of a kind of sexual altruism, and she quotes the French expression "One need not die an idiot." This sounds like the equivalent of "not being in a rut."

As I'm putting on a dress to go meet N. for coffee, I'm suddenly struck by the strangeness of what I'm about to do: try to convince a stranger to sleep with me and my husband. It's now real, and I'm nervous. I've only ever been on the receiving end of seduction attempts. How exactly do I convince a woman to take off her clothes?

Simon, who devoted years of his life to exactly this question, gives me a little pep talk.

"With women, you have to listen to all the stuff they say. They have all these complex emotional issues, and you have to try to figure out what they are. Just keep asking questions. Be pleasant and reassuring but also slightly mysterious." He's probably afraid that I'll back out, because he adds that, to keep life interesting, "sometimes you have to stick your neck out."

"It's not my neck that's going to be sticking out," I say.

I'm already sitting down when N. walks into the café. She's a pretty, slim brunette with a friendly face. I notice that her makeup is fresh. She's eager to make a good impression, too. I'm certain that my husband will like her.

I try to seem riveted as she describes her boyfriend woes, her life as a single mother and the health issues of her elderly father. Despite the peculiar circumstances, she's clinging to the conventions of female bonding.

I steer the conversation toward sex. She says she's never been with another woman and isn't sure how she'll feel about that. She doesn't mention the possible swap with her boyfriend. When I show her a picture of Simon, she just glances at it. For her, this is more about the two of us.

We part warmly with a chaste double-cheeked kiss. I wait several days before sending her a note explaining that she's been in my thoughts, and that I found her charming "in every way." She replies immediately, saying that she's very game for our adventure, but that she'd like to meet again to discuss our plans in more detail.

Plans? I'd imagined the threesome unfolding spontaneously. But now I'm goal oriented. If that's what she needs, I'll do it.

At our second meeting, her insecurities surface: Do I think this counts as cheating on her boyfriend? ("Of course not!") What kind of women does my husband like? ("Brunettes!")

We lay down ground rules for the threesome. To avoid it becoming too thrusty and pornlike, the two of us will be in charge. My husband won't make a move unless we allow it. She and I will go to the small, furnished apartment that he uses as an office, and he'll join us there once we're ready.

"Do you think he'll agree to these terms?" she asks.

"He'll just be grateful to be in the room," I say.

Everything seems to be settled, but again we part without fixing a date. I send the usual lovely-to-see-you follow-up. She replies that she enjoyed it, too, but that she'd like to meet again to talk some more about our plans. I'm beginning to doubt whether she really intends to go through with the threesome. I'm also getting tired of putting on makeup every time I go to meet her, and I'm running out of dresses. Maybe I should have bought the watch.

But when I complain to my husband, he assures me that this is the normal pace of seduction.

"Obviously she's not ready yet," he says. "She has some sort of hesitation. You need to work out what it is and help her through it."

On the way to my third meeting with N., I decide to loosen up and become less calculating. I tease her about all the planning we're doing, and joke that I'm going to have to script our threesome using storyboards and cue cards. I confess that this is all a rather big deal for me; she says the same. For a while, I even forget that I'm trying to get her into bed. We coquettishly call each other N. and P.

This new playful mood seems to be what was missing for her. After about an hour, she takes out her calendar. We schedule the threesome for a week later, the twentieth, over lunchtime.

When I get home, Simon is waiting up for me.

"I decided to just be myself," I tell him.

"Oh, no," he says.

I share the good news that we have an actual date for our three-some. To keep his expectations in check, I mention potential glitches, including the fact that her father is eighty-six.

"So? He won't be there, will he?"

"You know there's a possible problem," I say.

"He might hand in his dinner pail? Drop off his perch? Buy a one-way ticket? The best for us would be if he checked out of the hotel on the twenty-first, earliest."

A week later, N.'s father is fine and I'm getting ready to meet her. "I have a threesome in two hours," I keep telling myself. I'm not going to die an idiot.

I meet N. at a café for a quick coffee, then we head to my husband's office around the corner. On the way, I insist that we stop at a little food stand to buy supplies, in case we work up an appetite later. Clearly, I'm shopping to calm my nerves.

But when we get up to the office, it's N. who's nervous.

"You're in charge, okay?" she says. I don't especially want to be the boss of the threesome, either, and we're both relieved when my husband arrives. They introduce themselves, and he's immediately very physical with her, which breaks the ice. We have a sort of group hug, and then we agree that he can take off both of our dresses.

My first surprise is that women are allowed to wear jewelry in bed. N. even keeps her large hoop earrings on. My second is that a three-some is so, well, sexual. I'd focused so much on the logistics and the catering, I had almost forgotten that we were all going to be naked.

My third surprise is that when you're detail oriented like me, three-somes are confusing. You quickly lose track of who's at which stage. There's a lot of ambiguous moaning. My husband tells me afterward that he got a little lost, too.

It's a polite threesome. I get the sense that we're all trying to divide our attention equitably, so there's no clear twosome or onesome. Occasionally, N. and I ask each other, "How are you doing?" like concerned friends.

After about forty minutes, I've had enough. I wonder whether I might check my email. N. is quite beautiful, but seeing versions of my own lady parts on her feels too familiar. I realize that part of what appeals to me about men is that their bodies are different.

I try to stay attentive—it's a birthday present, after all—but soon I'm just scratching both of their backs while they continue. When I glance at the clock again, I'm surprised to see that only an hour has passed. I had no idea that sex could last so long.

Finally, they tire themselves out. There's a sweet moment at the end when the three of us lie together under the covers, with the birthday boy in the middle. He's beaming. I'll later get a series of heartfelt thank-you notes from him, saying it was as good as he had hoped. "It affirmed for me how much I like the female form. When you have two, it accentuates that."

N. seems pleased, too. As we walk home together, she says she's surprised by how erotic she found the whole experience, especially being with me. She hints that she'd like a repeat performance.

I'm flattered, but I'm not planning on it. My own birthday is coming up, and I would like a watch.

You know you're a fortysomething *man* when . . .

- You're jealous of your young son's firm urine stream.

- A good night is when you only wake up twice to pee.

- Some of your favorite athletes are the sons of guys who used to be your favorite athletes.

- Your last friend who was still trying to pick up people in nightclubs has finally given up.

- You appreciate the beauty of people in their twenties, but you know for a fact that you'll have little in common with them.

- You're no longer willing to sleep on anyone's couch.

8

how to be mortal

AS A SEXUAL EXPERIENCE, the threesome is okay. As a literary experience, it's life changing. In my essay about it, I stop trying to sound like an omniscient narrator, which was always an awkward fit for someone like me. I focus instead on describing my limited perspective as precisely as possible. In other words, I just decide to be myself.

When I email the essay to my editor, she replies right away.

"People who read this will want to be your friend," she writes. I'm so excited by her response, and by finding this new way to write, that I decide to put my name on it. Simon considers this a small price to pay for the best birthday of his life.

The magazine runs the essay at three thousand words, practically without changing anything. Not every reader wants to befriend me. But something even better happens: after reading the piece, people feel like they know me a bit. I can't always connect with others in real life, but at least I've learned to be myself with them on the page.

There are awkward moments. A friend of my father's discovers the magazine in a dentist's waiting room and shows it to him. (My dad compliments me on the writing.) Simon's male friends and colleagues keep emailing to congratulate him, but his family—who I'd thought were comfortable discussing everything—never mention it. A few women I know complain that I've raised the bar on spousal gifts: their husbands are now demanding fortieth-birthday threesomes, too.

The essay also gives me a sudden sex appeal. Men who'd never even flirted with me now smile knowingly, or make lingering eye contact. Several women hint that they'd have been up for a threesome, had I approached them about it. ("I'm ready," my husband says about each potential offer.) Even my therapist seems to find me more interesting. When I change the subject from the threesome, he steers me back to it.

"You were saying how great it was," he says.

"I didn't say it was great," I reply. (He later admits that he looked up the essay online.)

Fired up from this experience, I spend most of the next eighteen months at my computer, finishing my book. It's about what I've learned from observing how the French raise children. I hardly see friends, I hand over most parenting duties to my husband, and I eat a disturbing amount of cake. (It's a little-known fact that writing books makes you fat.) For the first time since moving to France, I even skip the *soldes*, the twice-annual sales in Parisian shops. I don't even take time off to treat the head lice that I seem to have caught from my children. I just sit at my computer for hours, scratching my scalp.

One April day, after consuming an entire panettone, I press "send" on an email containing my entire manuscript. There will still be another six months of edits, but the bulk of the work is done.

Ten minutes later, I collapse into bed. For months, I'd been running on adrenaline and carbohydrates. Now I realize that my whole body aches, especially my back. I sleep for twelve hours and barely leave my bed for two days.

When I finally get up, the pain in my back is still there. I assume this is because I've just spent an unnatural amount of time hunched over my desk. I order a footrest and a new computer screen that forces me to sit upright. I also go across town to see my doctor, who advises me to get a massage.

I get many massages, but the pain worsens. Within a few months I can't lift my sons or turn my head more than a few millimeters to either side. Soon the pain keeps me awake at night. When one of the boys flings himself onto my lap, it hurts so much I weep.

At the end of August, lumps appear on either side of my groin. I go back to the same doctor who, four months earlier, had recommended massage. When she sees the lumps, she looks panicked. She immediately orders blood tests and sends me to an internist, who has the unruly hair and frazzled bedside manner of a mad scientist. He reads the test results and says, in heavily accented English, "You 'ave some-ting *veee-ry* seee-rious." He says he doesn't know what it is.

I spend the next few weeks getting more tests. I soon know the French for MRI—it's *IRM*—and I lie facedown on a table as a doctor extracts bone marrow—the impossible to pronounce *moelle osseuse*—from my hip. (The doctor is a ringer for the silver-haired Dominique de Villepin, France's foreign minister during the Iraq War.) A few days later, I watch as a different doctor carries away a glass dish containing one of my lymph nodes; it looks like a glistening red jelly bean.

I spend my days on the Paris *métro*, holding oversized plastic bags that contain my various scans. (In America the doctors keep them; in France the patient does.) Whenever I show the slightest worry, doctors offer me prescriptions for Xanax. Soon I'm sharing the little white pills with Simon, and neither of us can sleep without them.

As all of this is happening, I'm editing my book. On the same day that I send back the corrected proofs, I lie in a PET scan—in French it's called a *TEP scan-NER*—as a man's voice issues instructions in French: "Don't breathe." "Don't move." I've only just figured out how to be the decider. Inside that tube, I realize that I no longer am.

I arrive home from all these procedures in time to cook dinner. Even before whatever is happening happened, my husband and I were overwhelmed by our responsibilities. Now, when three children come rushing into our bedroom each morning at seven a.m., we face both the exhaustion of living through this and the terror that I won't.

Usually I'm keen to talk to Simon about everything, and he's irked by my endless need to analyze our relationship. Now all I can bear to discuss is the timing of my next appointment. For the first time, we've entered a realm where words can't go.

Finally, we're summoned to the hospital for my diagnosis. We sit in front of a large desk as two physicians, including the Dominique de Villepin look-alike, examine papers for several minutes. When the men finally speak to us, they describe my symptoms, but they don't say what I have.

Finally, I interrupt.

"Is it cancer?" I ask. (This is the same word as in English but pronounced "can*cer*.") Both doctors seem relieved that I've broken the ice. One of them says that, yes, it's a blood cancer called *lymphome non hodgkinien*—non-Hodgkin's lymphoma.

After he says this, I have the sensation that I'm falling back in my chair in slow motion. It's as if I'm sinking without moving. This must be what people mean when they say they're "reeling."

Though I've just spent several weeks in a state of terror, I still have to rearrange my brain to accommodate this new fact: I'm not in pain because I sat incorrectly at my desk. I'm in pain because I have cancer in the bones of my back. One of the doctors says I must immediately begin a three-month course of chemotherapy and immunotherapy.

Simon and I have never discussed the worst-case scenario. But in the courtyard of the hospital, I ask him to tell me what his plan is, in case I die. I know he must have one. He's quiet for a moment. "We'll move to London, to be near my sister," he says.

No one at my publisher has any idea that I'm ill, or that I've been editing my manuscript in doctors' waiting rooms. I'm afraid that if they find out, they'll panic and pull back on the publicity. And I reason that, thus far, my illness hasn't interfered with my work.

But I still need a photo for the book jacket, and I will have to take it before my hair falls out. So the day before my first round of chemotherapy, I meet a photographer at a café in my neighborhood. He snaps a picture of me reaching for a cup of espresso and staring confidently into the camera.

As a journalist, I usually over-research everything. But with this illness I don't. In fact, I barely grasp what's happening inside my body. I can't remember which blood cells I have too many of, and which I don't have enough of. Just as I'd been feeling more grown up, the illness infantilized me. I have no choice but to throw myself into the care of my doctors and trust them to heal me.

And yet, I also feel a kind of adult calm. I can see it in the jacket photo. This is the most consequential situation I've ever faced. The bad news isn't patio-distance away anymore; it's inside of me. And I suddenly know one thing very clearly: if it was just me, I could cope with dying. But it isn't. And because of that, I have to survive. I have to raise these children. I cannot leave Simon to do it alone.

When I learn that a public hospital near my house specializes in treating blood cancers, I ditch the fancy private hospital across town and go to the public one instead. Gone are the English-speaking secretaries and valet parking. The state hospital was built by Henry IV in the seventeenth century to house victims of the plague. It's no-frills, clean and efficient. My doctor there is a stern, pretty blond woman who listens patiently as I try to pronounce *lymphome non hodgkinien*.

I arrive for my first treatment—reassuringly called a *cure* in French—wearing a fashionable terry-cloth sweatshirt, shredded jeans and black running shoes. It's a deliberate fashion choice: I look like a hipster, and hipsters don't die. A secretary directs me to an outpatient unit called the *hôpital de jour*, which makes me think of soup. I watch American sitcoms on my laptop to distract myself, as a nurse inserts a needle into my arm.

One immediate effect of chemotherapy is that I lose weight. For the first time in my adult life, I can eat an enormous bowl of pasta in cream sauce for dinner, then wake up to discover I've lost a pound.

By my second treatment, I'm panicked over a hard bump that has appeared at the base of my spine. The on-duty oncologist inspects it, then laughs. "That's your bone," she says. "You were too fat to feel it before."

Getting ill is a crash course in other minds. I learn that there are people who secretly love bad news, and that certain women will be jealous of how skinny you are, no matter what's causing it. A surprising number of people urge me to get a pedicure. The woman who'd worn a white dress to my wedding doesn't contact me at all.

I'm surprised by the sheer variety of inappropriate reactions to my illness. Several friends note the exciting coincidence: someone they know died of exactly the same disease! A former classmate informs me that cancer is caused by "emotion," and that it can be cured by eating miso soup. One woman walks into my house, wails like Antigone in front of my children, then envelops me in a painful embrace. Another friend warns, "Don't read the statistics!" making it clear that he already has.

And yet other people, some of whom had been just acquaintances before my diagnosis, make me feel like they are literally holding me aloft above despair. I relate best to those who have been through major illnesses, too: a man who had a heart attack; a former colleague who was hospitalized twice for depression; a childhood friend who's being treated for breast cancer. They feel like wartime comrades.

And I'm moved to see that—though I can be awkward and distant—some people are fond of me anyway. A woman from my book group drops off a lasagna. Relatives in Florida send a cozy throw blanket for me to wrap myself in. (I highly recommend this as a get-well gift.) Even N., my threesome partner, offers to babysit, though I decline.

I hesitate to disclose my illness to my friend whose boyfriend writes for the *New Yorker* and who'd witnessed my failed fortieth birthday party. New York's literary world is tiny, and word could get back to my publisher. But when I finally tell her, they're both exceptionally caring. The boyfriend puts me in touch with an American blood-cancer specialist he knows. My friend gives me a soft black beret that once belonged to her grandfather.

I wear the beret everywhere, to cover my thinning hair. I've decided that, instead of shaving it off the way cancer patients do in the movies, I'll just let it fall out. I'd like to keep at least some hair as long as possible. And I like the poetic way that, in French, they say your hair is "falling."

Soon there's a very unpoetic coating of highlighted blond hair on all my coats and sweaters. It mostly falls from a circle on the top of my head, like male pattern baldness. The remaining hair is too fragile to brush or wash, so it gathers into ropelike clumps. By about eight weeks into chemo, I look like Larry David with dreadlocks. Simon is so unnerved by the sight of my uncovered head, he asks me to wear the beret to bed.

Every three weeks, I walk to the hospital for another *cure*. When an attending doctor discovers that I'm a writer, he gives me the manuscript of his novel. It's about a young woman with cancer who dies at the end of the book.

At my next *cure*, I hand the manuscript back to him. "Just one suggestion," I say. "Don't kill the protagonist."

The editor of my book still doesn't know about my illness, but she's growing worried about something else: publishing a parenting book by someone who's had a well-publicized ménage à trois. I remind her that the essay isn't a salacious exposé *about* me; it's an essay that I wrote about myself. There's hardly even any sex in it. (Curiously, the essay doesn't bother my British editor at all.) A publicist calls from New York to coach me on how to respond if journalists question me about the threesome. She suggests saying, "Yes, I tried that. But I didn't really like it."

I'm mostly worried about doing a book tour while bald. My mother flies to Paris and shops for wigs with me. At a store near the Paris opera, a saleswoman ushers us into a private room, then brings out a series of expensive real-hair wigs. She assures us that they're made from European hair, "not Indonesian," and she keeps forgetting what kind of cancer I have. I opt for a synthetic blond bob, both because it seems less racist and because it's a third of the price.

We also shop for clothes for my book tour. Before my treatment, I was an American size six—not overweight, but far from the Parisian ideal. When I tried on outfits, French saleswomen would ask neutrally, "What do you think?"

Now I'm barely a size two. When I emerge from dressing rooms at this size—even wearing the beret—they smile approvingly and suggest adding belts to sweaters and blazers. I'm used to choosing clothes based on whether or not they make me look fat. Now, for the first time in my adult life, nothing does. I buy a flurry of tight minidresses and belt-able jackets, simply because I can.

My mother and I discuss my illness a bit, but mostly she's just patient and present. I realize that there's something hopeful about shopping, the activity we've always done together. Buying clothes implies that there will be a future in which to wear them. Though when I choose a black dress—a short-sleeved sweater attached to a high-waisted silk skirt, which I'll wear in publicity photos—it crosses my mind that I might also be buried in it.

When the publicist calls to say that I'm booked on a morning TV show in America, the strain of keeping my secret becomes too much.

"I need to tell you something," I say. I deliver my news in a breathless, detached rush, since if I slow down, I'll cry. I explain that my chemotherapy is scheduled to end a few weeks before the book comes out.

Everyone at the publishing house is extremely kind. They're also still concerned about the threesome essay. I reassure them that if anyone grills me about the threesome, I'll pivot and mention the cancer.

Anyway, my parenting advice now boils down to two words: don't die. I've told my kids I'm sick but that I'm getting treatment to make me better. And this is true. Midway through chemotherapy, I'm no longer in agonizing back pain. For the first time in months, I can turn my head.

I wear the black beret everywhere. "My mother is bold," my awkwardly bilingual daughter announces, whenever she catches me without it.

In January, a few days after my final *cure*, I have another PET scan. It's the one that will show whether the treatments have worked. I lie in the tube and obey the Frenchman's voice. A week later, Simon and I head through freezing rain to drop the kids at their school. Then we rush to the hospital to meet with the blond doctor, who will give us the scan's results. When we walk into her office, she smiles for the first time since we met her. She begins talking before we even sit down.

"I have very good news for you," she says. I'm in *rémission complète*— complete remission. This time, I have no trouble understanding the French.

A few weeks later, I have my head shaved, which I instantly realize I should have done months earlier. Then I fly to New York to launch my book. I'm not used to wearing the wig, so just before I go on the morning show, I decide to put the beret on top of it. It's my comfort object, and makes me feel less jittery. (I may have just survived cancer, but I'm still nervous before going on live TV.) The combination of wig and beret makes me look like a Satmar Hasidic wife, or an undernourished Basque peasant. Viewers assume that I'm trying to look "French."

"Lose the beret," my agent texts me, as soon as I'm off the air. In the show's online chatrooms, strangers gleefully inform me that berets haven't been in fashion in France for seventy-five years. (As a resident of Paris for a decade, I did know this.)

But I'm cheered when one reviewer describes me—or at least my literary persona—as "likable." And I get notes from strangers who say that after reading the book, they feel like they know me. What I know is that I'm forty-one years old, and I'm alive. And I'm on my way to becoming a person.

You know you're in your forties when . . .

- You can tell when something is ridiculous.

- You can calm someone down.

- You realize that you can manipulate people, and that some of them have long been manipulating you.

- You're loyal but watchful.

- You know that extreme jealousy is a deal breaker.

- You're surprised to realize that someone is flirting with you. You had written yourself off too soon.

how to be an expert

TO MY ASTONISHMENT, my parenting book becomes an immediate best seller and takes on a life of its own. After a reading at a bookstore in Manhattan, two young women holding babies approach me with strange expressions on their faces. It takes me a minute to work out what these expressions mean: they're nervous about meeting me.

Not everyone likes the book, but it becomes part of the cultural conversation. I'm spoofed by the *New Yorker* and mocked by *Forbes* (in an article titled "No thanks. I'd rather raise a billionaire.") A TV news show in Oregon runs a segment about a mother who imposes all-French practices on her unwitting children, complete with forbiddingly gourmet meals. Online, I discover an animated Taiwanese video in which an Asian-looking woman in a beret, who's supposed to be me, drinks red wine and teaches her child to paint the *Mona Lisa*. A lady Skypes me from Mongolia to say that she wants to publish a translation there. People around the world write to ask me for parenting advice. Hardly anyone mentions the threesome essay.

It's a small jolt of minor fame. But it means that, practically overnight, I'm no longer an obscure journalist begging for work. I'm now considered an expert.

Am I really one? It's one thing to go on TV for a few minutes, to sum up my book for people who probably don't know much about France. But I panic when I'm invited to address the French department of a major American university. Can I convincingly make my case for an hour in front of actual experts? I did lots of research for the book, as a journalist. But at this talk, I'll be speaking to professors and graduate students, all of whom study France, and some of whom are French themselves. I'm an amateur anthropologist; some of them are real ones. I suspect that they've invited me there to humiliate me.

Just before the talk starts, I drink several espressos and stress-eat a package of M&M's. I hope to compensate, in caffeinated energy, for what I lack in academic rigor. The large room is packed with dozens of people. Some are standing in the rear. There are recording devices everywhere. I sit down at the front and a professor introduces me.

For the next hour, I answer questions from the audience and explain the main ideas of my book. Their tone is curious, friendly and even respectful. No one challenges my credentials or seems intent on skewering me. Soon there's applause, and the professor invites everyone upstairs for a glass of wine. At the reception, he's pleased, and says it obviously went well. Graduate students approach me with that same nervous look I'd seen at the reading.

I'm amazed. Is the bar for expertise lower than I'd thought? Are people projecting grown-up-ness onto me, to reassure themselves that someone knows what's going on? Or am I suffering from imposter syndrome, and I know more than I'd imagined?

Not long into my tenure as a so-called expert, I realize that some of the people whom I considered experts—and by extension grownups—are dogged by self-doubt, too. This is especially true in academia, where you're judged almost entirely on your intellect. Through friends, I meet a professor named Amy, who attended top schools, teaches at a major American university and regularly publishes in academic journals.

"I'm a fake intellectual," Amy tells me over a glass of wine. "I feel like I have a surface-level knowledge about a number of things. I can see this tiny little piece, like I have tunnel vision; I can't see the larger significance." She feels surrounded by people who know more than she does and who have a better grasp of their topics. "If what an academic is supposed to do is change the way people think about the world, I can't do it."

Amy is up for tenure soon but predicts she won't get it. "And I think they'd be right not to give me tenure; I'm not that good," she says.

Not all academics feel this way, of course. I meet another professor, Keith, who remembers exactly when he began to feel like an expert in his field, philosophy. As a graduate student, he considered his professors to be capable of a kind of intellectual alchemy. They could draw on both the history of the field and on the particulars of various philosophical problems. In lectures, they wove all these strands together. When you're a student, he tells me, "You don't see yourself as an immature version of them. You're like, 'How could I ever possibly become that?'"

About three years into his doctoral program, Keith was teaching a class of undergraduates when one of them asked him a hard question that was only tangentially related to the lesson. Without much effort, Keith responded with a thoughtful, layered answer that relied on a broad understanding of the field. He handled a follow-up question the same way. He was doing the same kind of alchemy as his teachers.

"I remember walking back to my office after that class and thinking to myself, 'Oh! That was a moment when I was an expert.'" He says he felt like a grown-up, too.

I'm cheered to meet someone who can pinpoint his own passage beyond apprenticeship. But when I retell Keith's story to some other academics, they're unimpressed.

"He's a grown-up because he knows how to bullshit?" an English professor says dryly.

My father-in-law, Simon's dad, tells me I've given too much credence to people with advanced degrees. "Competence in some kind of boring professional thing has no relation to mature insight into yourself, understanding the world, understanding other people. It's got nothing to do with being a grown-up."

Apparently, I've mistaken professional expertise for wisdom. It's not the former that makes you a grown-up, it's the latter. Or perhaps I've made a different error: I've mistaken being a grown-up for being a man.

Once I take the mystery out of expertise, I realize that I've done my research and I know enough to make my case. But I still feel a kind of sobriety and detachment. Very recently, I was lying in a tube wondering whether I'd survive. I'm still getting infusions of an immunotherapy drug every three months as a maintenance treatment.

I'm glad to be planning Dutch and Russian book tours, and to give a practically endless procession of interviews. I'm pleased each time a parent tells me that the French approach helped her baby sleep. And for someone who's socially awkward, a book is a useful letter of introduction. I don't have to struggle as hard to connect in social settings. People who've read it often feel like they've preconnected with me. My task is just not to muck up their good impression.

But I've just seen my life change in an instant, twice, so I'm careful not to grow attached to my new professional status. I'm facing my small success the same way I faced being in that tube: by listening to the voices and remaining calm.

What really affects me is the book itself. It's a relief to have finally done something well. When I was younger, people assured me that I had potential. In my thirties, I wondered whether I would ever realize it.

When I handed in my first book, in my midthirties, I immediately wished that I could start over and rewrite it. The reviews were mixed, and practically no one read it. Another book like the first one would probably have meant the end of being an author and back to begging editors for piecework. Simon later confessed that he feared for my career, and dreaded having a bitter wife who couldn't help pay the bills.

When I handed in the second book, on parenting, I felt that I'd written the strongest book I could. I didn't want to change anything. In my forties, I was no longer banking on my potential. I was finally doing my best work.

For all of the book's flaws, I'd also taken the adult step of having a perspective and defending it. For me, this was progress. I'd grown up learning never to get to the heart of things. And yet, I'd now gone deep into a complicated topic and pulled its strands apart.

And having been inside that tube, with my insides exposed, I know myself better. I'd spent my life imagining worst-case scenarios. Now I know that when one of those scenarios happens, I can handle it. I won't disintegrate. I walked home from my treatments and cooked dinner for my kids. I also didn't run back to America, assuming everything must be better there. I stayed in France, trusting another country with my very existence. And when it was over, I didn't want to change husbands or radically change anything. I emerged calm, and grateful for my life, and wanting it all even more.

You know you're in your forties when . . .

- You can detect when someone's lifestyle requires a trust fund.

- You understand that even a small job is important to someone, so you should do it well.

- Your retired high school teachers, who once seemed godlike, now want to network with you.

- When you watch *The Graduate*, you identify with the parents.

- When you meet someone extremely charming, you're not seduced—you're suspicious.

how to have a
midlife crisis

THE MIDLIFE CRISIS WAS INVENTED in London in 1957.

That's when a forty-year-old Canadian named Elliott Jaques stood before a meeting of the British Psycho-Analytical Society and read aloud from a paper he'd written. Addressing about a hundred people, Jaques claimed that people in their midthirties typically experience a depressive period lasting several years.

Jaques (pronounced "Jacks")—a physician and psychoanalyst—said he'd identified this phenomenon by studying the lives of great artists, in whom it takes an extreme form. In ordinary people symptoms could include religious awakenings, promiscuity, a sudden inability to enjoy life, "hypochondriacal concern over health and appearance" and "compulsive attempts" to remain young.

This period is sparked by the realization that their lives are halfway over, and that death isn't just something that happens to other people: it will happen to them, too. He described a depressed thirty-six-year-old patient who told his therapist, "Up till now, life has seemed an endless upward slope, with nothing but the distant horizon in view.

Now suddenly I seem to have reached the crest of the hill, and there stretching ahead is the downward slope with the end of the road in sight—far enough away it's true—but there is death observably present at the end." (Perhaps he was recalling the German philosopher Arthur Schopenhauer, who wrote in the nineteenth century: "When we are ascending the hill of life, death is not visible: it lies down at the bottom of the other side. But once we have crossed the top of the hill, death comes in view—death, which, until then, was known to us only by hearsay.")

Jaques didn't claim to be the first to detect this midlife change. He pointed out that, in the fourteenth century, Dante Alighieri's protagonist in *The Divine Comedy*—who scholars say is thirty-five—famously declares at the beginning of the book, "Midway upon the journey of our life / I found myself within a forest dark / For the straightforward pathway had been lost." Jaques called this "the opening scene of a vivid and perfect description of the emotional crisis of the midlife phase."

But Jaques offered a modern, clinical explanation, and—crucially— he gave it a name: the "mid life crisis."

As he addressed the meeting in London, Jaques was nervous. Many of the leading psychoanalysts of the day were sitting in the audience, including the society's president, Donald Winnicott, renowned for his theory of transitional objects, and Jaques's own mentor, the famed child psychologist Melanie Klein.

It was an acrimonious group, which had split into competing factions. Attendees were known to pounce on presenters during the questioning period. And Jaques wasn't just presenting an abstract theory. He later told an interviewer that the depressed thirty-six-year-old patient he described in the paper was himself.

When he finished reading the paper, titled "The Mid Life Crisis," Jaques paused and waited to be attacked. Instead, after a very brief discussion, "there was dead silence," he recalled later. "Which was very, very embarrassing, nobody got up to speak. This was new, this is absolutely rare." The next day, Melanie Klein tried to cheer him up, saying, "If there's one thing the Psychoanalytic Society cannot cope with, it's the theme of death."

Chastened, Jaques put "The Mid Life Crisis" aside. He went on to write about far less personal topics, including a theory of time and work. "I was certainly utterly convinced that the paper was a complete failure," he recalled.

But he didn't forget how it felt to be that troubled man standing on the crest of the hill. About six years later, he submitted the paper to *The International Journal of Psychoanalysis*, which published it in its October 1965 issue under the title "Death and the Mid-life Crisis."

This time, instead of silence, there was an enormous appetite for Jaques's theory. The midlife crisis was now aligned with the zeitgeist.

If you were a man born in 1900, you had only about a 50 percent chance of living to age sixty. The average life expectancy for men was around fifty-two. It was fair to think of age forty as the beginning of the end.

But life spans in rich countries were increasing by about 2.3 years per decade. Someone born in the 1930s had nearly an 80 percent chance of living until age sixty. That gave age forty a new vitality. *Life Begins at Forty* was the best-selling American nonfiction book of 1933. Walter Pitkin, the journalist who wrote it, explained that "before the Machine Age, men wore out at forty." But thanks to industrialization, new medicines and electric dishwashers, "men and women alike turn from the ancient task of *making a living* to the strange new task of *living.*"

By the time Elliott Jaques published "Death and the Mid-life Crisis" in 1965, the average life expectancy in Western countries had climbed to about seventy. It made sense to change your life in your thirties or forties, because you could expect to live long enough to enjoy your new career or your new spouse.

And it was getting easier to change your life. Women were going to work in record numbers, giving them more financial independence. Middle-class professionals were entering psychotherapy and couples counseling in record numbers and trying to understand themselves. People were starting to treat marriage not just as a romantic institution, but as the source of their self-actualization. Divorce rules were loosening, and the divorce rate was about to surge.

There was dramatic social upheaval, from the civil rights movement to the birth control pill. It wasn't just individuals who had midlife crises. The whole society seemed to be having one, too.

The idea that a midlife crisis is inevitable soon jumped from Jaques's academic paper to popular culture. And according to the new conventional wisdom, the forties were the prime time for this to occur. In her 1967 book, *The Middle-Age Crisis*, writer Barbara Fried claimed the crisis is "a normal aspect of growth, as natural for Forties as teething is for a younger age group."

The midlife crisis, which had scarcely existed five or six years earlier, was suddenly treated like a biological inevitability that could possess and even kill you. "A person in the throes . . . does not even know that something is happening inside his body, a physical change that is affecting his emotions," a 1971 *New York Times* article explained. "Yet he is plagued with indecision, restlessness, boredom, a 'what's the use' outlook and a feeling of being fenced in."

The crisis soon expanded from Jaques's original definition to include practically any inner strife. You could have a midlife crisis because you'd achieved everything you'd intended to, but couldn't see the point of it all. Or you could have one because you hadn't achieved enough.

Management theorists urged companies to be sensitive to their crisis-stricken workers. In 1972, a US government task force warned that midlife crises may be causing an uptick in the death rate of men aged thirty-five to forty. "A general feeling of obsolescence appears to overtake middle managers when they reach their late thirties. Their careers appear to have reached a plateau, and they realize that life from here on will be a long and inevitable decline."

Despite some biological claims, the midlife crisis was mainly viewed as a middle- and upper-class affliction. Classic sufferers were white, professional and male, with the leisure time to ruminate on their personal development and the means to afford sports cars and mistresses. People who were working-class or black weren't supposed to self-actualize. Women were assumed to be on a separate schedule set by marriage, menopause and when their children left home.

But women soon realized that the midlife crisis contained a kind of liberation story, in tune with the nascent women's movement: if you hated your life, you could change it. This idea found a perfect messenger in Gail Sheehy.

Sheehy was the daughter of a Westchester advertising executive. She had obediently studied home economics, married a doctor and had a baby. But that life didn't suit her. By the early 1970s, she was divorced and working as a journalist.

In January 1972, Sheehy was on an assignment in Northern Ireland when the young Catholic protester she was interviewing got shot in the face. The shock of this near-death experience soon combined with the shock of entering her midthirties. "Some intruder shook me by the psyche and shouted: Take stock! Half your life has been spent."

Researchers she spoke to explained that panicking at thirty-five is normal, since adults go through developmental periods just like children do. Sheehy traveled around America interviewing educated middle-class men and women, ages eighteen to fifty-five, about their lives. In the summer of 1976 she published a nearly four-hundred-page book called *Passages: Predictable Crises of Adult Life*. By that August, it was the *New York Times*'s number one nonfiction best seller, and it remained in the top ten for over a year. I remember seeing its rainbow-striped cover on my mother's nightstand.

Sheehy had gone hunting for midlife crises in America, and she'd found them. "A sense of stagnation, disequilibrium, and depression is predictable as we enter the passage to midlife," she writes in *Passages*. People can expect to feel "sometimes momentous changes of perspective, often mysterious dissatisfactions with the course they had been pursuing with enthusiasm only a few years before." Ages thirty-seven to forty-two are "peak years of anxiety for practically everyone." She said these crises happen to women, too.

With Sheehy's book, an idea that had been gathering force for a decade simply became a fact of life. Soon there were midlife crisis mugs, T-shirts and a board game that challenged players, Can You Survive Your Mid-Life Crisis Without Cracking Up, Breaking Up, or Going Broke?

But were midlife crises actually happening?

The anthropologist Stanley Brandes had his doubts. As he approached age forty himself, he noticed that all the self-help books in his local bookshop, in Berkeley, warned that he was about to experience a major life upheaval.

Brandes thought about Margaret Mead's classic 1928 book, *Coming of Age in Samoa*, in which Mead argues that Americans expect teenage girls to have an adolescent crisis, and many of them do. But she observed that Samoans don't expect the teenage years to be filled with emotional upheaval, and in Samoa they aren't.

Brandes reasoned that the midlife crisis might be a cultural construct, too. "It was kind of a trick that my culture was playing on me, and I didn't have to feel that way," he decided, laying out his theory in the 1985 book *Forty: The Age and the Symbol*.

Brandes didn't have much data to go on, but soon researchers were analyzing findings from studies including a massive one called "Midlife in the United States," or MIDUS, that began in 1995. What did all this reveal about the midlife crisis?

"Most people don't have a crisis," says Margie Lachman of Brandeis University, a member of the original MIDUS team. Lachman says midlifers are typically healthy, have busy social lives and are at the earnings peaks of their careers, so "people are pretty satisfied."

Some of those who report having a midlife crisis are "crisis prone" or highly neurotic, Lachman says. They have crises throughout their lives, not just in midlife. And about half the people who have midlife crises say it's related to a life event like a health problem, a job loss or a divorce, not to aging per se.

Just 10 to 20 percent of Americans have an experience that qualifies as a midlife crisis, according to MIDUS and other data.

As this data rolled in, most scientists abandoned the idea that the midlife crisis is caused by biological changes. They regarded it mostly as a cultural construct. The same mass media that had once heralded the midlife crisis began trying to debunk it, in dozens of news stories with variations on the headline "Myth of the Midlife Crisis."

But the idea was too delicious to be debunked. It had become part of the Western middle-class narrative, offering a fresh, self-actualizing story about how life is supposed to go.

Another reason for the idea's success, Margie Lachman says, is that people like attaching names to life stages, such as the "terrible twos" for toddlers. In fact, she says, "Most people I know say their two-year-olds are delightful." The midlife crisis persists, in part, because it has a very catchy name.

Elliott Jaques watched with amazement the avalanche that his paper caused. Requests for reprints of "Death and the Midlife Crisis" came in from around the world.

Jaques had long since moved on to other topics. He became a specialist in workplace relations, and devised a way to measure workers according to the amount of time they're given to complete tasks. He consulted for the US Army and the Church of England about their organizational structures, and wrote more than twenty books. He never wrote about the midlife crisis again.

Jaques died in 2003. His second wife, Kathryn Cason, who co-founded an organization dedicated to propagating Jaques's ideas about the workplace, told me that the midlife crisis was "a tiny little early piece of work that he did" and something Jaques "didn't want to talk about after twenty or thirty years." She urged me to read his later writings.

I have to admit that I never did. Jaques had lots of big ideas, but the whole world was mostly interested in his small one. The headline of his obituary in the *New York Times* read "Elliott Jaques, 86, Scientist Who Coined 'Midlife Crisis.'"

You know you're in your *mid*forties when . . .

- Your feet have mysteriously grown a size.

- People you consider to be old now treat you like a peer. They say things like "For us it doesn't matter anymore; but for our children it does."

- You know several people who are going through menopause.

- You still don't know what "perimenopause" is, and you'd rather not know.

- You tell younger friends who are angsty about turning forty that "Forty is for amateurs."

- People pretend to be surprised that you have three kids.

how to be jung

WHEN I THINK ABOUT THE FORTIES, I'm often reminded of the movie *Gravity*, in which Sandra Bullock plays a nervous astronaut on her first mission. She's a highly trained scientist and NASA has presumably decided that she's ready to be in space. But she's petrified. She gladly takes orders from George Clooney, the brash, experienced commander who's been in space many times before. They're literally connected by a cord.

But then there's an accident, in which their spaceship is hit by debris. To give Bullock a chance to survive, Clooney unhooks himself from her and floats away. She's lost radio contact, too. She's left dangling in space, alone, with no one to give her orders or rescue her. If she wants to return safely to Earth, she'll have to figure out how to get there all by herself.

I feel like Simon has unhooked himself from me. He's had enough of being my designated grown-up. It's an imperfect analogy. Simon can't even drive a car. We're still a couple, and he doesn't make a grand pronouncement about what he's doing. But gradually, I realize that he's no longer willing to consult on the wording of my work emails, or spend an hour helping me decide whether to take a two-day business trip. ("Just go if you want to go," he huffs.) He won't spend the evening helping me decode what someone meant when she called me "complicated," or nurse my ego after I've received an especially churlish tweet.

I'm sympathetic to Simon's new stance. After all, I'm a fully trained grown-up. I'm constantly doling out advice and instructions to my kids. Slightly older friends have started sending their children to me for career guidance. Apparently, several mothers in Mongolia consider me their personal guru. (I like to think of them in a yurt, teaching their toddlers to say *"merci."*)

My own guru, Simon, has his own problems. He can't sleep properly anymore, and he barely has time to finish his work. Plus he's been traveling back and forth to see his mother, who's living in a care home in London and getting worse.

And he's grown tired of being lionized and infantilized by me, all at once. I hang on his judgments about politics and people, but gripe about his lack of practical skill. "If I ever divorce you, it will be for someone who can hang curtains," I say one night, as I'm standing on a ladder in our living room.

And I've realized that, quite often these days, I don't agree with Simon or follow his advice. I still find him immensely perceptive, but he now seems less like someone with a direct line to Platonic truth and more like an intelligent person with a particular point of view.

I'm not alone in giving up my designated grown-up in the forties. It's a hallmark of the decade. This is partly because our parents—our primordial grown-ups—are getting old. Most conversations with them now involve health care. In a 2013 study of Americans ages thirty-seven to forty-eight, nearly a third had lost one parent, and about one in ten had lost both. One in five regularly cared for an older parent or relative. These days, I hear about a friend's parent dying at the rate of about one every few months. "How are your parents?" has suddenly become a question that my contemporaries ask each other, not as a social nicety but out of real concern.

We dangling astronauts need to cope on our own, but how? In *Gravity*, Sandra Bullock first gives up in despair, then realizes she has the training to operate a spaceship by herself. She eventually makes it back to Earth—though not before looking sexy in zero gravity in a pair of boy shorts.

How do people in real life make the passage to adulthood? To find out, I begin to read about Carl Jung. Jung makes it clear, both in his writings and his life, that going out on your own isn't just biologically inevitable. It's what a person has to do in order to grow up.

Jung, the son of a pastor, was born in Switzerland in 1875. As a promising young psychiatrist working at a mental hospital in Zurich in the early 1900s, he discovered the ideas of Sigmund Freud, who was just beginning to gain prominence. The two men struck up a correspondence and were soon building the nascent field of psychoanalysis together, Freud as its inventor, and Jung—nineteen years younger—as his heir apparent. (Freud was apparently pleased to have found a non-Jewish disciple.) By 1910, Jung was the editor of the main psychoanalytic journal and president of the International Psychoanalytical Association. He described his relationship with Freud as one of "father and son."

In 1912, Jung was thirty-seven, with a thriving private practice and a teaching post at the University of Zurich. He was married to Emma, the daughter of a Swiss watch titan. The couple lived with their children in a five-thousand-square-foot house overlooking Lake Zurich that Jung had designed himself.

But Jung's differences with Freud were becoming harder to reconcile. Freud was secular and rational, and wanted psychoanalysis to be considered a science. Jung, the pastor's son, had a mystical, artistic side, and he was increasingly drawn to ancient myths and the occult. Beliefs that he had suppressed in order to become a doctor and a disciple of Freud were resurfacing as he approached age forty.

Their father-son relationship frayed. "I realized how different I am from you. This realization will be enough to effect a radical change in my whole attitude," Jung wrote to Freud in November of 1912.

"I propose that we abandon our personal relations entirely," Freud replied from Vienna six weeks later.

When he broke with Freud, Jung was effectively shunned by many in the psychoanalytic movement, and he resigned as president of the psychoanalytical association. Jung was the astronaut cut loose who needed to strike out on his own. But he had only a vague inkling of what "his own" was.

At that point, it helped that Jung was married to an heiress. He resigned from his teaching job and scaled back his private practice. He decided that he would search for universal truths by investigating the inner workings of his own mind.

For roughly six years, starting when he was about thirty-eight, Jung plunged into an inner journey in which he summoned waking visions, listened to voices and wrote down what he experienced. Sometimes he feared that he was going crazy. When World War I broke out in 1914, he believed that some of his violent visions had been premonitions. He also acquired a mistress, a former patient in her twenties whom he insisted on bringing home for Sunday dinners.

Jung finally had a breakthrough: a recurring vision of an old man named Philemon. Jung would speak to Philemon while strolling in the garden. He gradually decided that the old man represented his own inner authority. Jung had given up Freud and found a new mentor within himself. (This self-guidance was imperfect; Jung was later accused of having anti-Semitic views.)

Jung spent the rest of his life trying to understand what had happened to him during that feverish six-year period. "It has taken me virtually forty-five years to distill within the vessel of my scientific work the things I experienced and wrote down at that time," he wrote in 1961, shortly before he died. "I hit upon this stream of lava, and the fires of it reshaped my life."

Jung essentially came up with a theory of how people become grown-ups. He decided that from puberty until about age thirty-five, we're ruled by our egos. This is a volatile part of ourselves that seeks social status and approval from others. During this phase we observe conventions and build our families and careers.

But something changes around age thirty-five or forty. Like Jung did, people at this age begin to confront a part of themselves that they've kept hidden and that they're ashamed of. They may have organized their lives around trying to hide it. Jung called this hidden aspect of the personality *der Schatten*—"the shadow." The shadow, he wrote, is "the thing a person has no wish to be."

I realize that I've seen people around me confronting their shadows. A friend who'd been claiming for a decade that she was writing a novel finally admitted that she would henceforth pursue her actual talent: jewelry design.

Another woman I know, who was married with two kids, admitted to both her husband and herself that she had never been attracted to men.

Facing your shadow can be chastening, and not everyone succeeds. A brainy friend who'd shown great intellectual promise when she was younger tells me, over dinner, that she now knows that she lacks the attention span to do sustained hard work. "I'm forty-seven years old and I haven't done any of the things that people told me I would do when I was twenty-five," she says.

But facing your shadow can be energizing, too. At a talk by a forty-year-old author, someone in the audience asks him why he decided to write a detective novel. "Because I realized I'm never going to write a novel of ideas," he replies.

A friend who works in finance had been pursuing handsome, tall men for decades, in vain. In her forties, still single, she bought several vials of a handsome, tall man's sperm and used it to get pregnant.

Jung believed that once you acknowledge your shadow and bring it into the open, it loses some of its power. Your ego recedes, and another part of your personality can emerge: the self. Unlike the ego, the self is unchanging. It's a fixed, core part of a person. He calls this process "individuation."

Not everyone manages to individuate, but I've seen it happen, with good results. My friend's jewelry design business is booming. The lesbian mom divorced her husband and now has a wife. My single friend is the mother of two enormous children.

None of these people had a Jungian-style six-year crisis. It was more that, around age forty, they reckoned with the gap between their aspirational and their actual selves. They asked questions like "What is possible?" "What am I truly good at?" and "What do I actually like?" They dropped the pretense of doing what they thought they were supposed to do. And as a result, more than anything, they seem relieved.

I haven't individuated, but I've at least started to admit my shortcomings. I tell a new friend, over lunch, that I may not actually have a personality, or any fixed qualities at all. I feel that's something she should know about me before our friendship advances any further.

I brace for rejection, but instead she disagrees.

"You have qualities," she says kindly.

For now, I'll take it.

In my new status as a local author, I'm invited to a cocktail party for a library in Paris. I arrive to an unusual sight: apart from the waitstaff, I'm one of the youngest people in the room. (Most of the other guests are retirees who've donated to the library.)

I drink my first glass of champagne while listening to a speech about the Marquis de Lafayette. I'm standing near the bar nursing my second glass when I strike up a conversation with a handsome British man in his seventies. He's a local author, too.

I know exactly who he is. I read one of his books in college. When he was in his forties, and at the peak of his swagger and success, I suspect that he would have barely noticed me.

But age and the fact that I'm fizzy from the champagne have papered over the fact that he's a seventysomething "nine" and I'm a fortysomething "six." He laughs at my jokes and inquires about my writing. His attention makes me feel young and desirable, a feeling I realize that I haven't had in years.

I tell him that I'm researching the forties, but that it's a hard decade to pin down. Usually people draw a blank when I say this, but the writer's eyes light up as if he's suddenly channeling Jung.

"The forties are when you become who you are," he says. Then he leans in and adds, in a stage whisper, "And if you don't know by your forties, you never will."

We stand at the bar, smiling at each other, as gray-haired couples stroll past in evening wear. At that moment, I realize that the forties are something else, too: they're the decade when, in order to feel like the belle of the ball, you have to flirt with elderly men.

You know you're in your forties when . . .

- You've become more realistic about what things will be like. You watch videos of Burning Man, but you know that you will never actually attend Burning Man.

- You realize you're never going to be someone who sees a bowl of apples and decides to "whip up" an apple crumble.

- You've stopped pretending that you're the sort of person who meets people for drinks. You just meet them for dinner.

- You've decided that eight hours of continuous, unmedicated sleep is one of life's great pleasures. Actually, scratch "unmedicated."

12

how to get dressed

I MAY HAVE STARTED TO ACCESS my inner authority, but soon I have another problem: I no longer know what to wear. I've gained back the weight I lost during chemotherapy, but that's not the issue. It's that my body has reorganized itself. Nothing looks right on me anymore. Tight dresses look lumpier. Thin shirts look skimpier. My arms, once an asset, feel like they've been swapped with those of an aging aunt.

For the first time in my life, the wrong clothes can age me dangerously. A certain type of patterned jacket makes me look like I'm on a canasta team.

And I can no longer wear anything ironically. The printed T-shirts and a-toddler-could-wear-them-too sandals that I've sported for years now look childish beneath my midforties face. Yet innocuous basics, like a plain black dress, suddenly seem *too* basic. Anything flimsy or very cheap looks like I just fished it out of a discount bin. Most mornings, I end up standing half-naked next to a pile of discarded clothes.

I'm not alone. Friends report that more and more of their body parts need to be covered. "I have old lady legs," my friend Lucy whispers into the phone, from work, when we make a date to shop for pants.

Men my age are at a fashion crossroads, too. "Every day I pull out nine shirts with these awesome patterns, but they're all a little too tight in the gut," a forty-year-old Philadelphian tells me. (He's been jogging and keeps hoping that one day they'll fit.)

These are new problems, and we're unsure how to tackle them. Have we aged out of our own closets? Aren't we still too young to have to "dress our age"? And what would that mean if we wanted to do it? What exactly are we fortysomethings supposed to wear?

I live in one of the world's great fashion capitals. So I start looking for clues in the women my age whom I pass in the supermarket or notice at school drop-offs.

This doesn't help. The women flash by too quickly for me to discern the guiding principles of their outfits. And even when I sit opposite someone stylish for hours, I can't figure out how she conjures so much *je ne sais quoi* with a sweater and a cocktail ring.

I don't want to copy these women exactly, anyway. And even if I did, I doubt whether the same looks would work on me.

Nor can I fall back on my birthright: shopping. Though I've lived in Paris for years, I've never quite figured out how to shop here. The American boutiques I grew up with—including my mother's—were a cross between a sorority house and a therapist's couch. While trying on clothes, you'd tell the saleswoman everything you hate about yourself. Fellow shoppers would join the conversation, and soon you'd know all about their vacations, diets and divorces. Everyone understood that it went no further.

It's still that way. An American saleswoman tells me that one of her menopausal customers once lined up tubes of vaginal lubricant near the cash register, ranking them according to which ones she liked best.

"What size jeans do you wear?" a saleswoman once shouted to me from across a store.

"If I go to the bathroom first, I think I can fit into a twenty-six," I shout back.

"That's what all my customers say: 'I'm a poop away from a size twenty-six,'" she replies.

No discretion is required. In American boutiques, we women are all comrades in an epic battle to look decent. When I was a teenager, someone once walked past my mother's storefront, having gained weight and gone gray. The women inside remarked that she had "given up"—a reminder of what can happen if you surrender.

This isn't how it works in Paris. Salespeople here are courteous but distant, murmuring sizes discreetly and using the formal *vous*. Customers don't launch into neurotic soliloquies in the changing room. When I hand back a skirt that I've just tried on, and tell the young saleswoman that I'll need to lose two kilograms (about four and a half pounds) before I buy it, a chilly silence comes over her. I've apparently revealed something way too intimate.

There's practically no solidarity between customers, either. I once emerge from a dressing room at the same time as a woman who's trying on exactly the same outfit as me. As we examine ourselves, like twins, in the mirror, she doesn't even make eye contact. In French shops, women are each in their own trench, doing battle alone.

I once read that there are two kinds of shoppers: those who just see what they like and buy it, and those who need to see every possible option before they can decide. French shoppers mostly seem like the first kind. They home in on a single jacket or pair of pants, examine themselves silently in it, then either buy it or not.

And shopping isn't just for ladies here. A woman's husband might observe from a couch while she tries on clothes, then discuss the merits of a jacket with her in hushed tones. It's not emasculating to opine on a blouse. Whereas, when I return from my shopping expeditions, Simon glances at my purchase for about a second, mumbles "nice," then turns back to his book.

Someone tells me that Parisiennes typically acquire one "signature piece" per season—a jacket or a pair of shoes that they can weave into their existing wardrobes. I resolve to do this, too, but I can't decide which piece to anoint: The green suede boots? The jumpsuits that are big this season? Perhaps a vintage fur? If I did lose those two kilograms, perhaps I could try a menswear-inspired look, like Diane Keaton in *Annie Hall*? I buy one signature piece, then another. Soon my closet is stuffed with failed attempts to find my *pièce de résistance*.

I'm the second kind of shopper, who needs to see all options. Buying clothes feels like an exploration of all my possible selves. I might walk into a store looking for jeans. But an hour later I'm in a dressing room piled with tops, shoes, dresses and bathing suits. I try on anything that strikes me, from wide-leg pants, to long dresses, to pleated skirts.

French salespeople rarely see anyone shop like this, and they're giddy at the prospect of a huge sale. But after forty-five minutes in a changing room, submerged in clothes and unexpressed self-loathing, I either rush out apologetically without buying anything, or I feel so guilty that I pluck a random sweater from the pile and pay for it.

The next day, seized with regret, I almost always want to return the sweater. In America, no one is surprised when you walk back into a store, having changed your mind.

In France, however, returns are technically permitted but actively discouraged. When I once try to return an unworn scarf at a French department store, the salesman dramatically sniffs the length of it for evidence of my scent, then demands to know what the problem is. I eventually discover a retort—usually a lie—that instantly silences French salespeople: my husband didn't like it.

The net result of all this buying and returning is many wasted hours, with little to show for them. I still can't figure out what to put on in the morning.

———

Then I meet Bryn Taylor. Taylor is a New Jersey native who travels around America coaching men and women on how to dress. She has come to Paris to observe French fashion, and we agree to meet for coffee.

I'd expected a tiny, whiny stylist in oversized sunglasses. But Taylor is sturdy, unpretentious and tall. (Both her father and uncle played professional basketball). She has cropped black hair and wears a no-nonsense blue blazer. She says she mostly dresses her clients—many of whom are in their forties—in midpriced brands. "I came from New Jersey. We grew up in malls. I'm not really a luxury person," she explains.

Taylor says her clients often start out by insisting that they want to look "unique." "'Unique' is a word I hear more than you'd want to imagine," she tells me. But usually they can't explain what they mean by "unique," and they send Taylor photographs of outfits that have little in common with each other. "You get this whole collage of their brain, essentially. A lot of it is disjointed, not realistic. They don't know what they're responding to."

Her clients' closets sound a lot like mine. They're the accumulation of failed attempts to look unique. A woman might own twenty pairs of black pants, all of which she describes as "wrong."

And like me, Taylor's clients "say they get completely lost and confused when shopping. They are overwhelmed," Taylor says. They're no longer sure what's age appropriate, and they frequently have body-image issues. "Stomach, arms and butt are the three big ones," Taylor says. "Post-forty, I would say the majority of my clients do not like to show their arms."

Her clients are so hyperaware of what they dislike about themselves, they're not sure what they *do* like. "It's almost like they're living in a body they don't understand or recognize," she says.

This is a cultural problem. In the US and Britain, there's "anxiety at the core of fashion," writes the anthropologist Daniel Miller, who studies clothing and consumption. In our version of feminism, women expect to "make choices for themselves and not be dictated to by external pressures." In fashion, as in other realms, we don't want to be bound by our origins, our station in life or even our own bodies. Of course I don't want to buy what's on the mannequin, and Bryn Taylor's clients insist that they want to look "unique." Somewhere deep in our American (or British) minds, we think we're supposed to invent a style from scratch.

That's a tall order for ordinary women without design degrees. Most of us have trouble even describing which clothes we like. And we've created an obfuscating haze around our bodies, making it hard to see what we really look like. In one study, more than 90 percent of female college students said they did "fat talk," described as "a back-and-forth conversation where each of two healthy-weight peers denies the other is fat while claiming to be fat themselves."

And unlike in France, in the Anglophone world there's a sense that shopping for clothes is a trivial, guilty, girlish pleasure. You're not supposed to take it too seriously. When a customer can't make up her mind, I've heard a saleswoman in an American shop remind her, "It's just a dress."

We're on a quest to find ourselves through clothes, and to be unique. But we're ashamed of our bodies, too, and we suspect that caring about clothes at all is a slightly shameful secret. It's no wonder that we buy twenty pairs of the wrong pants.

Bryn Taylor's solution to the "uniqueness" problem is to ignore it. Instead, she focuses on her client's budget and body type. When she discovers an especially well-cut blazer, she might put several different women in it. If a blue blazer looks good on someone, she might add a blazer in white or in leather. (Blazers, I'm gathering, are the signature item for fortysomethings.) Likewise, if a client feels great in sheath dresses, Taylor will look for another sheath dress with a fresh detail.

A unique look eventually emerges from this process, simply because of the woman's stature, coloring and accessories. And anyway, once a client is wearing clothes that suit her, "the 'unique' thing flies out the window," Taylor says. "They were grasping at 'unique,' but they didn't know what they meant. I think they just wanted to look good."

I realize that, in her New Jersey practicality, Taylor has seized on an approach to clothes that's essentially Parisian, too. There are plenty of French women who make shopping blunders and who want to hide their upper arms. But certain cultural messages in France make shopping less traumatic.

For starters, I've never heard a Frenchwoman say she's striving to look "unique." Women here almost always say that they aspire to look "elegant" and "chic."

This is partly because French feminism aims for equal rights, but with all the codes of elegance and seduction left intact. In one TV clip, an interviewer asks Simone Veil, the French feminist who helped legalize abortion, whether she'll undo her trademark chignon so the audience can see her long hair down.

"Right away, if you'd like," Veil says with a coquettish smile, then starts removing the bobby pins.

There's nothing demeaning or superficial here about taking your appearance seriously. "For me, a loss of interest in dressing well and using makeup is a form of depression," explains Inès de la Fressange, a well-known model in her sixties who embodies the conventional wisdom of well-heeled Parisians.

Christine Lagarde, the Frenchwoman who heads the International Monetary Fund, doesn't mind discussing her fashion influences. She tells an interviewer that early in her career, she learned to dress well from a Belgian boss who was "very strong and elegant" and "always very attentive to how she looked."

Lagarde says that Americans offer a cautionary tale. "When I came to America and saw a lot of working women in the 1980s and 1990s who always dressed like men, that had an influence on me, too—to not do that."

Aiming for elegance instead of uniqueness takes off some of the pressure. There are established formulas for looking elegant and chic, in much the same way that there are recipes for making a chocolate cake. Unless you're a full-time fashion professional, why try to invent the recipe for elegance from scratch? You would probably end up having a nervous breakdown in a dressing room.

Parisiennes don't all get it right, of course. And they think it's natural to pass through periods of experimentation in your twenties and thirties. But they say that, gradually, "you find your style."

You do this, in part, by knowing your own body. Forget the blurring of fat talk. Especially as they enter their thirties and forties, French women are encouraged to make cold-eyed, pragmatic assessments of their assets and deficits. No one believes that they can wear all possible pants.

"I am lucky because I had parents who are tall and slim, and my own size has not changed," Lagarde tells an interviewer. (In her twenties Lagarde was a synchronized swimmer on France's national team.)

Carine Roitfeld, the former editor of French *Vogue* who's now in her sixties, does a similar self-critique. "I don't have a generous cleavage, but I do have nice legs and ankles, so I wear skirts," she explains. "I don't have a beautiful mouth, so I apply makeup to my eyes and don't wear lipstick."

It's easier to be a focused shopper once, like Roitfeld, you've ruled out whole categories of clothes. "I love large coats, but they're not for me—I would just look lost in them," she says. "In the end, my style comes down to a skirt closely fitting my slim waist, seamed stockings, high heels and a sweater."

Finding your style isn't just about making a spreadsheet of your strengths and weaknesses. Agathe Buchotte, owner of a Parisian boutique called AB33, tells me that it's also about "mastering your own image." This means having a sense not only of your own shape but also of your own qualities, and of what other people see when they look at you. Whatever you look like, you know it and you own it.

This explains why some women could conjure so much allure with so little. They understand themselves and they make confident, specific choices. This becomes more critical in your forties. If you're unsure where your body starts and stops, you don't know what others see in you and you're trying out all possible versions of yourself, it shows. A fortysomething who doesn't know her own shape will have trouble getting dressed in the morning.

Buchotte doesn't think it's easy to hit the mark. I've often walked past her store's front window and admired the outfits that embody the shop's haphazardly chic style. Buchotte says she often spends hours deciding what to put on the mannequins—which is all the more reason to lean on established patterns created by experts. She aims for ensembles that seem to have fallen together naturally. There's an overall harmony, but you can't point to the planning.

And the French don't just think aesthetics are important for their own sake. They assume that there's a symbiotic relationship between what you wear and your well-being. When you know yourself and you're comfortable in your own skin, it's easier to choose the right clothes. But once you're dressed in a style that suits you, you feel better.

This explains why, in the forties, classics like a "little black dress" suddenly seem *too* basic. They lack personality and definition, and make us seem like we lack these qualities, too. Now that our skin is blotchier, we can also get lost in wispy, flowery dresses and be dwarfed by prints.

Solutions vary, but one reliable choice is modern, structured clothes with clean lines and unexpected details. They should neither be too generic nor too off-the-wall. A few well-chosen details make the difference: the collar of a patterned shirt peeking out of a well-made sweater; a slouchy satin blazer that you can wear with everything. (Yes, I've bought into the cult of blazers.) If the forties have a signature color, it's navy blue.

The guidelines are similar for men. "I used to want clothes that say something about me. Now I just want to buy really solid stuff that fits great," the Philadelphian tells me. He describes with awe a "crazy over-priced sweater-blazer" that he wouldn't have noticed five years ago, because it's a solid color and low-key. But it fits him perfectly. "There's nothing amazing about it, but now it's one of my favorite things to wear," he says.

I notice that French shoppers and salespeople focus on *la silhouette*—the outlines of the whole ensemble. There are formulas for that, too. If you're wearing a bulky sweater, match it with slim pants. Baggy pants probably need a slimmer top. An A-line skirt looks better with a small heel. Once you've nailed the overall shape, each individual element is less important. You can buy cheaper versions of most tops and pants, as long as the silhouette is just right.

All this elegance can be stifling, of course. In Paris, there's never a time when you're allowed to just wear sweatpants to the supermarket. Parisians look so good, in part, because it would be humiliating not to. Clothes aren't just self-expression here, they're also a kind of armor, creating an impenetrably chic facade so that you can't be mocked. Even inside your own house, around your immediate family, social codes require that you look decent.

But there's an existential payoff for following the French rules: when you know your body well, you come closer to knowing yourself. "Who I am is certainly part of how I look, and vice versa," wrote Ursula K. Le Guin, an American (though she studied French literature and married a Frenchman).

"I want to know where I begin and end, what size I am, and what suits me," wrote Le Guin, who died at eighty-eight. "I am not 'in' this body, I *am* this body. Waist or no waist."

The experts say that once you've cracked your personal fashion code, you shouldn't stray too far from it. Your style will evolve over the years. (The mistake that ages you is *not* changing your style, Inès de la Fressange says.) However, says Buchotte, "it must always resemble you. You have to stay close to yourself."

L iberated from my need to create a fashion persona from scratch, I march into my favorite boutique and throw myself at the mercy of the saleswoman there. I'm so desperate, I don't worry about being overly confessional. (Though I have strategically had my fashion crisis during one of France's twice-yearly sales.)

"I need help," I tell her. I explain that I'm surrounded by brigades of fashionable women, but that I don't know what to wear.

She looks me in the eye to make sure I'm serious. Then she tells me exactly what's wrong with my outfit: My sandals are "juvenile." My sequined handbag is *moche*—a rather severe word for "ugly."

Then she walks around the store pulling clothes off the racks: some cropped black skinny jeans, a printed blue tank top and a navy blazer with three-quarter sleeves. I'd never noticed any of these items before. They don't exactly call out to me.

But when I emerge from the dressing room and slip on the wedge heels she hands me, I see a new person in the mirror: a member of the chic Parisian army.

The jeans fit perfectly, with just the right amount of flattering stretch. The patterned top keeps the ensemble from being too plain. The jacket tones it all down, and the three-quarter sleeves give it surprise and verve. They are all well-made basics that are neither boring nor screaming. The colors go together, but they don't exactly match.

The heels are flattering, but I could walk reasonably long distances in them. For the first time in my middle-aged life, I harmonize.

I suddenly realize that I've wasted hundreds of dollars and countless Saturday afternoons trying to discover something that any Parisian could have told me instantly: I'll never look like Diane Keaton. I'm a small-boned, wide-hipped, high-waisted Ashkenazi woman who looks good in skinny jeans, blazers and a small heel. I will later add a ponytail and some bracelets.

I have another epiphany, too: I have nice ankles. Before I entered my forties, I never once considered my ankles to be an asset. Now they and my calves are the only parts of my body that still look good from every angle. Henceforth, I'll plan whole outfits in order to give my ankles maximum play.

My new look isn't especially unique. I soon notice that some of those stylish women I see around Paris are wearing versions of the same ensemble. They have my body type, so it works on them, too. And yet—because we're different people, and choose different colors, fabrics, shoes and hairstyles—this uniform looks different on each of us. At most, we're fashion cousins.

I'm not sure I've mastered my image, but at least I've found my style. And I've worn variations on it ever since. I stray from it at my peril. By not trying to look unique, I finally look like myself.

Rules for dressing in your forties . . .

- If you buy three items at the same time, one of them will be a mistake.

- That long pleated skirt that looks great on the hanger will never fall that way on your hips.

- If you like the outfit on the mannequin, buy exactly what's on the mannequin. Do not try to re-create the same look by yourself.

- Whatever bothers you when you're trying something on will always bother you. If the shoes hurt even a little bit in the store, they will be excruciating on the street.

- The occasional splurge is worth it, if the item gives you a feeling of well-being and confidence *every time you wear it*.

- Pare back on the rest. Buy fewer items of better quality. Men, invest in one pair of hand-stitched brogues that you wear with everything. Shoes and handbags needn't be by high-end designers. Says Inès de la Fressange: "A pileup of luxury labels can be fatal after forty-five."

how to age gracefully

I'VE FIGURED OUT how to dress like myself, but I have yet another problem: I don't look quite like myself anymore. My frown line—those two vertical slashes between the eyebrows known as "the eleven"—no longer disappear after I wash my face in the morning. When I walk around Paris, I suddenly feel as if I've developed a skin condition. Strangers seem to be staring, not at me exactly, but *at my age*.

Apparently this feeling isn't unusual. A Canadian sociologist writes that some older women feel a vast disconnect between how they look and who they truly are. She describes a seventy-one-year-old who imagines that when neighbors see her, they think, "That's an old lady walking her dog." Whereas, in fact, "I'm still me inside, the outside is sort of a shell."

I don't feel like a shell. I feel like myself with an eleven superimposed on my forehead. But I can feel the mind-body disconnect beginning. I suspect it starts in the forties, then widens. It explains why I'm so jolted when waiters call me "madame." "Madame" means my looks are detaching from my essence.

No one wants to have an older essence. I know Americans in their sixties who still cringe at being called "middle-aged." At a certain point, you're practically obliged to say that you feel much younger than you are. To actually feel your age would be to admit that you're tired, staid and unable to operate electronic devices.

It's unnerving to feel this disconnect. It's not a midlife crisis, but it's a steady ache. I could handle looking older sometimes. But I look like a lady in her midforties all the time, everywhere I go. It's not a disguise that I get to remove sometimes. When I pass women who seem to be about my age, I look at them in silent solidarity, and wonder how they cope.

After a few months of feeling this way every time I leave my house, I have an epiphany about why those strangers keep staring at me. It's not because I look old. It's because I look terrified.

Women are supposed to dread getting old. And this dread is supposed to begin when we're young.

I remember feeling proud, in seventh grade, that I still looked like I was in sixth. I did arm exercises as a teenager so that I would never get "bat wings." (I got them anyway.)

When I was in my twenties and thirties, the cultural message was clear: I was peaking and would never look this good again. Women are supposed to be nostalgic for this brief phase of youthful beauty *while they're still in it*. In one published study, women twenty-five to thirty-five were more concerned about becoming less attractive with age than those in any other age group.

Finally entering our forties is like the scene in the horror film when the heroine realizes that the monster is *inside the house*. The loosening and thinning and wrinkling that we've been fearing for decades, and trying to keep at bay, has come for us anyway.

Women I know—and a few men—describe what's happening to

their bodies as if they're narrating scenes from *The Exorcist*. The changes would seem to require special effects.

"My butt and my belly have changed places," one woman tells me.

"My skin has become *papery*," another says.

"I have not only a double but a TRIPLE chin!! Stop the insanity!!!" a forty-year-old friend writes, after I innocently send him a cheerful snapshot of the two of us. (Naturally, I'd only made sure that I looked good in the picture.)

To hear people older than us tell it, the movie is about to get even scarier.

"Forty to fifty is great, enjoy it," a woman in her fifties tells me. "But at fifty, your face falls." (I picture the face-melting scene in *Raiders of the Lost Ark*.)

Women seem to cope with aging in two ways. The first way is to watch it happen. (People in this camp probably have no trouble watching scary movies.) When I mention the topic of aging to a friend who's forty-four, she instantly catalogs all the recent changes to her face: incipient jowl, eye bags, neck wrinkles ("and I always despised people with that creepy neck thing," she adds) and a "frown" between her eyebrows. She blames herself for her eleven, saying, "I must have started doing it in my teens because I thought it would make me look intelligent."

I deal with getting older the same way I deal with horror films: I avert my eyes. I can't help but notice my eleven because it shows up in every recent picture of me. (Smartphones are the enemies of aging.) But I try to only look in mirrors without my glasses on—one benefit of waning eyesight is that you effectively Photoshop yourself. I'd always scoffed at actresses who made a surprised "oh" expression in pictures so their features would look taut. But I now instinctively assume this expression whenever I look at myself. My daughter calls it my "mirror face."

Not everyone seems to mind looking older. In psychological research, lesbians and African American women are less concerned about becoming less attractive with age than heterosexuals and whites are, respectively. When I run into a German woman I haven't seen in years, I see that she has morphed into an aging earth mother, at ease with her rays of laugh lines and her long blond hair that has gone at least halfway gray. A lawyer I know has eagerly switched into I've-become-my-father mode: he announces, age forty-one, that he will henceforth no longer wear T-shirts.

But most people I know are distressed, and for the beautiful ones it's even worse. A handsome gay man tells me that he used to know instantly which men were homosexual because they routinely flirted with him. Getting older has thrown off his gaydar.

A very pretty woman in her midforties says she used to get bumped up to business class on flights, just by flirting with the fellow behind the check-in counter. She didn't even have to plan vacations; men would invite her to travel on their yachts. In recent years, however, the upgrades and invitations have ceased. She still flirts with the check-in guy, but without results. I sense she walks around feeling like she's missing a limb.

What's a fortysomething to do? One approach is to sow confusion about your age. A Texan tells me his grandmother's tactic: tell people you're seven years *older* than you are.

Me: So if I say I'm in my fifties . . . ?

Him: People will say you look fantastic.

Me: And if I say I'm thirty?

Him: No one will believe you.

There is also, of course, the strategy that I grew up with: fight all signs of aging with early and frequent medical interventions. In Miami and some other places, middle-class women are practically obliged to get a face-lift, followed by regular injections of Botox and fillers, or they risk looking freakishly natural. I know a gorgeous Miamian in her fifties who's considered an eccentric simply because she's never had work done.

Elsewhere, even some of the most salt-of-the-earth feminists I know admit that they've had at least a few injections. Done with moderation, these look pretty good.

I tell Simon that I'm thinking of getting a touch of Botox, too, to make my eleven less prominent.

"Don't do it," he says. I had no idea that he had views on female skincare. But he says that he's been observing older women, and thinks that the trick is to stay slim and age naturally but with elegance.

I think this must be what another friend of mine means when she says she's following a philosophy called "Aging Gracefully." She explains that this involves "accepting the body's natural changes." When I prod her for more details about this philosophy, she confesses that she isn't sure what else it involves; she just feels inspired by the name. Then she tells me about her liposuction.

I want to age gracefully, too. And I suspect that this doesn't mean squinting past mirrors, charting the spread of my eye bags or believing the "madame" isn't the real me.

And I don't want to spend the rest of my life pining to look thirty again. It's antifeminist and futile. It might even be bad for my health. One American study found that young people who held "negative age stereotypes" were more likely to have heart troubles over the subsequent four decades. I suspect that feeling your body is just a shell makes it harder to get out and exercise, and to avoid binge-eating cookies.

But what's the alternative? Is there a different, healthier, saner way to think about my eleven?

Perhaps. If there's a secret, it's in the mind, and it's related to the secret to dressing well. You have to bridge the gap between the shell and the self. In other words, you must own your age and even be proud of it.

I'm probably idealizing the French a bit. But I've noticed that women here take a slightly different tack than I do, as an American. Like Hélène, the sexy sexagenarian, many tell me that they aim to be *bien dans son âge*—roughly, to wear their age well and be comfortable in it.

I realize that the women I meet who seem to actually be aging gracefully do look their chronological ages. They don't appear magically younger. ("Trying to look young is the quickest way to look old," Inès de la Fressange says.)

But these women share certain qualities. They all seem to be immersed in their lives and at ease in their bodies. They don't look terrified or detached, or like they're starring in their own personal horror film. Sure, they wouldn't mind having their twenty-five-year-old bellies back. They're not thrilled about their elevens, either. But they're not in permanent mourning for a previous version of themselves. They're fully inhabiting, and enjoying, their current bodies and ages (and spending a lot of energy maintaining them). To be *bien dans son âge* is to live out the best version of whatever age you're in. I know not-at-all-beautiful women who do this, and they look radiant.

Just as dressing well in your forties entails making choices that reflect who you are, and not just wearing generic basics, looking good as you get older requires accentuating and enjoying what's specific to you rather than striving for cookie-cutter perfection.

Part of the appeal of smooth-skinned young women is that there's no obvious story written on them yet. In theory, you can project anything you want. As women get older, they look like they have a story. The French adjustment is to treat that story not as unwelcome baggage, but as part of a woman's specificity and allure. It would be odd to reach the forties, or older, without having this.

Some French women do get face-lifts, and they have all kinds of injections and procedures. But the objectives tend to be modest. "I'm trying to take off five years," one Parisian woman observed. Whereas Americans "are trying to take off twenty."

"The beauty is to see the humanity of someone," explains Elsa Weiser, founder of the eponymous Elsa Weiser Beauty Institute in Paris's tony Sixth Arrondissement. She warns that smoothing out your features too much eliminates your uniqueness, too. Especially after a certain age, "We don't want to look like we come out of a box. We're not frozen, we're alive."

I have a breakthrough about my own specificity when, at a dinner, I'm introduced to an American woman who looks just like me, except that she's taller and—I soon learn—she grew up in the Church of Jesus Christ of Latter-day Saints. She's basically my Mormon doppelgänger. We stare at each other for a moment, acknowledging the likeness.

She's not gorgeous, or flawless, or especially skinny. But her combination of qualities is appealing. I can imagine someone caring about her more than anyone else in the world, despite the existence of millions of other objectively more attractive women.

I'm struck by this. For the first time, I can see why someone could want me simply because I am, specifically, myself.

"Oh my God, I understand why someone would want to sleep with me!" I tell her.

Even in France, being "comfortable in your age" doesn't happen automatically. It's a deliberate, adult act. It requires believing that your particular shape, mind and assortment of qualities—including your age—have a valid place in the world. It means making a choice about how you're going to age. And it means believing that the person in the mirror is you.

You know you're a fortysomething *woman* when . . .

- Friends who refuse to dye their hair or shave their armpits for political reasons no longer look charmingly rebellious; they look scraggly.

- People on the street only notice you when you're fully coiffed. But they have started to appraise your daughter.

- You've attended a "pool party" in which almost none of the women wore swimsuits, and the few who did wouldn't stand up.

- You see the hidden costs of things. You realize that behind every glamorous, itinerant childhood, there's a mother who handled the school enrollments and the packing.

- You're losing patience with "imposter syndrome."

how to learn
the rules

EVER SINCE I WAS A KID, I've been collecting rules of life. These are compact truths about how the world works. I heard my first rule when I was nine or ten and riding home from school in the backseat of a neighbor's car. I'd just told the neighbor—Mrs. Gross—that it was okay to turn into our street, since she had the right-of-way.

Mrs. Gross didn't budge. Instead, she looked at me in the rearview mirror and said, "You can have the right-of-way and be dead."

She said this with such seriousness and conviction, I knew I'd be foolish not to take heed. And it struck me that every adult probably has a few such truths inside them, distilled from their life experience. I was desperate to understand the world and how to navigate it. If I could gather key lessons from lots of people, surely I'd be prepared for almost any situation. These rules wouldn't make me wise, but they would nudge me in the general direction of wisdom. At least I'd do some things right.

I soon noticed that people rarely say profound things when they're supposed to. Each Saturday, the rabbi stood before our congregation and whispered a secret into the ear of the child getting bar mitzvahed that week. I assumed he was imparting advice that would guide them into adulthood. I longed to know what it was. But when my own turn came, he whispered something like "This is an important day," then the organ played.

In fact, rules tended to emerge when I didn't expect them. Often someone would just blurt one out. When I got older, my ears perked up when someone mentioned that "a man will tell you what he wants on the first date" or that "any woman who's very thin spends a lot of time working at this." These felt like facts that any grown-up should have in her arsenal.

I was suspicious of clichés. I liked truths that seemed self-evident, but that were so slender and specific hardly anyone noticed them. "Keeping your tush clean is the key to good health," a boyfriend told me once, when emerging from the toilet. "Don't get divorced," a colleague said, after an acrimonious exchange with her ex-husband.

Tips on how to socialize were immediately useful. I heard a comedian say that when you're stuck in a boring conversation with someone, "Ask them questions to which the answer is a number." A businesswoman told me that she forbids three topics at her dinner parties: children, jobs and real estate. (I'm partial to rules that come in threes.)

I also collected rules with no obvious utility. These made me feel prepared for an uncertain future—my own equivalent of a basement stocked with water and ammunition. I got excited when a producer explained on the radio that low-budget movies shouldn't have many speaking parts, since you must pay actors more once they talk. (He said that's why waitresses in low-budget restaurant scenes usually just stand silently with their notepads.)

My litmus test for whether a rule deserved to be in my personal pantheon was whether it could work as a person's last words. Could I imagine someone on his deathbed, surrounded by loved ones, saying, "You're fluent in a language once you can explain to someone—in that language—how to tie his shoes"? (I can.)

I also considered it fortuitous when someone repeated a rule that he had heard from someone else. A woman whose boyfriend had slept with her friend told me her therapist had a very reasonable explanation for this: "People sleep with people they know." (These struck me as excellent last words, in a pinch.) Someone else repeated a rule passed down from a friend that I suspect might contain the formula for modern marriage: a woman must sleep with her husband every seven to ten days, or he goes a little nuts.

I was partial to rules that contain numerical formulas, perhaps because they seemed scientific. "Cute is two-thirds," a friend told me once, meaning that something is cute when it's two-thirds its normal size. (This was his main takeaway from his brief marriage to a short, adorable woman.)

When I started to travel abroad, I began collecting expressions, too. Foreign sayings had the advantage of being vetted in their own countries, but sounding fresh to me. As an exchange student in Japan, I learned that "even monkeys fall from trees." (I've since found many occasions to say this in non-Japanese settings, though I often get quizzical looks.)

I liked the explanatory power of the Italian phrase "The appetite comes with eating" and of the world-weary French expression "Only friends can disappoint." When something comes too late, the Dutch say that it's "like mustard after the meal."

I can't always tell whether something is an established foreign expression or just something a foreigner happens to say. "Better the wrong place with the right people than the right place with the wrong people," a Parisian tells me once. I later learn that this is just something her husband once muttered on a bus.

It gradually occurred to me that I was gathering these bon mots not to learn about life, but to disguise my ignorance. It seemed a bridge too far when, in my twenties, I began repeating phrases that a Hollywood talent agent might say while smoking his after-lunch cigar, such as "Dress British, think Yiddish" (attributed to Lew Wasserman), or "Show me a beautiful woman, and I'll show you a man who's tired of fucking her."

My desire for life rules left me susceptible to superstitions. The hostess of a luncheon told me that if a slice of cake falls over while it's being served, the recipient won't get married for six years. Thereafter I stuck to desserts like brownies, with a low center of gravity. Years later, I realized what she was probably trying to tell me: if I wanted to find a husband, I should eat less cake.

I was also susceptible to religion. What's a religious practice, if not a collection of small rules for daily life? When I investigated Judaism in more depth in my twenties, I quickly realized I'd stumbled onto the mother lode of life rules. Observant Jews don't just follow hundreds of commandments in the Old Testament, they also study centuries of rabbinic commentary on how to apply them in myriad situations.

—What if a man falls off a roof and accidentally lands on— and has sex with—someone other than his wife?
—What if you've purged your house of bread products to observe Passover, but moments before the holiday starts, a piece of bread flies through your kitchen window and lands in your vat of soup. Can you still eat the soup?

I learn that there's a prayer to say before you eat a doughnut, and another one to say before you bite into a peach. The blessing over a potato is different from the one for a potato chip, because the chip no longer resembles the original spud. (There's a lively rabbinic debate about Pringles, since they still look quite potato-ish.)

I loved all this minutiae. It was like communing with my ancestral OCD. No wonder I collected tips on low-budget films I'd probably never make. I descended from people who were obsessed with unlikely scenarios.

I didn't follow all the religious rules, but I kept adding more. If I believed that God didn't want me to eat stone crabs, shouldn't I also accept that he doesn't want me to play tennis on Saturday afternoons? (More experienced practitioners knew where to draw the line. I dated an Orthodox man who followed every edict except the one banning nonmarital sex.)

In the end I backed away from intense religious practice. I was self-conscious enough without fretting about which blessing to say over peanut butter (there are separate ones for chunky and smooth). But mostly it was that, for someone who was already drawn to rules, being semi-observant didn't feel spiritual, it felt compulsive.

I went back to seeking everyday solace in my assortment of secular principles. But the older I got, the flimsier these seemed. My random life rules weren't making me feel more adult. They didn't give me judgment, compassion or an understanding of other people. Surely being a grown-up didn't just mean vacuuming up other people's stray insights and beauty tips. It was time to forge some insights of my own.

The Ten Commandments
of the Forties

1. Never wave at someone while wearing short sleeves.

2. Do not buy the too-small jeans with the expectation that you will soon lose weight.

3. Don't suggest lunch with someone you don't want to have lunch with. They will be far less disappointed than you think.

4. When you go to meet someone who works in the fashion industry, do not wear your most "fashionable" outfit. Wear black.

5. "Nice" isn't a sufficient quality for friendship, but it's a necessary one.

6. If you're wondering whether she's the daughter or the girlfriend, she's probably the girlfriend.

7. If you're wondering whether she's the mother or the grandmother, she's probably the mother (especially if she has twins).

8. There are no grown-ups. Everyone is winging it; some just do it more confidently.

9. Forgive your exes, even the awful ones. They were just winging it, too.

10. It's okay if you don't like jazz.

how to be wise

THINGS CHANGE IN YOUR FORTIES. I now laugh with genuine surprise at the punch lines of jokes I know I've heard before. At airports, I look at my gate number on the screen, then seconds later I've forgotten it. I recognize my children's teachers by sight, but I couldn't tell you their names. (In my defense, they're French, and one of them keeps remarrying.)

But something else changes in the forties, too. It might even compensate for those evaporating gate numbers. Lately, when I'm confronted with a new situation or problem, a sort of mental index card pops up in my brain. This card contains other, similar situations that I've encountered before and how they turned out. Based on this index card, I have a decent idea of what to do next.

Let me be clear: I haven't become an oracle. And my range is limited. I don't have index cards for Chinese politics or nuclear proliferation. But faced with once-vexing situations in daily life, I often feel quite clear about how to handle myself. I spend less time paralyzed with doubt and regret and more time efficiently proceeding with my life. Often, I'm not even tempted to ask Simon what he thinks.

I'm glad to have this new card catalog in my head. And I've noticed that other people my age now seem to have them, too. What do all these index cards amount to? Are we finally becoming wise?

People have pondered wisdom for millennia, but the first modern researcher who tried to study it was a New Yorker named Vivian Clayton.

Clayton was born in Brooklyn in 1950. Her mother taught shorthand at a high school. Her father was a freelance fur designer. From an early age, Clayton was struck by how different her parents were from each other.

"My mother was low on emotional intelligence, and her level of compassion was much lower than my father's. She tended to make decisions impulsively, and sometimes they were very hurtful," Clayton tells me on the phone, from her home in Northern California.

Her father was far more even-keeled and would take time to reflect before making a decision. Sometimes he'd decide that the best move was not to do anything. He was very alert to how his choices would impact Clayton, and in general he seemed to understand how other people were likely to react and feel. "His strongest suit was compassion," she recalls.

Clayton's father, Simon, wasn't a financial success. When she once spent the day at work with him, they had lunch at his worktable, then he unrolled a sleeping pad and took a nap on the table, too. She was struck by the smallness of her father's life. "That was the size of his space, that was it."

And yet he was content with his circumscribed world. For years he wrote a weekly column, "Simon Sez," for a fur-trade newspaper, describing the foibles of life in the four square blocks that comprised Manhattan's fur district.

And Clayton noticed that, whereas her mother rarely got what she wanted by acting impulsively, and usually out of anger, her father's approach often succeeded. "Over time he would come up with a decision, and it seemed to have benefited from the time he took to make it," Clayton says.

He also had an unusually precise understanding of himself. "He knew he was not an ambitious person. He knew what his flaws were. He sometimes would apologize for not being perfect."

Clayton was still trying to understand this elusive quality of her father's when she wrote a paper about wisdom for an undergraduate psychology class. That paper led to a doctoral program in psychology, where she studied wisdom full-time. As far as she knew, she was the only person investigating this topic.

That meant Clayton first had to define what wisdom is. Looking for common themes, she read sources ranging from the Bible, to ancient Roman playwrights, to Henry David Thoreau, to the speeches of John F. Kennedy. She asked law professors, lawyers and retired judges to describe wise people they knew.

Beginning in 1978, Clayton published a series of groundbreaking papers positing that wisdom is a decision-making process in which someone analyzes knowledge using their intellect and emotions, and then reflects on it. She determined that wisdom is distinct from intelligence. Intelligence tells you *how* to do something. Wisdom, because it has moral and social dimensions, allows you to decide whether to do it or not.

Clayton realized that, to be wise, you don't need to be brilliant. You need an "adequate intellect" in order to understand all the factors involved in a decision. You also need to feel compassion, and to have that compassion "enter into the mixture, when you finally come up with a decision or judgment." And since wise decisions require reflection, they're usually made slowly.

In other words, Clayton's definition of wisdom sounded a lot like her father.

On the strength of her research, Clayton was hired to teach at

Columbia University in New York. It was a triumphant return to the city where her father had slept on his desk.

Her research began to unleash interest in the study of wisdom. Journalists called her for interviews. Higher-ups at Columbia wanted to know when she would publish next. Colleagues and competitors showed up at her office to sniff out her progress. Could she measure people's level of wisdom? Could she teach it?

But wisdom was an elusive subject. Intelligence is "the ability to think logically, to conceptualize and abstract from reality," Clayton wrote in a 1982 paper. Whereas wisdom includes "the ability to grasp human nature, which is paradoxical, contradictory, and subject to continual change."

At age thirty-one, Clayton made a decision that surprised everyone around her: she resigned from Columbia. Wisdom was overwhelming. She didn't want to study it forever. And Clayton knew herself. She was slow and plodding, and didn't respond well to external pressure. "I realized I was not by nature a true academician," she told me. "And if I wanted to make anything of my life and make a living, I better get the hell out of there and get retrained and get to work."

After Vivian Clayton left the study of wisdom, many others picked up the baton. There was soon the "Berlin Wisdom Paradigm," the "balance theory of wisdom" and the "Emergent Wisdom Model." A psychologist at Yale launched a project to teach wisdom to middle schoolers.

There were also many competing definitions. Some researchers defined wisdom in practical terms, as an expertise at solving common problems. Others defined it more esoterically as the pinnacle of personal growth, or as "a deep understanding of life and a desire to see the truth." Still others considered wisdom to be an ideal that people should strive for, but that they're unlikely to attain.

While there was never a consensus definition of wisdom, eventually some common—or at least overlapping—descriptions emerged:

Wise people can see the big picture. They're able to look beyond the problem at hand to grasp the wider context and longer-term implications. They're not swept up in the group mind.

And yet they know that their own knowledge, judgment and perspective are limited. They're humble. They realize that all decisions are made with imperfect information and will have imperfect outcomes.

They know that life is ambiguous and complicated. They see nuance rather than absolutes. They know that most people and situations have both good and bad elements, and they're adept at identifying what these are. The legendary Dutch soccer player Johan Cruyff pointed out that someone might seem like a bad player. But when you analyze his various qualities—his left foot, right foot, head shot, speed, etc.—you might see that he can do some things extremely well.

They know that, in any situation, multiple outcomes are possible. Actions have unforeseen consequences. Even good solutions have hidden transition costs. When I show my husband a listing for a new apartment that's bigger and cheaper than our current one, he refuses to even consider moving. He claims that the upheaval of moving, and of adjusting to a new place, could easily outweigh its benefits.

Wise people know themselves. They've made a candid assessment of their own good and bad qualities. They have a decent understanding of their own family history, and of the historical era in which they live. When Angela Merkel was Germany's chancellor-elect, she met British prime minister Tony Blair. Blair's chief of staff recalls that "Without being starstruck, the soon-to-be chancellor plonked herself down in front of [Blair] and said disarmingly, 'I have ten problems.'" She then listed them, starting with "lack of charisma." Blair was impressed.

But they're not self-centered. They acknowledge other people's points of view and accept that others have goals and values that differ from their own. Neurotics are unlikely to be wise, even if they're very smart, because they're preoccupied with themselves.

They're good at reading people. They have insight into how others think and how they're liable to act in various situations. They grasp people's motivations and emotional states, and they can predict how their own actions and decisions will impact others.

This knowledge of other people isn't just academic. Someone who's wise genuinely cares about other people and acts out of empathy, generosity and compassion. They favor conflict resolution, compromise, generosity and forgiveness, and they believe in charitable giving. When Nelson Mandela was president of South Africa, he would stand up every time the tea lady entered his office, and remain standing until she left. Mandela decided not to run for a second term so his newly democratic country could experience a peaceful transition. Wise people are driven not just by their own advancement, but also by a desire for the common good.

They're pragmatic and adaptable. They can manage life's uncertainties. When reality contradicts their beliefs, they change their minds. "Wise people are able to accept reality as it is, with equanimity," explains sociologist Monika Ardelt. They don't aim for the unattainable. They can change. I once heard someone explain why Barack Obama was a wise politician: he only wanted what he could get.

They have experience. This includes "rich factual knowledge and rich procedural knowledge," the psychologists Paul Baltes and Jacqui Smith wrote. You can't be wise yet ignorant. You need data points to feed your judgment. Wise people draw on this data to know which elements of a situation to focus on and which to overlook.

They're resilient. They learn from negative experiences and recover from setbacks. In the face of adversity, they maintain their emotional balance and sense of humor. They focus on the positive, without dwelling on past grievances. But they don't go around irrationally convinced that they're about to strike it rich.

They know when not to act. In general, people have an "action bias": when there's a problem, they want to do something about it. Wise people know that sometimes the best option is to do nothing or to wait, even if people are clamoring for them to act. As chancellor, Angela Merkel once asked French president Nicolas Sarkozy to stop pressuring her to choose how to tackle a problem. She pointed out that in some cases, if you don't make an immediate decision, the problem you're trying to solve changes or disappears. "I'm someone who gives time to time; because I've seen, in slowness, there is a vast hope," she said.

When I was on an operating table about to deliver twins, the obstetrician inspected my cervix. He was surrounded by a team of people in surgical scrubs who were eager to proceed and to perform a cesarean if necessary. The doctor was scrubbed in for surgery, too.

He could have pushed the babies out or cut me open and pulled them out. Instead, he decided to do nothing. He told everyone to come back in twenty minutes. He knew from experience that, just by waiting a bit longer, the twins would probably descend on their own and come out the old-fashioned way. Twenty minutes later, they did.

When wise people make a judgment about what to do, or not to do, they often make the right call. All of these good qualities only count as wisdom if, quite often, you turn out to be correct. Wise people have "a willingness and exceptional ability to formulate sound, executable judgements" in the face of life's uncertainties, Baltes wrote. Or as the neuroscientist Elkhonon Goldberg explains, they have "not only a deep insight into the nature of things, but also—and even more so—a keen understanding of what action needs to be taken to change them."

Once researchers had a working definition of wisdom, they could test people to see whether they are wise or not. And they could measure whether wisdom really increases with age. Are fortysomethings wiser than, say, people in their twenties?

If you use a very broad measure of wisdom, the answer is: not necessarily. "Most wisdom researchers would concur that wisdom does not automatically increase with age and that it is relatively rare even among older adults," Ardelt wrote. She found about as much wisdom in college students as in people over fifty-two. (Though older people with college degrees had significantly higher wisdom scores than the students did.)

Vivian Clayton found that the older people got, the less they associated wisdom with age, and the more they associated it with understanding and empathy. "There is wisdom at each age, even childhood," she told me, echoing the Latin writer Publilius Syrus, who said, "Bright faculties are the source of wisdom, not length of years."

And yet, while overall wisdom doesn't automatically come with age, "it appears that wisdom *can* increase with age," Ardelt observed. She said that becoming wise requires "motivation, determination, self-examination, self-reflection, and an openness to all kinds of experiences to do the necessary inner work."

And when researchers test for individual aspects of wisdom, they find that many of these do improve by midlife. People in their forties and fifties are more positive than younger ones, better at controlling their own emotions, less focused on themselves and better at reading other peoples' moods. Perhaps as a result, they're also better at reasoning about social conflicts.

Those in midlife also have more of what researchers call "crystallized intelligence," such as the ability to draw conclusions, make judgments based on their experiences and apply their knowledge to new situations.

This sounds a lot like those index cards popping up in my head, reminding me how similar situations turned out. They're just one element of wisdom, but I'll take it. We fortysomethings could have used these index cards earlier, but we definitely need them now. They've come just as we're juggling growing children, aging parents and busy careers. We've never had more responsibility and less free time.

We're also increasingly called upon to make decisions and give advice. When a friend told me that her husband had confessed to sleeping with several other women, she was pretty sure this meant that their marriage was kaput.

I didn't see it that way. An index card popped up in my head with examples of marriages that have come back from all kinds of brinks. I told her that I'd seen traumatic events become part of a lifelong love story, not necessarily its finale, and I urged her not to make an impulsive, irreversible decision.

This may have been terrible advice. I'm still far from wise and I live mostly in the small picture. But being slightly less clueless is an improvement, and I'll take it. My index cards have made me happier. They're the start, at least, of what I craved while growing up: to have more knowledge, less regret and a better grasp of what's happening.

After Vivian Clayton left Columbia, she moved to California and retrained as a geriatric neuropsychologist. She opened a private practice in which she assesses whether elderly people are fit to make legal decisions for themselves. It's the study of decision making from a new, real-life angle.

Clayton watched, from afar, as the field of wisdom research that she started became its own branch of psychology. She can tick off the names of wisdom research centers at several major universities. But nearly forty years later, Clayton is certain that, when she left New York, she made the right choice.

"I have never looked back," she tells me. "I did what was important to do, and it was time to step off. I just knew it."

You know you're in your forties when . . .

- You know that not all old people are wise.

- You still turn to older people for advice, hoping that they know more than you.

- You see people's good and bad qualities, and know that someone who's very smart in one domain can be useless in another. You've seen that there are "smart idiots" and "amiable rogues."

- You can be aware of someone's flaws and nevertheless still like them.

- You realize that you've been moving at the speed of your generation all along, even if—for a long time—you didn't know what that speed was.

how to give advice

A FEW WEEKS after I turn forty-five, I get an email from the dean of an American art and design school in Paris. She wants me to give the commencement speech at the school's graduation ceremony.

The ceremony is about a month away, so I sense that I may be a last-minute choice. Also, the school has just thirty-five graduates, and the speaking fee won't even pay for the dress I'll need to buy to deliver the speech in. (Many of the graduates are studying fashion design.)

Nevertheless, I accept. Giving advice to the next generation—or at least a tiny part of it—seems like a crucial step in my slow journey toward adulthood.

But what exactly will I tell these students? They don't want to hear about French parenting. And I can't rely on my own experience with commencement speeches. When I graduated from college, a US senator delivered his stump speech on Poland, then wished us luck.

I watch lots of commencement speeches online to get ideas. After I've seen about a dozen of these, I realize that there are three key rules: The best speeches are under fifteen minutes. It's a plus if the speaker can do celebrity impressions. And the fact that someone once starred in a hit sitcom does not mean that she has any worthwhile advice.

I also discover that commencement speeches are mostly an American phenomenon. The British hold graduation ceremonies, but they don't bring in outside motivational speakers. (My husband's graduation from an English university was conducted almost entirely in Latin.)

French universities usually don't even have a ceremony; they just mail your diploma. A professor at one of the top schools in Paris tells me that she once showed her class Steve Jobs's 2005 commencement speech at Stanford. Jobs describes how he dropped out of college and studied calligraphy, which seemed pointless at the time but later became the basis for the fonts on Apple computers. He concludes that when you follow your passion, all your strange choices gradually make sense, and the great narrative of your life emerges.

Her French students were unmoved by the speech, calling it "completely disconnected from reality" and "so Californian."

That puts me in a tricky spot. The whole point of a commencement speech is to say something encouraging. Most of the ones I watch boil down to: Yes you can. Here's how. But I'll be in Paris, speaking to a graduating class that's only a quarter American (the school's roughly two hundred students hail from forty-eight countries). If I say anything too uplifting, I'll seem deluded. The message of a French commencement speech would probably be: No you can't. It's not possible. Don't even try.

A few days before my speech, I attend the school's end-of-year fashion show. As I'm waiting for it to start, I strike up a conversation with the student sitting next to me, and he asks me why I'm there.

"I'm a writer, and I'm giving the commencement speech on Saturday," I say. He looks surprised. He has never heard of me or read anything I've written. "I was flattered and surprised to be asked," I add.

He listens thoughtfully, then says, "Well, I guess at a certain point in your career people just start asking you to do things. And you think, 'Well, I've never done that before, but I'll give it a try.'"

Now I'm surprised. At age twenty-two, he knows this already. Millennials seem far more emotionally evolved in their twenties and thirties than my generation was, perhaps because they've grown up meeting like-minded people in internet chat rooms, and watching TV shows with names like *Awkward*. In my day, you didn't get to discuss being awkward. You just were.

Two days later, I put on my new purple dress and ride the *métro* to the hotel where the commencement ceremony is being held. There are about 125 people in the hotel's gilded ballroom, including parents who've flown in from around the world. I realize instantly that I should have pocketed the speaking fee and worn something from my closet. Practically everyone is wearing black.

The graduates aren't writers. But, like me, they will probably spend a lot of time alone in rooms struggling to make things. So in under fifteen minutes in that room, though without celebrity impressions, I share my advice on how to cope. Much of it applies to any creative work:

You're qualified. Or rather, you're not the only imposter out there. That student sitting next to me at the fashion show was exactly right. You never feel completely ready to do your next job. No one else does, either. Just carry on.

Everything that happens is potential inspiration for your work. Or as Nora Ephron put it, "Everything is copy." When someone tells you a story, you notice a recurring theme in conversations or you turn a corner and see something that moves you— use it. In fact, when you're deep into a project, information about it will pour into your life.

Seek out inspiration, too. Read and watch the work of artists you admire. "Most of what I do comes from seeing someone else's work and thinking: I can do that. I want to do that," the writer and director Miranda July says.

Stay in the room, offline. It needn't be an actual room. You can be alone in a busy café. I've gotten ideas while walking or riding the Paris *métro*. (I recommend line eight.) Figure out your clearest, most productive time of day to work, and guard this time carefully. Much of life consists of the dead time between events. Don't fill these interstitial moments with pornography and cat videos. You need to be blank and a little bit bored for your brain to feed you ideas. In solitude, "one's inner voices become audible," the poet Wendell Berry wrote.

When you have an idea, write it down immediately. Do not trust yourself to remember it. Always carry a pen and a notebook, plus something good to read.

You needn't reinvent the wheel each time you create. It's not cheating to fall back on established forms. My husband likes to quote an editor who said, "You can write it any way you like, but I'm going to put it back together chronologically."

Grow where you're planted. Yes, this sounds like it should be printed on a mug. But it's essential. Embrace whatever weird talents or expertise you've ended up with. Treat your assignment, whatever it is, as the most important job in the world.

It's the research, stupid. An architect tells me that he's never nervous about creating a building from scratch. "I just keep gathering information, and the building takes shape," he says. Often, the reason you can't move forward, despite weeks of trying, is that you don't yet know enough about your topic. Go back and find out more.

Embrace anomalies. When I was starting out as a journalist, an older reporter told me that when researching a story, you will inevitably discover some fact or detail that muddies the clean narrative you had imagined your story would follow. This fact is irritating and inconvenient, and you will be inclined to ignore it.

Instead, pay attention to it and see where it leads. Doing this will make your work richer, truer, less predictable and more airtight against objections.

"Don't be too silly or too profound." The singer Jarvis Cocker says this is a key to writing rock 'n' roll songs. (If you're too profound, "you'll be embarrassed when you're older," he reasons.) He also warns not to be a "rhyme whore." His example of this: "I don't want to see a ghost / It's the thing I fear the most."

Be generous. Many of the people you meet at the beginning of your career will still be around decades later. If you were a jerk early on, they'll remember.

Pay attention to what you're doing on the side. When I was a financial journalist in Brazil, I took samba dancing lessons. Eventually, I wrote a brief article about this for the arts section of my newspaper. My bosses hardly noticed it, and I'm pretty sure no one read it. It would be years before I got to write that way for a living. But it was the first piece I'd ever written that lit me up inside.

Ignore the naysayers. People with other kinds of jobs will say, "I don't know how you do it," or "I could never sit alone in a room all day." They will think you are an irritating obsessive who jots in notebooks during dinner. Just keep going. You're the lucky one. And though you can't tell, you're probably getting better.

You control the work, but you don't control whether other people will like it. A writer I know once described his Zen-like approach: total commitment to the process, total equanimity about the outcome.

Done is better than perfect. Get over your fear of finishing. Being able to complete tasks doesn't just matter in kindergarten; it's a key skill for grown-ups.

It's okay to be an obsessive. They're the ones who do good work. The late Garry Shandling once recalled that when he was making a TV show, he ran into another comedian who was making one, too. Shandling asked how it was going. "He said, 'This is so much easier than I thought. I'm having so much fun.' And I thought, 'Oh my God.' Then of course, he was out." Doing routine work gets easier with time, but doing your best work doesn't.

This Herculean extravaganza is worth it. For most people, getting married or having a baby are peak moments in their lives. But when some mysterious place in you churns up a sculpture, or a dress, or a scent, or a graphic design, and other people respond to it, that's a peak moment, too. "It's not about working toward a specific, correct goal; it's just about working," said the artist Maira Kalman. "To care passionately about your work will keep you— dare I say it—happy."

Even if you follow all these rules, your first attempt will be terrible. A large part of the creative process is tolerating the gap between your glorious vision of what you want to create and the sad thing you've just made. Remember that everything good you see started out as someone else's bad first draft. Version number twenty of your work may still not be brilliant. But version number one almost definitely won't be.

I leave the graduates with two final thoughts. The first is the best creative advice I ever got from Simon: when you get out of a bus or a taxi, look back at your seat to see if you've left something behind. If you lose your portfolio, you won't get the job.

The second is a French expression that is optimistic but not grandiose: *vous allez trouver votre place*—you will find your place. I love the idea that, somewhere in the world, there's an empty space shaped just like you. Once you find it, you'll slide right in. (I don't mention that this search might take several decades.)

Then, feeling very adult, I get back on the *métro* and go home.

You know you're in your forties when . . .

- You've gotten a lot better at one or two things.
- People in their twenties ask you for advice, and actually seem to follow it.
- You give worthwhile advice, and many of your friends do, too.
- You know that most people are just as clueless as you are.
- Your parents have stopped trying to change you.

17

how to save
the furniture

RIDING HIGH FROM MY COMMENCEMENT SPEECH, I'm invited to give
a talk in Brazil. I'm excited to go back there. I'll be speaking at an event
called the International Seminar of Mothers in Belo Horizonte, a mid-
sized Brazilian city. It's best known as the place where Brazil suffered
a national humiliation: in the 2014 World Cup semifinal, Germany
beat Brazil's national soccer team 7–1.

I'm supposed to talk about French parenting, so I'm not that worried. I only start to think about my speech a few weeks beforehand,
when one of the organizers informs me that they're expecting a thousand mothers to attend my talk. That will be the largest live audience
I've ever addressed.

I also realize that they want me to speak for an hour straight and
then take questions. I've never given such a long, uninterrupted talk.
(At the U.S. university it was mostly a discussion.) My stump speech on
the topic only lasts twenty minutes.

"The public is expecting a lot," the organizer—a Brazilian mother
herself—writes. I press her for details on what, specifically, she'd like

me to talk about. I have trouble imagining what might interest Brazilian moms. And I've given lots of speeches at this point, so I'm tired of repeating myself. I feel a mounting sense of dread.

"It would be very interesting if you can talk a bit about the mother/woman perspective," she writes back.

That's all she says. I find an online speech calculator, and learn that if I speak at an average pace, I'll need to say five thousand words. So I paste together five thousand words from various talks I've given and organize them.

Then I board a plane to Brazil. The fact that I'll soon be in front of a thousand mothers feels ominous and unreal. During the overnight flight, I have an anxiety dream in which someone discovers a sex tape of me. When I wake up, I'm in Belo Horizonte.

In the airport's arrivals area, I meet another of the speakers. She's an American grandmother who has written parenting books, too.

"Did they ask you to speak for an hour?" I ask her, as we're wheeling our suitcases to the taxi.

"I know, it's nuts," she replies. I'm relieved that she also struggled with the assignment.

At the hotel, I meet the organizers in person. They're a group of Brazilian veterinarians who have gone into the conference business. This is their first. One of the women is tall and glamorous, with long black Charlie's Angels hair.

"Are you a veterinarian, too?" I ask.

"I'm a pig specialist—swine," she replies.

I want to go upstairs and work on my speech, but instead, I'm escorted into a press conference filled with journalists and Brazilian "mommy bloggers." One of the bloggers, a blond woman in a furry vest, is telling the group that today is the first time she's ever been away from her baby. Her comment unleashes a wave of emotion. Soon everyone in the room—except me—is in tears.

Later I sit behind a table and greet some of the mothers attending the conference. They're mostly middle-class dentists, marketing consultants and stay-at-home moms. Each wears a name tag with a picture of her young child on it. Some of the pregnant women wear a picture of their fetal sonograms. I'm struck by how young they all look. When my book came out just a few years earlier, I looked like one of them. Somehow, I've now morphed into their elder.

Practically every woman hugs me. I'm hugged more during three days in Brazil than during twelve years in Paris. Many also want a photograph of us together, with our heads touching. If there's an outbreak of French lice in central Brazil, I'll be patient zero.

These mothers seem to have a hard time managing their kids. I learn that there are many words for "tantrum" in Portuguese: *manha* is whining and complaining; a *chilique* is a full-scale meltdown. I'm reminded that *mimada* means spoiled, that a *babá* is a nanny and that a *folguista* is the nanny who comes on your regular nanny's day off.

I try to edit my speech more, but I barely have time. The next morning, I head downstairs to deliver it. One of the organizers—a cattle specialist—tells me that an earlier speaker described how her husband died two months before she gave birth. "The talk was incredible," she said. "We were all in tears."

I walk into the double-wide ballroom where the grandmother is giving her talk onstage. A thousand Brazilian mothers wearing headphones are listening, rapt, to the simultaneous translation.

Clearly, it's going well. The mothers are buzzing with interest and chuckling on cue as the grandmother answers questions. She is sincere and sensible—and clearly relishing her role as a teacher and expert. She walks off the stage to warm applause.

A minute later, the editor of a Brazilian parenting magazine introduces me. I am suddenly facing a sea of Brazilian mothers. There's no podium, so I have to hold my seventeen-page speech, the slide changer and the microphone, and take my glasses on and off, depending on whether I'm looking at the speech or at the audience.

For the first five minutes, I'm fine. I introduce myself in Portuguese, and tell a story about arriving in Paris and feeling like an alien. I can feel that they're ready to go on a ride with me.

But then it all slows down. By the time I reach page six of the speech, the room is so still, I can practically hear the translation coming through the wireless headsets. It doesn't help that each time I turn a page, I turn my back to the audience and put down the microphone on a chair behind me. I'm severely testing everyone's goodwill. By page eight, I fear that some of the mothers might just leave.

As I'm speaking, I'm aware that in the movie version of my talk, this is the moment when I would stop reading, tear up the papers and speak from the heart about my struggles as a mother. But to do that, I'd need to be surging with adrenaline and inspiration. In fact, I'm just as bored as the audience.

I trudge on, as a polite, resigned silence settles over the room. When I finally finish, I answer some questions, then walk offstage to very mild applause.

There was no mass exodus from the conference hall. My speech was low energy and mediocre but not a disaster. As the French say, I saved the furniture. (This means that the house caught fire and burned down, but I managed to at least drag some furniture into the yard.) I feel terrible.

"Nice talk," says the grandmother, who's been watching. I assume she's feeling triumphant.

I compliment her on her talk. She smiles, and admits that she spent weeks preparing it.

That night, there's a dinner for the speakers. When a woman at the table describes the challenges of raising a son with Down syndrome, the whole table—again, except me—is in tears.

"What's with you Brazilians? Do you need to cry every few hours?" I ask, trying to lighten the mood. Everyone looks at me like I'm a monster.

Just then, I finally understand—too late—what all those Brazilian mothers wanted from me, both during my talk and at this dinner. They weren't just looking for parenting tips. They wanted to take part in a shared emotional experience. They were ready to be brought to tears. Crying is the mark of a successful gathering in Brazil and a sign that you've connected. ("The communal emotive experience is very Brazilian," the Brazilian American writer Juliana Barbassa explains to me a few weeks later.) The veterinarians took for granted that I knew this, and didn't think to explain it.

When our main course arrives, the magazine editor who'd introduced me that morning—a charismatic woman in her fifties—brings up my speech. "I felt that you were sometimes not happy with what you were saying," she says delicately.

"Yes, I felt I had something much more interesting to say," I reply. I admit that I'm tired of repeating the same facts about French parenting.

She puts down her fork. She's angry now.

"Never do this again," she says. "Forget what the audience expects. Just give the best speech you can, and trust that they'll come with you.

"They just want to see who you are," she continues, practically shouting now. "It's all about having a moment of connection." She scolds me for becoming bored with my own material. "*Respect the work.* Keep changing it. Grow with it. That's maturity!

"Also," she adds, "next time don't read."

By the time she stops talking, I'm in tears. I'm touched that, though I'm in my forties, she's willing to look past my mediocre speech and see my potential. I'm also moved that she cares enough to say this to me, even though it's too late for me to fix my speech and she may never see me again. No Parisian has ever held me to account like this, unless it's to scold me for failing to say *"bonjour."* I've chosen to live in a place where people keep their distance.

I'm crying, too, because I suddenly see my missed opportunity.

Standing up in front of a thousand people—even thousands of miles from home—is a chance to create something and to forge a connection. Instead of respecting the audience and trusting that they would come with me, no matter our differences, I treated my talk like a sad obligation and squandered it. I wish I could redo it.

It's energizing when something goes well. Even a small success creates goodwill and opportunity. (Afterward, the grandmother is invited back to Brazil repeatedly. I am not.) But when something goes badly, the opposite happens. For months after my speech in Belo Horizonte, thinking about it saps my confidence.

The morning I leave Brazil, the editor comes to my hotel lobby to say goodbye. I feel bonded to her after our emotional experience at dinner, and she promises we'll stay in touch. But I never hear from her again. We had our moment. I saved the furniture. And now it's gone.

You know you're in your forties when . . .

- You're living through the second renovation of public spaces and friends' kitchens.

- You accept that you love midcentury Scandinavian furniture, even though it's a generational cliché.

- You wonder whether you still qualify for a "midcareer" fellowship.

- You're now the "older lady" in the improv class.

- You have Googled everyone who was ever of any importance in your life. You sometimes forget this and Google them again.

how to figure out
what's happening

AFTER MY DAUGHTER WAS BORN, I joined an English-speaking "baby group" of women with similarly aged infants. We met once a week at one of our homes. I quickly decided that I had little in common with most of the other mothers. I attended the group for the company and the potty-training tips, but I didn't make an effort to be popular. I kept accidentally calling one woman by her baby's name (both started with "B"). When another woman said she planned to vote for a far-right candidate in the American presidential race, I said something to the effect of "Are you nuts?" The woman looked stricken and insulted. The following week, I got a message saying that the baby group was canceled, then I heard that the mothers had met in a local park without me.

I really didn't mind. I figured that, in a big city, there are always lots of new people to meet. What I failed to consider was that as you get older and more settled, the same people pop up in your life, just as they do in work settings. This is especially true when you have kids the same age. Plus the Anglophone world in Paris is tiny. I run into the baby-group mothers for years, at the Halloween party, the Anglo quiz night and the English-speaking soccer league. Each time, I'm aware that they hate me.

When my daughter starts junior high, I discover that the woman whose voting plans I'd insulted sends her kids to the same school. Not only that, she's a pillar of my new community. I spot her at the parents' night, when she gets a round of applause for planning the Christmas party.

I've made some strides since being shunned by the baby group. As a fortysomething, my emotional regulation has improved. I get into fewer sticky situations, and I'm now capable of thinking something without blurting it out.

I also don't like the thought of being at close range with someone who despises me, so I resolve to clear the air between us. When the parents' meeting breaks up and everyone heads into a classroom for drinks, I work up the nerve to approach the baby group mom.

"Hi," I say with cautious friendliness.

She looks at me with confusion.

"It's me, Pamela," I say, still waiting for her quizzical look to morph into dislike.

"We were in the baby group together?" I offer. She stares at me for another beat, then there's a small flicker of recognition.

"Wait, were you friends with Kara?" she asks finally. There's no emotion attached to this statement, just a polite straining to connect with the near-stranger in front of her.

I was indeed friendly with Kara. And this is apparently the sum total of what she remembers about me. She doesn't loathe me; she barely knows who I am.

I've advanced as a human being in the past few years, but I'm still lacking in one key component of wisdom: understanding what other people are experiencing. I long to better grasp social dynamics, and to be able to detect people's motivations and emotional states.

In my defense, this isn't easy. For Buddhists, learning to perceive the world clearly is the main task of life. It's why we're here. And they say it's critical to succeed at this. You can experience brief pleasure without understanding what's happening around you. But for sustained happiness and well-being, you must observe your own life and surroundings with great clarity.

Becoming less clueless certainly seems critical to my happiness. And it seems critical to being a grown-up, too. Real grown-ups seem to understand what's happening around them. They can detect social dynamics and grasp people's motivations and feelings.

People my age are supposed to have improved at this. On average, forty- and fifty-year-olds score highest of all age groups in a test called "Reading the Mind in the Eyes," in which subjects look at a series of photographs of people's eyes, and select which emotion each person is feeling. This ability remains stable, at a high level, between ages forty and sixty.

This is a crucial twenty-first-century skill, as everything from taxis to taxes becomes automated. The ability to read other people and understand their emotional needs is one task that humans can still do better than computers. In a few years, "people reading" jobs might be among the only ones left.

But how exactly does one do this well? What is the secret to seeing clearly? I've improved, but I still miss a lot of what's happening. Can I hone this skill, and if so, how?

I realize I have an in-house expert on exactly this topic. My husband is so good at reading people. I sometimes suspect that he has psychic powers. When we leave a meal or a conversation, my first question for him is always "What just happened?" At a party once, we met a woman—a former journalist—who seemed to suddenly grow cold while we were speaking to her. I assumed I'd said something to upset her.

Simon had a different take. He said that, while speaking to two journalists, she was suddenly embarrassed that she'd left the field. The chill had settled just as she described her new job in public relations, he noted.

Simon is no longer willing to act as my full-time interpreter of other people. But he has entered a teach-me-how-to-fish phase, in which he'll discuss his own techniques.

I've observed one of these already: he listens very hard to what people are saying. Sometimes he listens so hard, they think he's scowling at them. Friends have approached me, privately, to ask, "Does your husband hate me?" (Usually, he doesn't.)

Simon explains that he's listening—and watching—for certain clues. The first is, when does the person lose interest? He notes when someone looks away because she's bored. (To his irritation, he catches me doing this often.) He also notices when she changes the subject. "When people say, 'That's interesting,' it's a classic line to kill off a topic," he adds.

Simon also listens for what the speaker *does* care about. What topic does she keep bringing up? Which phrases does she repeat? He says people often have a recurring message that amounts to a kind of personal motto. They're trying to get you to believe something about them, and this underlies much of what they say. Their message might be "I have a relaxed parenting style!" "I earn in the low six figures," "I'm authentic and don't try to project an image," or "I have loads of friends."

"They're not lying," says Simon, "but most people have some story about themselves that they've assembled, and that they sort of believe. And you have to understand what their story is and not buy it."

I usually buy into people's mottoes without realizing that I'm falling for interpersonal propaganda. I leave conversations thinking, "What a relaxed parent, and with so many friends." I'm still easily dazzled by how people look, or distracted by concerns about what they think of me.

Perhaps because I'd grown up without analyzing anyone, it rarely occurred to me to examine people while they're speaking and try to detect patterns in how they behave. I'm too swept up in the experience to notice much about it.

Once I start doing this, I realize that I've been ignoring lots of crucial information. Just as a man will tell you what he wants on the first date, people are constantly shedding data about themselves. If you simply pay close attention, you can scoop it up.

To be able to do this, you must stop obsessing about yourself. That clears the channel of excess static so you can receive the information. Simon isn't a clairvoyant. He just doesn't fret constantly about what other people think of him. That frees up his brain to understand their motives, qualities and goals. ("If you don't act weird and you ask questions, people will like you," he assures me.)

Fortunately, in midlife it gets easier to turn down the static in your brain. On average, we're at least moderately less neurotic than younger people, psychological studies show. That means we don't project our own anxieties onto others quite as much, and we're less cluttered with worry about what they think of us.

I gradually start to decode people a bit, instead of taking them at face value. When I meet a pretty mother from my son's school, I no longer think, in a pointless loop, "She's so pretty, she's so pretty, she's prettier than me." Instead, I study her while she's talking and think, "She's pretty, and yet she seems shy, and she's possibly a bit dim."

It's an improvement. But I was still blindsided by my interaction with the baby-group mother. What was I doing wrong?

"Hamlet," Simon says.

I ask him to clarify.

"Neurotic people think that life is like *Hamlet*, where they are Hamlet, and everyone is looking at them and judging their psyche in a good or a bad way," he explains. In fact, everyone is his own Hamlet and views other people as minor characters in his personal drama. Most people don't evaluate everything you say in a constant referendum on your character. Even when they do pay attention, how you come across isn't terribly important to them. They're busy worrying about the protagonist in their own drama: themselves.

"You make much less of an impression on people than you think, because you're not the most important character in their story," he says.

Simon tells me about a long-ago girlfriend who made a presentation to his journalism class. For the first thirty seconds of the presentation, she was so nervous that she froze. She finally stammered a few sentences, then she left the room in shame.

Afterward, she came to Simon's room in tears, convinced that their classmates would forever think she was an idiot. Simon replied with an early version of his *Hamlet* speech.

"I said, 'Nobody's thinking about you. They're all thinking about their own talk, and who they fancy, and their own problems. Everyone's forgotten your talk. Nobody cares.'" Apparently, she was relieved.

I listen hard as Simon describes this scene, and think of other girlfriends he has mentioned over the years, including the one who had never heard of either Stalin or Chairman Mao. Suddenly, I realize my husband has a type: he likes his women, including me, to be a little bit clueless.

When I tell this to Simon, he immediately denies it. I think I've caught him by surprise, both because I had the insight and because it's true.

My other insight is that, in my quest to see the world more clearly, I don't need to depend entirely on my husband. There are world-renowned specialists in exactly this skill. Some are doctors.

There's a tradition of physicians as expert seers. The writer Arthur Conan Doyle was a doctor before he created Sherlock Holmes, the detective who can deduce a man's profession just by studying his hands or notice the crucial missing element of a setting. When Holmes's sidekick, Watson, marvels at this ability, Holmes scolds him, saying, "You see, but you do not observe."

Another expert seer is a real-life dermatologist named Irwin Braverman.

Braverman, who's now in his eighties, is an emeritus professor of dermatology at the Yale School of Medicine. In 1998 he and a Yale museum curator developed a course that helps medical students become more perceptive. The course is now required for Yale's first-year medical students, and it's taught at more than seventy medical schools around the world. The New York Police Department and Scotland Yard have used versions of it, too.

Growing up in Boston in the 1930s, Braverman didn't plan to spend his life looking at skin. He dreamt of becoming an architect or an archaeologist.

"I'm a visual person," he tells me by phone from New Haven. "I enjoyed going to museums and looking at paintings. Ever since I was a kid, I enjoyed looking at things."

Braverman's family—Esperanto-speaking Russian Jewish immigrants—vetoed both professions. "My uncle said to me, he never heard of a Jewish architect or an archaeologist in 1930 or 1940, which was true. My parents said, doctor, lawyer, businessperson, *maybe* journalism."

As an undergraduate at Harvard, Braverman liked working in a laboratory. So he picked medicine and eventually specialized in dermatology, where "90 percent of the time it's a visual diagnosis," he says. In dermatology, just by looking at someone's skin from the outside, you can detect diseases that are happening deep inside of them. (In his forties, Braverman authored a classic medical school textbook called *Skin Signs of Systemic Disease*.)

After he'd been teaching and seeing patients for many years, Braverman realized that his students were very good at memorizing information, but they weren't very good observers. They would look at slides of various rashes, then glance at a patient to see which slide he matched. But medicine isn't just about memorizing slides. "At least once a day I see something new I haven't seen before," he explains.

And students sometimes had trouble describing skin lesions, or they overlooked other important features of the patient. They might only look at what's flagrantly "abnormal." Or they would limit their attention to the patient's main complaint, but not take the time to examine everything else about him. "Sometimes in those normal features there are clues that actually tell you what this is all about," he says.

Like Sherlock Holmes, Braverman eventually realized what was missing from many of his students. They lacked a skill that a good physician has, and that he himself had acquired over years of seeing patients: you look very hard at a person or an image and keep looking at it until you see more and more. You don't just glance at something. You keep going back and forth over it until you've mined it for all there is to see. It's an intensive way of looking that Braverman calls "visually analyzing."

Like Simon, Braverman listens hard, too. "If you listen carefully and let the patient talk, usually the answer is in the history," he tells me. "What is the person saying? How is he saying it? What is he not saying?" Clues sometimes emerge at the end of an appointment, as an afterthought, when the patient casually mentions—for instance—that she's just been hiking in the countryside and hopes she wasn't bitten by a tick.

Braverman concluded that the solution to his students' shortcomings lay not in medicine, but in his old passion—art. He began taking first-year medical students to look at nineteenth-century oil paintings at the Yale Center for British Art. In one exercise, students spend fifteen to thirty minutes looking at a single painting, usually of people. Then they describe all of its features to the class. After that, they use these observations to interpret what's happening in the painting.

Typically, a few students in each class don't become better observers, even with practice. And a few are already so skilled at seeing, they don't need any help. But most students are somewhere in the middle. With training, they get better at visually analyzing the paintings. And afterward, their ability to observe skin problems improves, too.

"The students come away, they say, 'I realize I only look at things superficially. I come to conclusions before I've seen everything,'" Braverman says. "Anyone can benefit from this. It's not just a doctor thing."

I'm very taken by the idea that as you keep looking at things, you see more and more in them. This seems like a signature quality of the forties. By this age, you've seen that there isn't an infinite variety of people, problems and situations. Many of these recur. The world seems, at once, less infinite and unpredictable, and yet even more interesting. You look at the same things you've seen many times before and see new layers in them.

It's what Arthur Schopenhauer said: "The first forty years provide the text, the next thirty provide the commentary."

I'm too busy to go to a museum and stare at paintings, but I take Braverman's lesson to heart. I want to keep looking at things until I see more and more in them. As an experiment, I decide to rigorously observe the person I have the most contact with: myself. I'm still not keen to visually analyze my own face in the mirror, but I begin keeping lists of the things I do and don't like.

Things I Like:

Improv.
Own goals. (That's when, in soccer, you accidentally kick the ball
    into your own goal.)
Hoop earrings.
Croutons in soup.
Lesbians.

Sweaters.

Dresses that come with belts.

The metallic first sip of a cold can of Perrier.

The word "shimmy."

The word "boobies."

Baths.

Irish accents.

Tea with milk.

The fact that when someone in Germany has two PhDs, she's called "Frau Doktor Doktor."

Justice.

Jokes.

Understanding a joke in another language.

The fact that at his 1968 trial for conspiracy, Abbie Hoffman spoke to the judge in what sounded like gibberish but turned out to be Yiddish. (He called the judge "a front man for the WASP power elite.")

The fact that when archivists at the University of Texas were going through Isaac Bashevis Singer's papers, they found half a sandwich.

Coffee in the morning.

Having the whole day ahead of me.

Cake.

Salad.

Spotting lettuce in someone's teeth.

Noticing that someone bites his nails.

Deciding that someone is shifty.

Detecting that someone's handbag is a fake.

Being less nervous than the other person.

Knowing the subtext, but not saying it.

Having time to scrutinize a fashionable woman, unnoticed.

Short nails.

Sharpened pencils.

The first glass of champagne.

The moment when you stop texting and call.

Getting back from vacation.

My counterfactual life in which I hang out with comedians
and curse.

Having something great to read.

Having written something.

Pancakes.

Confidence.

Thai food with beer.

Finding out that someone else comes from Miami.

A feeling of shared understanding.

Singing show tunes with friends.

Things I Don't Like:

Small spaces.

Clutch purses.

Sweetened soy sauce.

Meanness.

Rejection.

Surprise parties.

Suspense.

People who complain about jet lag.

People who get angry when you mistake the gender of their pet.

People who say they "don't need nature."

People who want you to plan their visit.

People who walk into your home and immediately ask for your
WiFi code.

People you can't trust.

Injustice.

Suffering.

My own prejudice.

Hipster couples who aren't attractive.

Hipster couples who are.

Ardent atheists.

Voicemail.

The word "middle-aged."

Indifference.

Rushing.

Waiting for someone who's late.

You know you have a fortysomething mind when . . .

- You've spent forty-eight hours trying to think of a word.
- That word was "hemorrhoids."
- You no longer leave conversations wondering what just happened.
- When you speak to people in their twenties, you feel a gap in confidence and experience that you wouldn't want to have to bridge again.
- When you speak to people in their sixties, they don't feel the same way about you.
- You've learned that when you worry less about what other people think, you can pick up an astonishing amount of information about them.

how to think
in french

ANOTHER TOPIC I'VE BEEN LOOKING AT, over and over, is my own country. It helps that I'm living outside of America and comparing myself to people from other places. I'm starting to suspect that my issues might be cultural.

I have an epiphany about America when a friend whose family moved from Seoul to California when she was small says her Korean parents often complain that she lacks *nunchi*. *Nunchi* (rhymes with "moon-chi") literally means "eye measure" in Korean. It's the ability to notice things well. People with *nunchi* can pick up on unspoken signals and infer other peoples' states of mind. They're good at reading situations and social cues.

There's no exact English translation. When my friend Rebecca's kids are making a commotion in a quiet restaurant one night, she just scolds them to "read the room." (They don't.)

Apparently, Korean parents often complain that their American-raised offspring lack *nunchi*. This skill, which goes by various names, is a prized quality in East Asian countries. "The requirement is to 'read' the other's mind," the psychologists Hazel Rose Markus and Shinobu Kitayama write in their landmark 1991 paper, "Culture and the Self." This requires "the willingness and ability to feel and think what others are feeling and thinking, to absorb this information without being told, and then to help others satisfy their wishes and realize their goals."

In America there's a different emphasis. Instead of tuning in to other people, we're encouraged to tune in to our own feelings and preferences and to express these. "American culture neither assumes nor values such overt connectedness among individuals," Markus and Kitayama write. In the US, "Individuals seek to maintain their independence from others by attending to the self and by discovering and expressing their unique individual attributes."

This starts from birth. When writing about parenting, I notice that Americans—including me—assume that each child has his own unique sleep needs and his own taste in food. We're suspicious of day care because an institution can't possibly accommodate our child's unique rhythms and preferences. If a toddler doesn't like rice, oranges or avocados, it's his right to express this. We want schools to emphasize self-expression, too.

Researchers find that by the time they're adults, Americans and East Asians actually perceive the world differently. A metastudy concluded that, in general, East Asians are "high context," believing that in order to understand a situation, and the behavior of any individual in it, you must consider the interaction of all the different parties. And since a lot of information is conveyed nonverbally, it's crucial to pay close attention to subtle unspoken clues. In other words, you need *nunchi* to figure out what's happening.

Researchers say that Americans are typically "low context." We focus on individual actors and their choices, not on what everyone in a situation is doing. And the individual actor we focus on the most is ourselves. Instead of clueing in to other people's emotional states, we clue in to our own unique preferences, asking questions like, What kind of foods do I like? What's my personal sense of style? Am I self-actualizing?

This can make some conversations resemble a succession of self-promotional monologues. At a gathering recently, I asked an American woman what her job was. She responded with a ten-minute speech describing her entire professional history. She was following the cultural imperative to express herself, and didn't realize that everyone was getting bored.

No wonder Korean parents worry that their American-raised offspring lack *nunchi*. We're not trained to listen carefully to others and to pick up nonverbal clues. French people "often complain that Americans are 'boring,' that Americans respond to the slightest question with a 'lecture,'" anthropologist Raymonde Carroll writes in *Cultural Misunderstandings*. A 2014 American study led by a psychologist at Yeshiva University found that when researchers crossed two unrelated instant-message conversations, as many as 42 percent of the participants didn't even notice.

In other words, my cluelessness isn't entirely my own fault. I can't even blame my parents. It's part of being an American.

One needn't be Asian to have *nunchi*, of course. And this ability comes in different varieties. David Ben-Gurion, Israel's first prime minister, was apparently skilled at reading signals from other countries—he had geopolitical *nunchi*—but he was terrible at reading individuals. (His wife had interpersonal *nunchi*. She would sit in on meetings, then explain the dynamics to him afterward.) A woman I knew in college had a kind of *nunchi* transference. She told me that when she walks past another person, "sometimes I feel like I *am* them."

My British husband has classic *nunchi*, and I can see that our daughter, Bean, inherited it from him. While fetching her from a summer sports camp, I chat with two teenagers who are getting ready to play soccer. They seem friendly, but Bean keeps yanking me to leave.

"Couldn't you see that they were mocking you?" she asks, as soon as we're in the car. I'd apparently mistaken their snickering at a middle-aged mom for friendliness.

Bean may also have picked up this skill in France. I'm starting to think that my adopted country has its own version of *nunchi* that's both interpersonal and introspective. You're supposed to be able to read the room, but you're also expected to have a very precise understanding of yourself. Someone who lacks these skills is said, pejoratively, to have *la confiture dans les yeux*: jam in the eyes.

I didn't move to France to have the jam wiped from my eyes. I came here for Simon (who had himself come here to escape London's real-estate prices). But after a few years in Paris, and gradually improving French, I realize it's no accident that the English word "clairvoyance" comes from the French for "clear-seeing." Figuring out what's happening—within your family, your workplace and your social circles—and understanding your own response to all this, is one of the central pursuits of French life.

This starts in childhood here. State preschools emphasize an awareness of others. Mothers say their main parenting technique is to observe their children carefully, to understand them. Later, they launch into detailed descriptions of their children's characters, including their many contradictory qualities.

French elementary schools are a lesson in naming and ordering experiences. My children don't just learn how to read a clock; they must define what time itself is. In the hands of French educators, human history seems like an orderly procession of events. Students learn it in chronological order, from prehistoric times onward, and graduate with a sense of their own place in human events. My children's elementary school report cards rate them on dozens of specific skills, including esoteric ones like their ability to "adopt a critical distance from the language."

From an early age here, kids learn to detect surprising, paradoxical qualities. I realize that my younger son is truly French when, after I've been bugging him to wear a jacket, he turns to me on the street and says, "Mommy, I like to be a little bit cold." My older son explains that he's ready to get rid of his high chair; he'd assessed it and decided it was "more comfortable but also more babyish."

Parisians notice visual stimuli with far more precision than I'm used to. In daily life they seem to be constantly visually analyzing. When I bring a poster to my local framing shop, the salesman describes the exact effect that each frame would have on the poster. In boutiques, salespeople don't say "that's adorable" or "take it off"—the kind of comments I used to get in America. They say that a certain color sweater looks more "luminous" on me, that one red handbag is more versatile than another because it has more blue in it, that a pair of tan sandals clash with my skin tone (this is true, but it hadn't occurred to me) and that the glasses I'm trying on "eat my face." No one here actually says that something has *je ne sais quoi*. That would be too vague.

French adults often describe the social dynamics in their lives with the same novelistic precision. I'm used to American celebrity interviews in which actresses wax about how hard they work and how they're devoted to their children. In equivalent French profiles, actresses barely discuss their work or their offspring. Instead, they try to show that they've achieved a precise understanding of their own minds, and that they've organized their lives to accommodate this.

This is especially true for actresses over age forty. When French *Elle* profiles Charlotte Gainsbourg after she moves from Paris to New York, Gainsbourg is blunt about herself and her new life.

"I'm not an easy person. I don't think I'm very open, I don't speak easily," she says.

Gainsbourg, then forty-five, says she hasn't made any new friends in America, but that she didn't socialize much in Paris, either, because "I don't think it's in my nature to be very festive." She says she spends a lot of time walking around New York alone. "I also love to be a little bit unstable," she adds.

To an American reader, this might sound morose. But in the French context, it's high status. It's proof that Gainsbourg observes herself clearly, and that she has arranged her life to correspond to who she is.

Of course, one reason the French are so intent on figuring out what's happening is that they assume that a lot goes unsaid. France's mannered culture sometimes values elegant facades over transparency. Jean-Jacques Rousseau complained about this in the eighteenth century, noting in a letter that "The only frankness of your polite society is never to say what you think except with qualifications, civilities, double-meanings and half-truths."

Rousseau didn't manage to change much. "Being too explicit can be perceived by the French as being naive or impolite," the French academic Pascal Baudry explains.

If this sounds confusing, that's because it is. You're supposed to know yourself precisely, but you only reveal this knowledge selectively. People expect artifice in some contexts and precision in others. "Live hidden, live happy," the French expression goes.

Becoming attuned to when to expose your true self, and when not to, is a big part of growing up here and of learning to adapt as a foreigner. It's crucial to be precise among your friends and in selective magazine interviews. But real-estate advertisements highlight apartments that have no *vis-à-vis*, meaning that no other apartment has a view into them. Your home is private, and it's best when strangers can't see inside.

After a dozen years in France, and of living with Simon, my *nunchi* improves. I can now tell when I'm boring someone, and when they're treating me with disgust or contempt. (I've taken an online course in how to read micro-expressions. These two emotions are easy to spot because they're signaled asymmetrically on the face.)

I've also learned to compensate for my own limitations. Whenever I think a handsome man may be hitting on me, I remind myself that he's probably a solicitous homosexual. And when I have the urge to lend a new friend my apartment, I consider this evidence that the person might have a personality disorder.

But more and more, I feel like I have a handle on what's happening. When Simon and I are walking up the stairs of our building one day, we pass a neighbor who's standing outside his apartment. The man doesn't greet us, then he dashes inside.

"Unfriendly" is Simon's analysis. But I see it differently. "He was wearing his bathrobe, and he was embarrassed," I explain. Simon thinks about it and concedes the point. I've finally started to see.

You know you're in
your forties when . . .

- Hardly anyone you meet is twice your age.

- No matter how late you ate breakfast, you will be shaking with hunger if you have not had lunch by two p.m.

- That baby-faced friend from high school, who you thought would never look his age, now looks his age.

- The only songs you know all the words to are at least twenty years old.

- Most women who are pregnant seem *very* young.

- Despite its terrible backstory, you've grown fond of Thanksgiving.

how to make friends

ONE ENORMOUS ADVANTAGE of becoming less neurotic is that it's easier to make friends. I used to be the second kind of shopper with people, too—the kind who needs to see all options before she makes a choice. Only instead of needing to see all possible shoes, I needed to meet all possible people before deciding which ones to befriend.

It took me some time to learn that, unlike sneakers, people take offense when you're standoffish. In my forties, I've realized that it's a gift to find someone I adore, no matter who else is out there.

It's not just me who's gotten better at friendship. Much of my peer group has, too. This is partly biological. Since we're at a peak in conscientiousness (this includes traits like "hardworking" and "orderly"), it's easier to make plans with fortysomethings and to know they'll follow through on their obligations. Even my flakiest friends now seem more responsible and focused.

People in their forties are also more "agreeable," on average, than those in younger age groups. And having made it this far together—through the same songs, hairstyles, new technologies and national tragedies—there's a feeling of kinship that didn't exist in our twenties and thirties.

Taken together, this means that my contemporaries are easier to spend time with. At my twentieth high school reunion, my former classmates were competitive and a bit cold. I didn't go to my thirtieth reunion—a consequence of living outside the country. But from what I gather from the run-up, and from the gushing messages and cozy snapshots, the whole tone was warmer and people were nicer to each other. They had stopped pretending to be who they're not and just wanted to enjoy each other's company. (We've all realized that one of the great consolations of aging is that you get to do it with your friends.)

If the early forties have a slightly panicky now-or-never mood, the later forties feel more resolved. People who were anxious about not having children, or the right job, or a suitable partner, have either come up with solutions that satisfy them or they've reoriented. They might not have the life they planned for. But they've found one that they can live with or that they've grown to like.

And becoming less neurotic lets us see how much we have in common. We can join the group mood, confident that we're having a shared experience. After years of feeling exceptional, suspicious and out of sync, we realize we're quite a lot like other people. Knowing this is a bit of a disappointment, and a bit of a relief.

I've also benefited from seeing the French model of friendship.

American friendships can ramp up quickly, progressing within a couple of weeks from coffees to lunches, and before long to dinners. If someone is your neighbor, or your children are in the same class, and you find each other reasonably interesting, it's natural to meet for coffee and take it from there.

We do this wherever we are. For a while, when my hair was growing back after chemotherapy, I had a Jean Seberg–style bob. An

American expat whom I met briefly one night during this period—and who didn't know the backstory of my hairdo—emailed me soon afterward. "I saw you and thought, I want to know that woman, she looks cool," she wrote. We met soon afterward.

The French rules are different. Proximity alone doesn't imply that there will be any intimacy. After ten years, I don't even know the names of most of my neighbors, and I still address the couple next door using the formal *vous*. Keeping people at a polite, protective distance—so they don't intrude on your privacy or create obligations—is a French specialty. There's little requirement to do social chitchat. If you don't feel like talking to someone, you don't talk to him.

The French sometimes make fast friends, too. But in general, friendships progress cautiously here. It takes more than a haircut to get things going. You can know someone socially for months or years and slowly grow to like them without ever proposing that the two of you meet alone. There might be years between the first encounter and the first coffee.

I initially found this slower French pace strange. By the time someone warmed up enough to signal that they were ready to befriend me, I resented them for having been so distant for so long. I suspected that they were being the second kind of shopper with me, and looking to see if there was someone better.

In fact, they were just gradually getting to know me. And I've learned that this slower pace of friendship suits my spoon brain. I've started to apply the French rules to non-French relationships, too, even though I can tell that some Americans find me aloof. Though I trust my assessments of people more now, moving slowly means that I don't need to rely on adrenaline-filled first impressions or plunge into friendships before I'm ready. I can get to know people over time and test my hypotheses about them.

The French friendship rules also suit my tendency to be blunt. American friendships can involve lots of reassurance and mirroring. When a friend gets into trouble or has a setback, you're supposed to "make him feel better by finding extenuating circumstances, by reminding him of all his good points, and by helping him to have confidence in himself again," Raymonde Carroll writes.

Under the same circumstances in France, however, you're supposed to tell your friend the truth. "My friend is there to tell me out loud what I tell myself confusedly," Carroll writes. "He or she 'shakes me up' out of affection for me without, in doing so, judging me." Afterward, you thank your friend for her bluntness, saying, "I feel much better, I knew it was time for me to let you set me straight."

There are different expectations of the trajectory that friendships take. Some American friendships endure, but others are quite fragile. I had one drink with the lady who liked my haircut, during which she told me all about her life. But then we never met alone again. Even if you reach the dinner stage with someone, the friendship can end abruptly when one party changes cities, has a baby or simply becomes disappointed or fed up. (No wonder I felt like I was perpetually auditioning. I was.) As a general rule, we expect balance and reciprocity, and become concerned when one friend hosts more dinners or asks more favors. Friends are supposed to be there for each other in a pinch, but they shouldn't ask too much and risk overtaxing and alienating the other person.

The French might also lose touch with someone who leaves town or changes jobs. There's still risk of a rupture. But in general, once you've passed through the long trial period and someone is your *copine*, it's expected to endure. By that stage, you're said to "know them by heart." The screening process has been so extensive, you can be confident that you have the part in perpetuity.

This feels safer to me. Friendship comes with a kind of tenure.

Slowly, I've made real friends and solidified some old ones. My social anxiety hasn't disappeared, and others sometimes notice it (though being a foreigner is a good cover for being awkward). But that's rare now. These days, when I have a plan to meet someone and a voice comes into my head asking, "What will we possibly talk about for three hours, and what if she discovers how unlikable I am?" I shush the voice and see the friend anyway. I trust that I have qualities, and that I needn't constantly entertain people in order to be liked.

And now that my own mind is quieter, I've realized that there are people all around me who have worse social anxiety than I do. A woman I know confesses to me over lunch that she finds books far easier to cope with than humans, and that most of what she knows about people comes from reading nineteenth-century novels. Whenever she meets someone, she tries to decide which character from Jane Austen best explains him.

I've figured out that I have some basic requirements in a friend. One is that the person has a sense of humor. (The Jane Austen lady does, and despite her best efforts I've befriended her.)

I don't expect constant comic monologues or exchanges of quips. Someone can be serious and have a sense of humor. But nowadays, when humor is missing entirely, I notice. This quality isn't trivial or just about having a laugh. A humorless person is stuck in her own head and doesn't have much distance from situations or from herself. Occasionally I'll meet someone who's impressive and smart, but who—for reasons I can't immediately put my finger on—I never need to see again. Afterward, I'll realize what it was: he was humorless.

I've also learned to watch for whether someone listens. It's a basic skill, but it's not always there. (Simon will sometimes say of an elderly person, "He doesn't have a hearing problem, he has a listening problem.")

Having become more relaxed with others, I've loosened my grip on them. I realize that not everyone stays in your life. There are unforgettable people with whom you have shared an excellent evening or a few days. Now they live in Hong Kong, and you will never see them again. That's just how life is.

And I've gotten better at spotting members of my tribe. Jerry Seinfeld once said that his favorite part of the Emmy Awards is when the comedy writers go onstage to collect their prize. "You see these gnome-like cretins, just kind of all misshapen. And I go, 'This is me. This is who I am. That's my group.'"

My group consists of former misfits who like to read and write. And it turns out that there are quite a lot of us. One day, apropos of nothing, I propose to two new friends that we go away for the weekend together. They both agree, and we spend three days in a hotel sharing meals, swimming and talking into the night in each other's rooms. We describe what it's like to grow up not quite belonging, and then to finally find a life that suits us. At several points during the weekend, we all break into song.

Along the way, there are confessions. One of my new friends reveals that a Holocaust survivor taught him how to masturbate. (This was all aboveboard; apparently the survivor was a sex educator at his school.) I tell my friends that, in college, I had a class assignment to make a video about anything. I decided to make a documentary about myself, and went around interviewing people in my dormitory about what they thought of me.

After I say this, I wince, certain that my friends will judge me. Surely I've gone too far in revealing the ugly truth about myself. But the opposite happens.

"Oh, I love that, it's *so you*!" one of them says with great affection. I realize that while the story doesn't reflect especially well on me, they like me more for having told it. Perfection isn't a requirement of friendship, but showing people who you are definitely is.

You know you're in your forties when . . .

- You are capable of listening without judgment.
- You no longer accept one-sided accounts of relationship agonies, or obediently validate friends' stories. When you recount how someone has wronged you, you now add, "This is from my perspective, of course."
- You no longer need your friends to share your tastes.
- You know that among all the people whose company you enjoy, there are some who matter deeply to you. You actually remember the things they say. You treasure them, and will always make time for them.
- Sometimes these same people do not treasure you.
- You don't want to be with the cool people anymore; you want to be with *your* people.

how to say no

IT'S GREAT TO FINALLY HAVE CLOSE FRIENDS. I just wish I had time to see them.

If there's one word that describes the modern forties, it's "busy." I've never had so many small tasks to accomplish. My current to-do list is eleven pages long and contains tasks ranging from panicky ("insurance renewals!") to the aspirational ("read Stefan Zweig") to the paralyzingly daunting ("print and organize family photos"). There are endless emails to return and thank-you notes to write. Friends of friends visiting Paris want to know where to eat and whether we can meet for a leisurely drink. Even the simplest of these tasks requires a twenty-minute slot of time that I don't have. Oh, and there's housework.

I know these are privileged problems. I'm grateful to have them. But Dutch economist Lans Bovenberg correctly describes the new "rush hour of life," when work and child-rearing peaks collide, and some people are looking after aging parents, too. ("My mom thinks she's pregnant," a friend from Connecticut reports. "She lives in a retirement home, and she keeps saying, 'This is going to be a terrible place to raise a child.'")

Psychological researchers call this busyness "role overload," and say they have trouble recruiting midlifers for clinical studies (college students and the elderly have far more free time). Never mind having an existential crisis; it's been years since we've even been to the movies.

I can't claim to be handling all this gracefully. When I chastise my daughter for singing in the kitchen instead of helping me clean up, she says I lack "joy of life" (it's her English translation of *joie de vivre*). I'm taken aback, but I get it. It's hard to conjure joy of life when, in a single morning, I have to arrange for the unclogging of toilets, the selection of an orthodontist and the buying of multiple, appropriate birthday presents, while also submitting work projects on time.

Managing all these tasks requires constant triage. You must decide what to prioritize and—crucially—when to say no. The ability to refuse everything from playdates to freelance assignments is a core skill of the decade, without which you will drown in tedious conversations and what the British call "personal admin." Just as busyness is the signature predicament of the forties, saying no is its signature defensive move.

I realize I'm no good at this when, on a freezing winter night, I'm standing outside a party thrown by an American food blogger I barely know.

I don't especially want to attend this party. I'm feeling fluish, and I've missed spending the evening with my family. But I don't want to miss the party, either. What if something excellent happens there? What if I say no and the blogger feels I've snubbed her? When there was no door code on the invitation (you need one to get into most Parisian buildings), I figured that she might live in a mansion that opens onto the street. I don't want to miss seeing that mansion. And surely the food will be fabulous.

I arrive at the address on the invitation to find a typical Parisian apartment building that requires a door code. For forty-five minutes I stand on the street, sniffling and freezing. I can see the party through a window, but the people inside can't hear me shouting up at them. Because she's hosting, the blogger doesn't answer her phone. Why did she even invite me? I've only met her once. Then I get it: I've become someone else's aspirational friend.

Finally, a man comes out on her balcony to smoke, and calls down the door code to me. Upstairs, the blogger greets me, gestures to some sad-looking food on paper plates, then walks away. The guests are mostly other middle-aged American expatriates with the depressive air of people whose lives sound glamorous to friends back home, but who are in fact disappointed and underemployed.

One woman describes her son's speech therapy to me at great length. Another introduces herself aggressively as An-*dreh*-ah, as if I'm to blame for everyone who's ever mispronounced it. Then she demands to know, "What's your story?"

I retrieve my coat and flee, not even saying goodbye to An-*dreh*-ah or the blogger. The next day I agonize about whether I've made things worse by leaving abruptly. Should I email the blogger to apologize?

"You know what I think when I hear these stories?" Simon says. "I think how hard it must be to be you having these interior monologues."

Chastened, I realize that I need to get better at saying yes to things I want to do, and no to the ones, like this party, that on balance I don't. But how do I tell the difference in advance? What if I miss brilliant soirées in mansions, or I say no too often and the invitations cease?

I gradually learn some key lessons on how to edit my own life, both in leisure and work:

> **Know your own habits.** If going out to lunch derails your workday, don't meet anyone for lunch, period. Track your slots of discretionary time. When my kids go to bed at nine o'clock, I have two hours before I need to sleep, too. Spelling this out for myself

precisely—instead of being vaguely aware of it—helps me to use this block of time the way I want to.

Be lucid about the trade-offs you're making. Economist Tim Harford points out that saying yes to one thing means saying no to something else that you could have done with that time: "Will I write a book review and thus not write a chapter of my own book? Will I give a talk to some students, and therefore not read a bedtime story to my son? Will I participate in the panel discussion instead of having a conversation over dinner with my wife?" He recommends filtering future plans through a simple test: If I had to do this today, would I agree to it?

Follow your verve. When you're trying to decide between several options, pay attention to which one energizes you and which one makes you feel tired just thinking about it. (I learned this from a life coach, Janet Orth.) This isn't always feasible; practical factors can intrude and there are things you must do. But it's worth weighing the "energy" factor, too. Even as a grown-up, it's okay to choose the option that seems like more fun.

Do small things immediately, if you can. They'll swell in importance if you let them linger.

People—and even institutions—are usually flexible. "I used to twist my schedule around for people's invitations," a fortysomething teacher in Vermont tells me. "But I don't do that anymore. I've realized that there's much more room for negotiation in things than you think." If you don't like someone's proposal, propose something else that you can do with less stress.

A freelance journalist I know says that when he's ambivalent about accepting a writing assignment, he asks the editor for double the amount of money she offered. He finds that half the time, the editor agrees to this, so in the end he does half the work for the same amount of money. And he finds out how badly the other party wants him.

Don't let the internet eat your life. Rules help. A children's book author tells me that he only returns emails on Thursdays. Another writer tells me he never goes online between nine a.m. and five p.m. ("If I look something up, it's an hour.")

Focusing on the long term helps, too. The British writer Zadie Smith got a flip phone and installed internet-blocking software on her computer once she realized that she didn't want to be eighty-six "and think that a large part of the life had been spent on Mr. Jobs, in his universe, on his phone, with his apps. I didn't want that for my life."

Prioritize your own project. No one else will. People will come to you with their problems and imply that you're the only one who can solve them. This is almost never true. Unless the problem is life-threatening or the person is a very close friend, you don't need to derail your own work to solve it. Don't volunteer to do someone else's small, draining tasks out of guilt. You can do favors, but you get to choose which ones.

It's okay to be a little bit ruthless. When a neighbor wanted me to sell her the little closet attached to my apartment so she could build herself a bathtub, I agonized. I needed the closet, but surely she needed to take a bath. Then I consulted a friend—a man—about my dilemma, and he couldn't believe I was even debating this. "I'd just say, 'Sorry, I want my closet,'" he said. And so I did.

Have a plan. This makes it harder for others to derail you, and easier to determine what's part of your agenda and what isn't. The Chinese general Sun Tzu said that nothing will ever go according to plan, but if you have no plan you will definitely fail.

Say no nicely. Present your explanation plainly and honestly. "I'd like to, but I'm busy with work" is a perfectly reasonable—and true—explanation. If people don't like the answer, or they misunderstand your intentions, there's not much you can do. Sometimes they respect your directness even when you're turning them down.

"Thanks so much, and well done on saying no to things—you're a beacon of fortitude for us all!" an acquaintance wrote, after I'd told her that I was too busy to help her friend.

Just do what you want more often. At a friend's fortieth birthday party, there's a delicious Lebanese buffet. I finish my first plate, then tell my Parisian friend Julien that I'd like to go back for seconds, but that I don't want to be rude. Not everyone has eaten.

Julien replies with a lesson that applies to more than just the buffet (and makes me realize that he and I are becoming friends). "You must do what you want, what you feel," he says. "When you do that, everything goes better, everything works." Obviously, some people don't need to hear this message. But for those of us who fret about small transgressions, it's liberating. People aren't crushed if you don't go to their party. And when you do go, they're pleased that you're enjoying the buffet. Paradoxically, when you stop worrying about whether you're offending people or breaking rules, occasions take on a more natural flow.

Remember that this, too, shall end. When I ask a Californian in her fifties what has changed since her forties, she says that, for the first time in many years, she actually has free time. One of her children has finished high school and the other is nearly done. She doesn't quite know what to do with herself.

I won't have that problem ten years from now. I'll be writing Obama-era thank-you notes and going back for seconds at the buffet.

You're in
your forties when . . .

- You know how to disappoint someone.

- You've stopped spending time with people who make you feel terrible.

- You know that if someone wants to spend her leisure time with you, there's a good chance she genuinely likes you.

- You have so little time that you sacrifice sleep, but you need sleep in order to get everything done. This paradox makes you perpetually unproductive.

- You know that most marital conflicts are caused by either a lack of sex or a lack of sleep.

- You know that making a small change in your life can make a big difference.

how to control
your family

AS I GET ON IN MY FORTIES, I start to feel that I've cracked the code in many parts of my life. But paradoxically—given that I've just spent four days lecturing to Russian mothers in Moscow—one realm where I still struggle is parenting.

Now that my kids are older and more autonomous, how much should I try to influence them, and when should I respect their preferences and let go? I face this on smaller questions: Should I insist that my younger son taste scrambled eggs again, even though he finds them revolting? Should I transfer one of the twins into his brother's class, which seems to have a better teacher, even though his brother wants to be alone?

I also face larger issues: I had planned to move around a lot when my kids were young, including to America. But neither they nor my husband is even willing to change apartments. When I broach the idea of moving to a new country, everyone—including Simon—revolts. I may be the queen of the family, but it's four against one.

It surely doesn't help that I'm a hapless immigrant, who can't even be trusted to help with fourth-grade homework. To bolster my status I take Bean to the Salon du Livre, an enormous annual book fair on the edge of Paris, where my French publisher has a stand. They've scheduled a two-hour slot during which I'm supposed to sit and sign books. Surely Bean will be impressed when she meets my fans.

She and I sit at a long, narrow table with a row of authors on one side. There's a pile of my books on the table, and a folded sign with my name on it.

The Francophone African woman to my left is plugging her memoir. A famous French diet doctor is on my right. Fans wait in long lines to see each of them.

A few people ask me for directions to the toilet. But for two hours, not a single person stops to buy my book or ask for my signature. I don't mind. I know that some events are like that. But Bean is shocked. It was a big deal for her to have come all this way and to sit alongside me.

"No one wants to read your book?" she whispers. She hadn't known my status outside the family. Now I can see it registering in her eyes: in the real world, I'm a loser. It seems pointless to try to convince her otherwise.

I'm not alone in feeling powerless over my family. My friend Florence, who has three kids, too, says she thinks of her household as a kind of jellyfish. She can nudge it in a certain direction, but she can't really push it or order it around.

My kids still haven't gone to American sleepaway camp. But America has entered their lives in other ways. Through my non-American husband they've discovered the Marx Brothers' movies, which I'd never seen. Now they go around our apartment holding pretend cigars and singing, "Whatever it is, I'm against it."

They may not have embraced all my interests, but I've been embracing theirs. I spend quite a lot of time watching professional soccer. I don't even balk when they call it "football." When my younger son said he was sad "because Samuel Eto'o is getting old," I knew he meant the thirtysomething striker for Cameroon.

"What's the name again of the team that invaded Mozambique?" he asked recently.

"Portugal," I replied. "And it's not a team, it's a country."

I do have a kind of "soft" power, based on my life experience and presumed wisdom. But even this is often tested. When I'm walking with Bean to take the entrance exam for a bilingual middle school, she's visibly nervous.

"What if I don't get in?" she asks me. I realize that it's my moment to come through as a grown-up. I'm supposed to say something that's both encouraging and reassuring. And she's a tough audience, so it also must be true.

"You're prepared. And if you don't get in, we'll cope," I say.

"That's not what I wanted to hear," she says.

"You're going to get in, you're going to do great?" I say.

She looks skeptical. That's not it, either.

"It doesn't matter whether you get in or not!" I venture.

Bean looks at me with either contempt or disgust. She can tell that these statements are like tosses at a basketball hoop; I keep shooting and hoping that something goes in.

As we get closer to the school, I suddenly think of a better answer.

"Just be yourself!" I say. "Focus on thinking, 'I'm okay, I'm me, I'm fine.'"

"You're just trying to say something to your daughter because you're the parent," she says, correctly.

Finally, I just ask her: "Okay, what do you want to hear?"

"That whatever happens, it will be okay," she says.

"That's pretty much what I said at the beginning."

"I know," she says.

I realize that she's still nervous, and that she's looking for what the

French call a "technique"—a tested practical solution to her problem. It's what Americans might call a "life hack."

"Just focus on your breathing," I suggest.

"When I think about my breathing, I start to breathe like this," she says, pretending to hyperventilate.

"If you're meant to get in, you'll get in," I say. She looks dubious. I'm spouting self-help drivel, and she knows it.

When we're about a block away from the school, she suddenly becomes joyful and starts skipping down the street. I'm reminded that children can change moods in an instant, and this gives me another idea.

"Just enjoy the test, have fun with it," I say. She likes this technique, but she knew it already. And she's not about to take pointers on *joie de vivre* from me.

When we arrive at the school, a gaggle of anxious children and their parents are milling around outside. I consider telling Bean that she's going to crush them. Instead, I make a final suggestion: "Trust yourself." She looks at me, and for the first time says nothing. Then someone calls her name, and she walks inside the school without looking back.

Two hours later Bean emerges, smiling, and says it went very well.

"I just kept thinking of what you told me," she said.

Which thing that I told her?

"To trust myself," she says, as if this is obvious. And apparently, she did.

Though I'm winging it, I've realized that everyone else is, too. Parenting starts out as a concrete project. You're full of ideas about how to shape your children. But you end up with this jellyfish of a family that you can't control exactly. All you can do is warm the waters and nudge it in the right direction.

I've started following some of my own advice, and trusting myself more. Instead of assuming a "parental" persona, I try to be myself. I've accepted that whatever my true story is, it's enough. The next time my kids chastise me because I've mistaken the gender of another French noun ("It's *le réfrigérateur*, mommy"), I reframe the problem.

"Do you know why I came to France?" I ask. "I thought it would be interesting to live in another country. I wanted to travel and have an adventure. And guess what? Even right now, I'm having it."

Bean, truly French in her ability to explicate, clarifies her feelings for me.

"I'm embarrassed of you sometimes, but I'm not ashamed of you. I never don't want you to be my mommy."

And when I ask her what she wants to be when she grows up, she says, as if it's obvious: "Maybe a lawyer, but maybe a writer, like you."

You know you're in your forties when . . .

- Your reaction to seeing a newborn baby has gone from "I want another one" to "I can't believe people are still doing this" to "Ah, the cycle of life."

- In the course of a year or two, you have morphed from ripe young mother to middle-aged mom.

- When looking at pictures of a high school friend on Facebook, you think she's her teenage daughter.

- You swear in front of your children, but they're not allowed to swear in front of you.

- You still use birth control, even though it's probably unnecessary.

how to be afraid

IT IS A PERFECTLY NORMAL DINNER PARTY until someone stands up, checks his phone and says: I think there's been an explosion at the Stade de France.

Simon is not at the dinner because he's at the Stade de France as a journalist, watching the France-Germany match. Everyone runs to their phones. I say something I've never said at a Parisian dinner party before, and that I even hesitate to say now: "Could we turn on the TV?"

Soon people are staring at their phones and calling out the names of familiar cafés where there have apparently been shootings. All of these places are between the dinner party and my apartment. I passed by one of them an hour or so ago, on my way to dinner. We hear that there are hostages at the Bataclan concert hall. When I walked by it earlier today, to take my older son to the eye doctor, there was a huge white tour bus out front. It's six minutes' walk from my house, where my children are at home with a babysitter.

No one on French TV—or any TV channel we turn to—knows what's happening. But our city appears to be under siege. The dinner-party guests are scanning Twitter and calling out estimates of the number of dead. There are apparently dozens of people being held hostage inside the Bataclan. What about inside the stadium?

To my surprise, I reach Simon on his phone. He says the explosions were outside the Stade de France. He's inside the stadium's press box, tweeting and being interviewed on Dutch radio. He's a scared Parisian, but he's also a journalist who has found himself at the center of the biggest story in the world. Soon all of us will hear him on television, explaining that even after the explosions (there were several), the match played on, and the fans cheered French goals and did "the wave."

He has spoken to our babysitter, who says the kids fell asleep before the attacks began, and they haven't woken up. Since the Bataclan is under siege and there are shooters on the loose, I've decided to stay put. Simon will wait and see. He says: "The key goal for our family is that we all survive tonight. The kids will almost certainly be safe in the flat. Let's not take risks."

No one knows what's happening outside the stadium, or what will happen next around Paris. The host of the dinner, an Italian, says the same band of people must be doing the shootings at different cafés. Where are they now?

A friend in New York who did security training sees on Twitter that Simon is inside the stadium. He texts me instructions about what Simon should do in case he comes under fire: "Stay as flat to ground as possible. If he has to move, crawl low." This doesn't apply in all situations; will it apply now? I email these instructions to Simon. He usually thinks I'm excessively cautious. Will he think so this time? (He later tells me that he didn't get the message.)

A couple from the dinner party is trying to reach their teenage children. I call my babysitter. I text my brother. I reply to a kind message from a man I know only from Twitter. Two other dinner-party guests get text messages from their exes, wanting to know if they're okay.

"This is worse than *Charlie Hebdo*," I say to the room of people. That was the attack ten months earlier at a newspaper near our house—

and then at a kosher supermarket—in which seventeen people were murdered. No one replies. Apparently the scale of tonight's attacks was already obvious to everyone.

A map comes on the BBC showing the sites of two of the shootings. It's basically a map of my neighborhood. It's not just Paris that's in the news—it's my small part of it, a former working-class district that's been overrun by "bourgeois bohemians" like me.

French people are tweeting #portesouvertes, to help those stranded on the streets. This sounds generous but risky: Who would open their doors right now? Police are warning everyone not to go outside.

My hosts makes up some extra beds for the night. The couple from the dinner party tries to figure out whether they can drive home. Their kids are fine, but now they're home alone. Simon is still inside the stadium.

The French president, who was at the France-Germany match, says France's borders have been closed. I learn the French word for curfew: *couvre-feu*. On the news they're reporting that dozens of people may have been murdered inside the Bataclan. The numbers are hard to fathom.

Simon was safe inside the stadium, but now he and some friends are heading home, back into central Paris. My kids are still asleep. Their babysitter isn't. All I keep thinking is: What will I tell them when they wake up?

In the end, I don't have to tell my children about the attacks. Their babysitter does. Having spent the night on our couch, she's sitting in our living room when they wake up. Simon is home, too; he arrived in a taxi at 2:00 a.m. I come home when they're having breakfast. I've barely slept. (I will hereafter add eyeshades and sleeping pills to the list of items I carry everywhere.) We decide to let the kids watch cartoons indefinitely. Paris is calm, but we're afraid to go outside.

I slowly learn that people I know had been much closer to the shootings than I was. My friend Carmela was eating dinner at home with her daughters when they heard gunshots outside. Her eight-year-old, primed from the *Charlie Hebdo* shootings, asked immediately, "Mommy, is it an attack?"

"No, I'm sure it's not, it can't be," Carmela replied. Then she looked outside her window and saw bodies on the ground at Le Carillon, the café on their corner.

Simon is coping with his fear the only way he knows how: by writing about it. I track his feelings by reading about them. "I am pessimistic," he writes in one article I find online. "I fear that fear and danger might become the new normal here. I do not know how to tell my children this."

French newspapers begin running articles on how to discuss the attacks with children. Their advice is to be honest. This springs straight from Françoise Dolto, the psychoanalyst who was the French equivalent of Dr. Spock. Dolto believed that parents should tell children the truth in simple terms and help them to process it, even in tough times. Kids don't need to be constantly happy, she said, but they do need to comprehend what's happening. As with adults, seeing the world clearly is critical to their well-being.

There's a lot of reality to take in right now. Children all seem to have the same question that we adults do: Will there be another attack?

The special kids' edition of one French newspaper tries to answer that: "What happened is very sad and very difficult, attacks are still very rare. But for now, we cannot say there won't be more."

Children "don't live on planet Mars," the editor of another children's newspaper tells me. "They live in the same world we do."

Bean wants to feel that this isn't an unprecedented horror, and that children routinely deal with such events. She asks whether it's "normal" to have two terrorist attacks in your neighborhood in less than a year. How many attacks were there near my house when I was growing up?

I know I'm supposed to tell her the truth, but I hesitate to say it: there were none. It's happening now, to all of us, for the first time.

24

how to know
where you're from

VERY SOON AFTER those men attack my neighborhood, I develop a fervent interest in my own genealogy. I've always been curious about my origins, but I haven't spent much time researching them. I've been busy working and raising kids.

Now, suddenly, I'm obsessed. I'm soon spending much of each workday and most of every weekend trying to map out my family tree.

I'm not sure why I'm doing this. Perhaps it's because soldiers are patrolling Paris, and I'm afraid to send my kids to school. Forget being called "madame"; I'm now worried that my café will be ambushed. My mother has been texting, urging me to move back home. The past seems relatively safe by comparison.

The attacks were also a reminder that if I'm ever going to learn my family's history, I need to get on it. All my grandparents are gone, and my mother's generation is falling into disrepair. As far as I can tell, none of my relatives have much interest in our ancestry, or in any bad news that might be buried there. If I don't uncover our history, it could be lost forever.

I've made some gains toward feeling like an adult. I can now spot narcissists before they ruin my life. But without much concrete information about my own past, I still feel like I'm that astronaut dangling in space. Spending hours on genealogy websites is a way of putting some solid ground under my feet. And as I've learned, understanding your own origins is an element of wisdom. It helps you situate yourself within a broader context, and shows the material that you were made from.

That material has always seemed a little strange to me. I do look like my relatives. But they mostly married locals, became merchants or small businessmen and stayed in the same American cities—or in some cases the same neighborhoods—where they grew up. I studied languages, married a foreigner and moved to France.

Is my wanderlust a genetic fluke, or does something in my ancestry explain it? Have our untold stories left traces on the present, and on me?

I have some leads, including several pages of notes I took years earlier while interviewing my grandparents. And a few years before my grandmother died, after I'd pressed her about whether anyone from our family had stayed behind in Russia, she emerged from her walk-in closet holding three sepia photographs with Russian writing on the back. She said these were pictures of some of those relatives. I put the pictures into a folder and brought them with me to France.

I quickly discover that the place in Russia that my great-grandparents were from—which my grandmother knew as "Minski Giberniya"—was a place called Minsk Gubernia. This wasn't a town, it was an administrative region covering the city of Minsk along with several hundred surrounding towns and villages.

It also becomes clear why my family is obsessed with clothes. It's in my bloodline. A chart I find online, called "Occupations of Minsk Gubernia Jewish Population," explains that more people worked in "garment production" than in any other job. Once I plot it out, I realize that three of my great-grandfathers were tailors.

My mother suggests that I contact her cousin Barry, a handsome retiree in his seventies who was, until recently, a men's tailor himself. He now lives in a condominium in coastal Florida. He and my mother aren't close, but she says he knows a lot about the family.

When I call Barry, he's friendly but cautious. He says he's been compiling a family tree himself, and that I should just email him whatever information I have. I get the feeling that we're reporters competing for the same scoop. He doesn't send me his tree. And perhaps to get me off the scent, he spends a lot of time telling me about his father, a kind man—and also a tailor—who wasn't my blood relative.

When I finally get a copy of Barry's tree (my mother finds one in a drawer), it's unclear why he was so secretive about it. It's a handwritten one-page chart that mostly contains the birthdays and anniversaries of Barry's children and grandchildren. I'm not on the tree, and neither, conspicuously, is the family of Barry's sister. The "family tree" is basically a chart of who Barry likes.

As I call more and more relatives, bits of bad news begin to surface. Don, a retired mental-health administrator whom I've only met a few times, says he's surprised that a family member is contacting him at all.

"None of my first cousins are interested in keeping relations," he says sadly. "The family has kind of fallen apart."

Don is the first person who confirms that, as a clan, we're oddly uninterested in our own history.

"It's a family that's largely written off the past," he says. "There's almost like a denial of history. They didn't know and they didn't want to talk about it."

As I speak to more relatives, I'm struck by how some peoples' whole lives are remembered in a sentence or two: one great-great uncle "danced with all the ladies at the bar mitzvahs." His wife "served shrimp cocktails in glass jars."

These people are the lucky ones; at least we're still talking about them. "Almost everyone in history is forgotten," says my husband, who's been observing my research with bemusement. It's chastening to see that there are death certificates for all my ancestors. This drives home the fact that, eventually, everyone dies. There are no exceptions.

Much about our history has evaporated, but traces remain. My cousin Donna mentions that, back in Minsk Gubernia, one of my great-grandmother Rose's sisters was kidnapped by a Russian Cossack and never heard from again. Donna assumes that I knew this story already, but who would have told it to me?

"It was during the period of the czars," she says. "There was a soldier riding on a horse. My mother told me. And my grandmother told her the sister was very beautiful." Another cousin, Jane, confirms that she'd heard the same story.

Did my sweet South Carolinian grandmother know that one of her aunts was kidnapped? My mother says she never mentioned it. But from the list of siblings my grandmother once dictated to me, I can deduce which of her aunts was taken: Esther. My grandmother was named after her.

I break through Barry's defenses by sending him copies of the sepia photographs and of an old family tree written by my grandmother, going back five generations. Finally convinced that I'm not a rival, Barry is soon calling me regularly to discuss our latest findings.

During one call, he reveals he has the silver candlesticks that Rose brought with her from Russia. He even sends me a picture. They're polished and sitting on his dining room table in Florida.

I call my mother to report on these developments, but she isn't interested in the family stories.

"Get the candlesticks!" she says. (She's convinced that Barry's children won't want them.)

I'm obsessed with the relatives who appear in those sepia photographs with Russian writing on the back. My grandmother claimed that she had merely "lost touch" with them. Who were these people, and what happened to them? I'm probably the only person on earth who cares, and I suddenly feel that it's up to me to keep them alive.

"You're finally interested in history," says Simon, who has a history degree.

"Yes, but it's the history of me," I say.

I make an online family tree and urge my relatives to add whatever details they know. When I cross-reference the tree with a late-nineteenth-century Russian census, I'm pretty sure I identify our village in greater Minsk. It's called Krasnoluki. It has probably been at least fifty years since anyone in our family uttered this word.

I'm thrilled, and email this tantalizing finding to all my cousins. No one replies.

It's similar when I suggest that we meet in real life. None of them are keen to spend any time with me. Indeed, after hours of calls with various relatives, I realize that almost no one has asked me a single question about myself—not how old my kids are, what I do for a living or why I'm calling them from France. If they've heard about my work, they don't mention it.

Thinking maybe they're shy, at the end of one call I ask a cousin if she has any questions. Is there anything she'd like to know about me or my life?

"No, not really," she says.

After more than a month of intensive research, I realize I've fallen into the genealogist's paradox: I'm so obsessed with my ancestors that I'm neglecting my immediate family. While I've been shut up in my office interviewing relatives and searching ancestry websites, Simon has been handling homework and family dinners.

He's irritated about this and dubious about my amateur sleuthing. He says families are prone to aggrandize their own stories and to leave out the unpleasant bits.

"In every family some eighty-three-year-old is wheeled out to tell a series of misremembered facts and lies," he says one night, as we're getting into bed. "And one day even this is completely misremembered." (He assures me this isn't true of his own ancestors, who were Lithuanian intellectuals.)

If what I'm discovering is the aggrandized version of my family tree, I'm not sure I'd want to know the real version. The further back I go, the more low status and unglamorous we get. I'd thought that at least we were tailors back in Russia. But Don says my great-great-grandfather was a "tinkerer."

"He would travel out during the week to villages, and fix people's pots and pans, and come back to the city," Don said. (He knows this because, as a child, he lived with the tinkerer's daughter.)

I don't discover any Nobel Prize winners among my living relatives, either. Many of my cousins work as modern-day tinkerers, repairing office computers across the eastern United States.

Fortunately, I learn that Simon's family was barely more illustrious than mine. One of his cousins tells me that most of the men in his paternal line weren't scholars, they were timber merchants.

I do find one relative whom I can identify with: my maternal great-grandfather, Benjamin, who arrived in New York in 1906, age nineteen. (Rose, his wife and first cousin, came on her own soon afterward.) My mother's cousins say that Benjamin was a cosmopolitan who viewed his adopted country as a great adventure. "He was a curious man and he wanted to be American. Learning about things was a way to practice that," Don tells me. He mentions that Benjamin read the *New York Times* daily, and that he carried around a pocket notebook to jot down observations, aphorisms and jokes.

This last detail floors me. I carry a notebook everywhere, too, to write down observations about France. Benjamin is only responsible for an eighth of my DNA, but hearing this makes me feel like there's earth under my feet; I sense a direct line from his notebooks to my own.

And Benjamin enjoyed being a foreigner. He spoke lots of languages—my grandmother said he was fluent in Russian as well as Yiddish. Once Benjamin got to America, he and Rose could have stayed near relatives in New York. But like me, he wanted to establish himself someplace entirely new, and so he ended up in South Carolina.

Unlike me, however, Benjamin emigrated because he had to. And underneath his increasingly prosperous American life, he worried about the people he'd left behind. Don says that, throughout the 1920s, Benjamin was in touch with his family back in Russia. I suspect that he would have gladly brought them all to America. I figure out that those sepia pictures were of Benjamin's and Rose's siblings. A note on the back, from his sister Rachel, says "Look and remember," repeatedly, as if she knows she'll probably never see him again.

Benjamin was at least sporadically in touch with his family in the 1930s, too. But my grandmother said that when they mailed those care packages to relatives in Russia before the war, he would say: "We're sending this. We hope it gets there. But we'll never know."

The last of the sepia pictures is dated January 27, 1938, in Minsk. In it, three attractive middle-aged women gaze pensively into the camera, probably in front of a backdrop at a photographer's studio. Russian writing on the back says that they're Benjamin's and Rose's sisters. The women probably had husbands and children, too.

Benjamin and Rose had four children by then, and had constructed an American cocoon for themselves. In a letter to my grandmother in 1936, when she was a student at the University of Richmond, Benjamin wrote: "All we want for you is to mix with the most intelligent class of young folks of your age and to enjoy College life and to get a broad view of life in general." In a P.S. he added, "Your pajamas will be shipped Monday." In my family, clothes were forever mixed with love.

Soon afterward, Esther met my grandfather Albert. Albert would later tell me that his own Russian immigrant parents weren't very expressive. In a 1938 letter to Esther, he marvels at how positive and joyful her parents, Benjamin and Rose, are. This seems to be part of Esther's allure. "You should be very proud of having such wonderful parents, so friendly, so natural, so full of fun, why, they act as if they are still in love as much as ever," he wrote.

When Esther and Albert got married in South Carolina in March of 1939, the *Columbia Record* named Esther its "bride-elect of the month." It reported on her many bridal showers and on the string sextet that played at her wedding reception. In the group wedding photograph I have, Esther is wearing a fitted dress ("white imported marquisette with lace insertion"), and she's beaming with joy. She and my grandfather—who's as tall and handsome as a Hollywood heartthrob— would soon take a honeymoon cruise to Cuba, then move into an art deco apartment on Miami Beach.

Benjamin is smiling in the wedding photograph, too, but I sense that there's worry in his eyes. It had probably been a while since he'd heard from anyone back in Russia. Germany had invaded Czechoslovakia a few weeks earlier. It would invade Poland six months later. Minsk lay just east of the Polish border.

About a year after my grandmother's wedding, Benjamin died suddenly at home. A death certificate cites his cause of death as "coronary thrombosis." But I learn that wasn't the family story, not even for my grandmother.

"My mother always said the Nazis broke his heart; he was unable to cope with that inhumanity," Don tells me. "My mother and your grandmother didn't agree on a lot of things, but they certainly agreed on that."

It's probably better that Benjamin didn't live to read about what happened next. In June 1941, German forces occupied Minsk. In July, they forced about 100,000 Jews into a ghetto on the edge of the city. Between August 1941 and July 1942, they murdered most of the ghetto's inhabitants.

When I go back to the Ellis Island website and try another spelling of my great-grandmother Rose's name, I finally get a match. She would later tell her daughter—my grandmother—that she came from "the Minsk region." But when she arrived in New York Harbor, perhaps with those silver candlesticks bundled in a Belorussian shawl, she told a clerk that she came from someplace much more specific: Krasnoluki. It says so right on the ship's docket.

The Jews of Krasnoluki weren't brought to the Minsk ghetto. According to records from Yad Vashem, on March 6, 1942, German soldiers and Belorussians gathered some 275 of them in a building, then forced them to walk to the quarry of a brick factory. This group probably included parents, children and old people. Anyone who couldn't walk to the quarry was murdered on the way. Once the remaining group arrived at the quarry, the German soldiers—aided by Belorussians—shot all of them to death. Local residents then buried them.

It was, in other words, a human slaughter like the one that took place at the concert hall near my home in Paris, though on a larger scale.

When I send out another message to relatives explaining all this, I no longer expect anyone to reply. Over the months I've been researching our ancestry, I've seen that some of these revelations are significant to exactly one person: me. And being a grown-up means that, all by myself, I can absorb facts and make them matter. Even as an audience of one, I'm enough.

The more I learn about my family's history, the more sympathy I have for the good-news cocoon that I grew up in. Why mention

Krasnoluki, a place where teenage girls were snatched by men on horses, and families were walked to the edge of town and shot? What's to be done about it? Why not focus on wedding dresses and cruise ships, and enjoy the cocoon while you can? Why not just say you came from "greater Minsk"? Everyone but me was coping just fine, without knowing the details.

My grandmother was one of the most cheerful people I knew, and also—I realize now—one of the most grateful. She was always saying how lucky she was. I don't think she was silently ruminating on all those lost relatives. But she kept their pictures on a shelf in her closet. And she understood, her whole life, that there was a parallel, unlucky world that one could fall into. It had swallowed up her aunts and their families. Esther's positivity wasn't naive; it was an act of will against that fate.

My mother was born in October 1941, around the peak of the extermination in Minsk. Eventually the backstory—the very existence of our murdered relatives—disappeared. What my mother inherited was an urgent need to keep things positive, and a sense that to do otherwise is dangerous. She learned that you must never discuss the thing itself, or even go close to it. It's best to stay on the surface and keep bad news at bay, because something terrible is lurking underneath.

And then I was born. And I couldn't understand why we weren't talking about anything. My grandmother always told me that she was sure I'd write a book one day. Perhaps she was hoping that it would be this one.

Now that I know our family's history, I'd like to have a physical trace of it. When Barry calls to tell me another story about his father, I work up the nerve to ask him for the candlesticks. I tell him that it would be very meaningful for me to have objects that my great-grandmother carried with her from Krasnoluki more than a hundred years ago.

Barry goes quiet on the phone. In that silence, I realize that I'll probably never get them. "You've planted the seed," he says. "I'll let you know."

You know you're in your forties when . . .

- Your retired parents Skype you in the middle of your workday, hoping to have a long chat.

- You no longer blame them for your flaws.

- There are certain family members you don't speak to anymore—not because you're angry with them, but because you've realized that you simply don't like them.

- There's now just one generation that's supposed to die before you do.

- That generation is your parents.

- You realize that no one cares whether you feel like a grown-up. Merely by staying on the escalator this long, you've become one.

25

how to stay married

I'M EXCITED TO TELL SIMON everything I've discovered about my ancestors and my family. I've finally cracked my personal code.

But he's not interested. He doesn't sleep much these days, so he wants to wind down in the evenings. When I begin my explanation before bed, he interrupts. "No new topics after ten p.m.," he says.

It used to be worse. At a wedding reception years ago, an older British gentleman found me sulking in a corner and explained that Simon and I were in the throes of a GES—a Ghastly Emotional Scene. We don't have GESs anymore. By your forties, these epic clashes seem tiring and pointless. You and your partner know your ritual arguments so well, you can get through them in a tenth of the time.

And yet, in your forties there's another problem: none of your partner's original flaws have been fixed. Your arguments are shorter, but you're astonished and irritated to see that you're still having the same ones. So I'm surprised when, over lunch one day, my French friend Claire tells me that her husband doesn't have any flaws.

This is odd. I know Claire's husband a little bit, and could easily list five or six things that are wrong with him. And Claire isn't exactly a wallflower: she's one of the most opinionated people I know.

But another friend who's having lunch with us says a French boyfriend used to tell her something similar. "He'd say, 'I love you for your faults.'"

I'm intrigued, but cautious. There's plenty of divorce in France. While that boyfriend may have loved my friend's faults, their relationship fizzled anyway. But maybe there's still a lesson here. Is there something in the French approach to coupledom that could help Simon and me?

I was raised with the modern American idea of the self-expressive marriage. This is relatively new. Up until the 1850s, most Americans got married in order to fulfill their most basic needs. Together, you and your spouse could grow food and keep intruders away, say researchers led by the psychologist Eli Finkel.

Industrialization changed this. Once people didn't need to sew their own clothes and churn their own butter, they could also marry for "sentimental" reasons like love, passion and a sense of belonging.

The "self-expressive era" began in the mid-1960s, and we're still in it, Finkel writes. We still choose partners for love and belonging, and to share the rent, but we also expect them to help fulfill our need for personal growth, self-esteem and "mutual insight."

When I got married, I took this personal-growth model for granted. (Though my strategy was to marry someone who was already self-actualized, then to spend years badgering him for advice.) The French anthropologist Raymonde Carroll writes that Americans view their spouses as a kind of in-house therapist and pep squad, who must "encourage me to surpass myself and support me in my efforts." Likewise, "I must encourage him in his wildest undertakings, even if I am the only one to do so, if the undertaking will make him happy."

And an American couple is a social unit. They expect to be invited out as a pair and not spend much time apart voluntarily. In the American context, Carroll writes, "Not inviting my partner is a refusal, a rejection, of me."

When this works, it's terrific. The best "self-expressive" marriages are even more fulfilling than marriages in the previous era, Finkel writes. But to mutually self-actualize you must spend lots of focused time together. Thanks largely to longer working hours and the demands of intensive parenting, Americans spend far less time alone with their spouses than they used to. And during this alone time, they're more stressed and distracted by screens.

The self-improvement model isn't very forgiving. If your partner isn't helping you self-actualize, you're within your rights to leave him. A Californian once told me, not very tearfully, that she was divorcing her husband because "I'm just not my best self with him." Her friends and family found this reasoning perfectly valid.

I assume that everyone wants to be in a self-actualizing relationship. But when I describe this idea to my French friends, they think it's bizarre.

"In terms of self-development I depend on myself," says Delphine, a scientist with two teenage sons.

Delphine loves her husband and says she's fulfilled, but they aren't involved in each other's work or social lives. When we meet for coffee early one evening, she's about to meet another friend to see a play. She does that often, since her husband doesn't like the theater.

"It's almost as if we have parallel lives, in terms of interest and self-development," she tells me. "I don't talk to him a lot about what I do, or what I like, and he doesn't, either, because he's very intense about his work, and I'm not that interested in what he's doing."

The pair don't even share many friends. "We share daily life more than interests," she says. "It's funny to tell you that. But I think we like it that way."

Delphine does want to self-actualize. She has many plans and projects, and an ambitious career. But like other middle-class French people I speak to, she doesn't assume that her partner will play a big role in all this. Personal growth is her own objective, not the main function of her marriage. And she's skeptical of couples who do practically everything together, noting, "They are an entity in themselves, and you feel a bit excluded."

So what do French couples look to each other for? Instead of being engines of each other's self-actualization, they see a couple as two puzzle pieces that either fit together or don't. And to know whether you fit with someone, you need to know yourself and the other person with great precision.

In general, French explanations of why relationships fail seem to rely less on moral judgments like "he was a jerk" and more on specific descriptions of exactly why the two peoples' characters clashed.

Practically every French female celebrity of a certain age seems to have an ex-husband from an early marriage whom she gradually realized didn't *correspond* to her. "I needed to find a man with a feminine side who made my own feminine side resonate," the talk-show host Alessandra Sublet explained.

To know what corresponds to you and what doesn't, you must understand your partner's qualities in great detail. Indeed, the French approach to coupledom is similar to the French approach to parenting. Just as you're supposed to observe your baby carefully, to get to know his habits and preferences, you're expected to observe your partner assiduously. Much like the dermatologist Irwin Braverman suggested, you keep looking at someone until you see more and more in him.

In French, people are usually described as having both *qualités*— good qualities—and also *défauts*—flaws. But it's assumed that these two are closely linked. Your *défauts* are the flip side of your *qualités*.

There's always the risk, or the possibility, that one will morph into the other.

Delphine says her husband's principal flaw is that he's a *rêveur*—a dreamer (Simon would probably call him a fantasist). It frustrates her that she's the one who files their taxes, pays their bills and handles the household's other administrative tasks.

But this same *défaut* is also one of his *qualités*, she says. As a dreamer, "I think he brings a lot of fantasy, especially in our sons' lives." He loves comic books and animated films, and watches them with the boys. "I would think that if they were only brought up by me, it would be boring," Delphine says. "The fact that we're very different is a good thing for our kids."

And crucially, in the French telling, you don't fall in love with someone just for his good points, or for his closeness to an imagined ideal. You love him for his unique mix of *qualités* and *défauts*—which aren't actually separate anyway, and which together form his *caractère*, his character. In other words, you fall for his specific combination of traits. And his flaws are an integral part of the whole.

Of course, the French can also be inflexible about what they'll accept about people. They have brutal codes for beauty. Obese people sometimes can't even find jobs. And there are some rigid ideas about the best way to do things. Practically the entire country sits down for lunch at one p.m. An American hosting a dinner party in Paris said that when she once tried laying out all the food at once, picnic style, her French guests organized the meal into courses anyway, waiting to eat the cheese and salad last.

And yet, the French can be surprisingly broad-minded. They tend to assume that anyone is lovable, even if he's highly imperfect, because he's uniquely himself. (In France, "even the most 'horrible' people—criminals, assassins and the like—can have friends," Raymonde Carroll writes.) It isn't just your partner whom you expect to have a mixture of *qualités* and *défauts*—it's everyone.

In other words, when my friend Claire told me that her husband didn't have any flaws, she didn't mean that there was nothing irritating about him. She meant that she sees the flip side of every *défaut*, to the point where they're just part of the package she loves—and so they're not really flaws at all.

I decide to try this with Simon, too. Maybe it's the key to being married in your forties. Currently, I love him for his *qualités*, but his *défauts* drive me nuts. I know, broadly, that on the plus side he's quite smart and intuitive. I also know that he can't operate a can opener, he's never voluntarily thrown away a newspaper and when anything goes wrong he thinks it's going to last forever.

But have I paid attention, specifically, intimately and meticulously, to what he's really like? Have I tried to study him, looking at him over and over, until I see more and more? Not really. I've floated above the surface of him, alternately viewing him as a larger-than-life intellectual, and a peevish, incompetent child.

I've also never considered that his positive and negative traits might be related, or that I could love him not despite his flaws, but because of them. Why not give this a try, and see what happens? Perhaps this small adjustment would make a big difference?

I begin studying Simon and listening carefully when he speaks. If a man tells you what he wants on the first date, maybe Simon will still be telling me this fourteen years later.

I quickly see that practically all his *défauts* are paired with his *qualités*. Sure, our house is permanently cluttered with books and newspapers, but that's because he loves to read and write. This isn't an earth-shattering realization, but reconceptualizing it makes it easier to tolerate the piles of paper on our dining room table.

When I accidentally wake him up early one morning, he assumes I'll do this every morning for the rest of his life (I think of this as his "slippery-slope" mode). But the same mode means that, as a columnist, he can look at present circumstances and extrapolate about the future.

All aspects of his personality seem to travel in pairs. True, he can't do basic practical tasks. (Once, when he couldn't strike a match, I had to light the candles on my own birthday cake, then run back to the table so he could carry it to me.) But in the time that most of us spent learning to blow up balloons and pack grocery bags correctly (he puts the strawberries on the bottom), Simon was reading. When I ask him about the Bosnian War, he gives me a lucid explanation of the entire conflict—on the spot.

I'm not sure Simon has personal-growth needs. Our book-filled apartment looks a lot like his childhood home, and he has practically the same values and politics as his parents. In baby pictures he has almost exactly the same face as he does now.

Nor is he on a voyage of self-discovery. Whenever I mention psychotherapy, he quotes a British novel in which a mother refuses to let her son describe his dreams: "There is only one thing more deadly boring than listening to other people's dreams, and that is listening to other people's problems," she says.

But it turns out that Simon does have needs. Once I listen to him more carefully, I finally realize that he's been saying more or less the same thing to me for fourteen years: *I want to work*. It's practically his mantra. He says it with varying degrees of frustration and anger. He doesn't need me to participate in his work, he just needs me to get out of the way or to look after the kids for a while. Thankfully, I've never forced him to listen to my dreams. But I've kept him so busy fulfilling my personal-growth needs, I haven't left much space for him.

Since he's a writer, I go online and read some of his columns. It turns out that basic information about my husband's psyche is on the internet. In an article for a men's magazine, he describes his counterfactual weekend: "You awake again at noon, coiled together with

Scarlett Johansson. Eventually you take her out for a long brunch with newspapers. You idly wonder what to do that afternoon . . . Around Sunday lunchtime, just as Scarlett is saying goodbye, your phone trills. It is Salma Hayek." Simon loves our life and our family. But unlike me, at every moment he sees its opportunity cost. In his forties, he's trying to accept what he has.

It worries me that we never discuss any of this. In the American model, couples prize transparency and think that people in healthy unions shouldn't keep secrets. But I notice that in France, couples assume that a bit of distance and mystery energizes a relationship. A French girlfriend tells me that she doesn't tell her husband some things that happen to her at work, so she can surprise him with those stories when they're with friends.

I practice this *technique*, too. When I accompany one of my sons on a school trip, a girl in his class explains to me, apropos of nothing, that her parents divorced, and that her mother—who's named Élodie— remarried a woman who's named Élodie, too. "So I now have two moms, and they're both named Élodie," she says.

It's the kind of story I would normally have told Simon right away, or at least before ten p.m. Instead, I save it, and tell the story when we're at dinner with friends a week later. Simon isn't overly impressed with the tale of two Élodies. It doesn't cloak me in an aura of mystery. But at least I have a story that he hasn't heard before.

And at the end of the day, I think he likes our story. As puzzle pieces go, we're not bad at all.

You know you're in a fortysomething relationship when . . .

- You lie about your spouse's age.

- Your how-we-met story feels like a fable.

- You used to only like some of your wedding pictures. Now you like *all* of them, because you look so young.

- It's been many years since you were invited to a wedding.

- At least five people who attended your wedding are dead.

- You've realized that "soul mate" isn't a preexisting condition. It's an earned title. They're made over time.

how to be a
femme libre

THERE'S THIS NOTION, in France, of the *femme libre*—the "free woman." Once I notice this term, I begin to see it everywhere.

"When was the first time you felt *libre*?" a French women's magazine asks a different celebrity each week. A thirty-nine-year-old actress tells *Le Monde* that she now plays more complex characters, not just the pretty blonde, and "I feel more *libre*, less like I'm limping. I'm no longer trafficking in who I am."

There are some young *femmes libre*s, but most are around forty or older. In her sixties, the British actress Jane Birkin is "a *femme libre* who has always claimed her independence, her outspokenness," an editorial in *L'Express Styles* explains. At seventy, Catherine Deneuve is "capable of everything and more *libre* than ever, the actress continues to surprise," says French *Vanity Fair*.

Men in France can be *libre*, too, and they're praised for being free thinkers. But *homme libre* doesn't have the same cultural resonance. It's mostly used to describe men who have just left prison.

But I count dozens of French books—many of them autobiographies and biographies—with *femme libre* in their titles. When a certain type of woman dies in France—often a writer, political activist or beloved performer—it's practically a given that newspapers will proclaim "the death of a *femme libre*."

Despite the term's ubiquity in France, there's little discussion of what *femme libre* means. I gather that its origins are political. An 1832 French pamphlet titled "*La Femme Libre*" made the risqué claim that wives should not take orders from their husbands. By the time Simone de Beauvoir published *The Second Sex* in 1949, the term had broadened to describe a woman with rigorous opinions on matters of the day. She isn't frivolous. "A free woman is exactly the opposite of a light woman," de Beauvoir wrote.

Today's free woman doesn't have to be political. She's closer to a free spirit, though without the new-age connotations. In a common French narrative, a woman's twenties and thirties are the period when she does what's expected. But by her forties, she becomes increasingly "free" by doing what truly suits her.

The sixtysomething newscaster Claire Chazal says her love life—including a relationship with a much younger man—is an expression of *liberté*. "It's the desire to be autonomous and to do what I want, perhaps even with a certain egotism."

There's an Anglo-American version of becoming more free as you age, but it's different. It's more extreme. The free-spirited older Anglo woman might claim to abandon the social codes entirely, and say she doesn't care what anyone thinks. In the beloved British poem "Warning" by Jenny Joseph, a woman says that once she's old, she'll binge on sausages, spit, plop down anywhere when she's tired and, famously, wear purple.

This might be liberating, but it hardly sounds like something to look forward to. It's as if the world has decided you're irrelevant, so you thumb your nose and just wear purple.

The French *femme libre* is a mix of freedom and conventions. She can make unpopular choices and think for herself, but she doesn't abandon all the social codes or let herself go. (French women described as *libre* are often quite elegant, though they don't have to be.) The freedom of a *femme libre* is mostly on the inside. She knows her own mind with great precision, and she has cleverly organized her life to match her needs. She feels that she still has a place in the wider world, and she doesn't wear purple.

And while the "free" time of life gets mentioned in the English-speaking world, it isn't venerated the way it is in France. It doesn't have its own name or come with as many role models. When the French economist Dominique Strauss-Kahn was accused of sexually assaulting a hotel maid, his wife—the well-known journalist Anne Sinclair—defended herself for staying with him.

"I'm neither a saint nor a victim, I'm a *femme libre*," she told French *Elle*. "I feel free in my judgments, in my actions, and I make decisions about my life in complete independence." She was also free to change her mind; the couple later divorced. A 2015 biography was called *Anne Sinclair: Une Femme Libre*.

It's as if there's a whole other stage of adult development that women aspire to here. And they're celebrated for achieving it. When I hear a young singer interviewed on French radio one morning, and the presenter asks, "How would you like people to describe you?" I can practically predict what she says next: "I don't know, I suppose as a *femme libre*." Becoming *libre* is France's feminine ideal.

There's something very grown-up about the "free woman." She has gravitas and a sense of purpose. She can make things matter. And yet, she doesn't take herself too seriously. She's at ease in her own body, and she knows how to experience pleasure.

It's not a bad thing to aim for, even if you're not French.

I'm not a *femme libre* yet (I'd like to think I'm still too young), but I've made some advances. I don't mind being called "madame" anymore. I've gotten used to it. When I showed up for a work breakfast recently,

I was the oldest person by a decade. But instead of wallowing in self-consciousness, I reminded myself to be "comfortable in my own age" and to own it.

I'm still an American inside. I can't imagine myself changing out of my garter belt in a parked car before going home to my husband, like that French grandmother in her sixties. But that's in part because I don't have a car, and because my husband would never notice my stockings. I also struggle to imagine sixty. But I am determined to be free in one key sense: I'll decide for myself how I want to age. And part of that, I hope, means accepting that the body I'm in is mine.

In my forties, I have come to see myself more clearly. I now accept that I have a spoon brain that needs time to dig into things. The CIA still hasn't tried to recruit me.

But I've become the first kind of shopper in all parts of my life (except, perhaps, for actual shopping, where I remain the queen of returns). Now, when I encounter a person, a place or a job that I like, I'm satisfied and I stick with it.

Like many of my peers, I've stopped wishing I was someone else, with a different set of skills or a different type of upbringing. So I was raised in retail? So my parents didn't discuss politics and philosophy at dinner? So what? I've learned to extract lessons from what I was given, and to appreciate my family's stability, specificity and warmth. Like the Brazilian editor told me: *Respect the work.* Keep changing it. Grow with it. That's maturity.

I've come to see that people raised by professors have problems, too. ("It was one endless conversation about socialism," a daughter of academics told me about her childhood.) Simon recently admitted that at his dinner table growing up, there were long discussions about history and ideas, but also constant arguments about who had done what to whom inside the family.

Schopenhauer was right that "the first forty years provide the text." In midlife, we have a critical mass of data and some distance. We can look hard at our lives and see more and more in them. But this same scrutiny reveals how much we have in common with other people. We can share a mood, and a meal, much more easily. And that makes it more fun.

I've realized that, like me, hardly anyone figures out a decade when they're still in it. There's always going to be a lag. But having now traversed most of the forties, I think I know what it means to be a grown-up:

> It's to be yourself with other people.
> It's to keep them at the distance you choose.
> It's to care for others.
> It's to love them for their flaws.
> It's to be good at something.
> It's to transmit what you value and know.
> It's to be honest.
> It's to be awed.
> It's to grasp what's happening and name it.
> It's to know your blind spots.
> It's to be a little bit wise.
> It's to merge your aspirational and actual selves.
> It's to find your tribe.
> It's to decide for yourself what matters.
> It's to stop thinking that grown-ups are coming to explain everything and rescue you.
> It's to wing it.
> It's to step up to the plate.

There are stages of becoming a grown-up. First, you definitely aren't one. Then you pretend to be one. Then you're sure that there are no grown-ups; that they're mythological and don't really exist. And then finally, maybe one day in your forties, you just are one.

This doesn't feel anything like you'd imagined. It's not all-knowing, omnipotent and large. It's humble, solid and small. But at long last, it feels like you. And you think, just then, that this is the best age of all.

You know you're in your late forties when . . .

- No one even feigns surprise when you reveal that you have three kids.
- You have attended several fiftieth birthday parties.
- Friends have begun to mention where they would like to retire.
- You've started to imagine where you'll live when your kids move out.
- You no longer consider fifty to be old.
- A feeling of well-being has crept up on you.
- Small decisions can still be paralyzing.
- You have stretches of feeling like an insecure twentysomething again.
- You feel a certain clicking past of the years, like stars rushing past in a space odyssey film.
- You can't fully account for the past decade.
- It still feels like it's your "day."
- You realize that, very soon, you will consider the forties to be young.

ACKNOWLEDGMENTS

Before I undertook this book, I consulted a psychic.

"I see the book just flowing out of you," he assured me.

It did not flow out of me. A two-year project became a four-year project. I ended up spending a lot of my forties trying to describe what the forties are like.

My editor, Virginia Smith Younce, not only tolerated this process, she made my struggle her own. Thank you Ginny for your unflagging enthusiasm and confidence and your preternatural common sense.

I am immensely grateful to grown-up incarnate Ann Godoff of Penguin Press, to the endlessly wise Marianne Velmans at Transworld and to my agent and favorite reader, Suzanne Gluck.

At Penguin Press, thank you also to Scott Moyers, Gail Brussel, Sarah Hutson, Matt Boyd, Tricia Conley, Darren Haggar, Christopher King, Karen Mayer, Caroline Sydney and the heroic Sharon Gonzalez.

Thank you Trish Hall at the *New York Times*, who ran the column that became this book, and Honor Jones, James Dao and James Bennet, who gave me time off from columnizing to finish it.

I am also grateful to Tracy Fisher and Andrea Blatt at WME, Joanna Coles and Anne Fulenwider at Hearst and Abigail Pesta.

Many experts generously gave me their time, including Stanley Brandes, Irwin Braverman, Vivian Clayton, Igor Grossmann, Douglas

Kirsner, Margie Lachman, Walter Mischel, Andrew Scott and Marcello Simonetta. Thank you.

It takes a village to write a book. Anna LeVine Winger and Adam Kuper gave me priceless feedback on the manuscript plus the confidence to finish it. Ken Druckerman offered advice and encouragement at key moments. Leah Price looked into a mush of ingredients and assured me that it would one day be soup. Benjamin Moser and Rachel Donadio: you are friends and readers beyond measure.

I am lucky to walk the earth alongside Adam Ellick, Nancy Gelles, Andrea Ipaktchi, Florence Martin-Kessler, Valerie Picard, Lithe Sebesta and Eric Van Dusen.

Merci to Alice Kaplan for her moral support and to Natasha Lehrer for her help with translations. Thank you, also, to Nathalie Amzallag, Noga Arikha, Donald Aronoff, Benjamin Barda, Philippe Benaroche, Erik Bleich, Sophie Bober, Jaime Bruck, Ingrid Callies, Linna Choi, Jason Domnarski, Marsha Druckerman, Shana Druckerman, Steven Fleischer, Marie Fontana-Viala, Andrew Gaines, Sharon Galant, Mark Gevisser, Marie Gossart, Hermione Gough, Ron Halpern, Laure Hekayem Bienvenu, Natacha Henry, Amanda Herman, Jane Kahn Jacobs, Renée Kaplan, Julien Karyofyllidis, Ruth Kuper, Danièle Laufer, Douglas Lavin, Mathieu Lefevre, Dietlind Lerner, Sabine Le Stum, Suzanne Litt Lyon, Joris Luyendijk, Kati Marton, Sabine Matheson, Spencer Matheson, William Milowitz, Enrique Norten, Janet Orth, Brooke Pallot, Carrie Paterson, Amelia Relles, Alan Riding, Marie Rutkoski, Julia Scott, Donna Joy Seldes, Jacqueline Shapiro, Ilana Simons, Michael Specter, Mark Stabile, Christine Tacconet, Gadi Taub, Amy Urbanowski, Emilie Walmsley, Patrick Weil, Elsa Weiser, Marta Weiss, Sarah Wilson and Barry Zell.

Thank you Jerome Groopman and Ronald Levy.

When I needed a place to work, a dozen people offered accommodations, warming me with their generosity. Thank you all.

ACKNOWLEDGMENTS

I double-dedicate this book to my grandparents Esther and Albert Green. You are remembered and adored.

To my gorgeous mother, Bonnie Green, thank you for your positivity, encouragement and *joie de vivre*. And to my father, Henry Druckerman, who started over brilliantly in his sixties, thank you for showing me how to live a creative life.

Joey and Leo: thank you for keeping the page count, tolerating my many absences and making me the happiest mommy in Paris.

To my wise daughter, Leila, who's not allowed to read this book until she's forty, thank you for being yourself, and for teaching me the French expression: the hardest thing is to start.

It may not always seem like it, but this book is a love letter to my husband, Simon Kuper, who shouted, cajoled, edited and praised me, while suspecting the book might never be written. Thank you for letting me tell our story, and for seeing me clearly but loving me anyway. Here it is, Mona. And for better or worse, it's me.

BIBLIOGRAPHY

***Introduction:* Bonjour, Madame**

Agarwal, Sumit, John C. Driscoll, Xavier Gabaix, and David Laibson. "The Age of Reason: Financial Decisions over the Life-Cycle with Implications for Regulation." *Brookings Papers on Economic Activity,* October 19, 2009.

Ashford, Kate. "Your 'High-Earning Years': Salary Secrets for Your 20s, 30s and 40s." Forbes.com, January 13, 2014.

Barnes, Jonathan, ed. *Complete Works of Aristotle, Volume 2, The Revised Oxford Translation.* Princeton, NJ: Princeton University Press, 1984.

Brandes, Stanley. *Forty: The Age and the Symbol.* Knoxville: University of Tennessee Press, 1985.

Brim, Orville Gilbert, Carol D. Ryff, and Ronald C. Kessler. *How Healthy Are We? A National Study of Well-Being at Midlife.* Chicago: University of Chicago Press, 2004.

Chopik, William J., and Shinobu Kitayama. "Personality Change Across the Life Span: Insights from a Cross-cultural, Longitudinal Study." *Journal of Personality,* June 23, 2017.

Chudacoff, Howard P. *How Old Are You?* Princeton, NJ: Princeton University Press, 1989.

Cohen, Patricia. "The Advantages of the Middle-Aged Brain." *Time,* January 12, 2012.

———. *In Our Prime: The Invention of Middle Age.* New York: Scribner, 2012.

Donnellan, M. Brent, and Richard E. Lucas. "Age Differences in the Big Five Across the Life Span: Evidence from Two National Samples." *Psychology and Aging* 3 (September 23, 2008): 558–66.

Gratton, Lynda, and Andrew Scott. *The 100-Year Life: Living and Working in an Age of Longevity.* London: Bloomsbury Information, 2016.

———. "Each Generation Is Living Longer Than the Next (on Average)." www.100yearlife.com.

Grossmann, Igor, Jinkyung Na, Michael E. W. Varnum, Denise C. Park, Shinobu Kitayama, and Richard E. Nisbett. "Reasoning About Social Conflicts Improves into Old Age." *Proceedings of the National Academy of Sciences of the United States of America* 107, no. 16 (2010): 7246–50.

Hartshorne, Joshua K., and Laura T. Germine. "When Does Cognitive Functioning Peak? The Asynchronous Rise and Fall of Different Cognitive Abilities Across the Life Span." *Psychological Science* 26, no. 4 (2015): 433–43.

Karlamangla A. S., M. E. Lachman, W. Han, M. Huang, and G. A. Greendale. "Evidence for Cognitive Aging in Midlife Women: Study of Women's Health Across the Nation." *PLOS ONE* 12, no. 1 (2017).

Knight, India. *In Your Prime.* London: Penguin Books, 2015.

Lachman, Margie E. "Mind the Gap in the Middle: A Call to Study Midlife." *Research in Human Development* 12, nos. 3–4 (2015): 327–34.

Lachman, Margie E., Salom Teshale, and Stefan Agrigoroaei. "Midlife as a Pivotal Period in the Life Course: Balancing Growth and Decline at the Crossroads of Youth and Old Age." *International Journal of Behavioral Development* 39, no. 1 (2015): 20–31.

"Looking for the One, Part 1: The Anxiety." Dear Sugar Radio, podcast episode 39, January 15, 2016. www.wbur.org/news/2016/01/15/dear-sugar-episode-thirty-nine.

Menting, Ann Marie, ed. "The Wonders of the Middle-Aged Brain." *On the Brain: The Harvard Mahoney Neuroscience Institute Letter* 19, no. 3 (Fall 2013).

Mortality.org

Mintz, Steven. *The Prime of Life: A History of Modern Adulthood.* Cambridge, MA: Belknap Press of Harvard University Press, 2015.

Oeppen, Jim, and James W. Vaupel. "Broken Limits to Life Expectancy." *Science* 296 (May 10, 2002).

Roberts, Brent W., and Daniel Mroczek. "Personality Trait Change in Adulthood." *Current Directions in Psychological Science* 17, vol. 1 (2008): 31–35.

Strauch, Barbara. *The Secret Life of the Grown-Up Brain.* New York: Penguin, 2010.

U.S. Equal Employment Opportunity Commission. "Age Discrimination." www.eeoc.gov/laws/types/age.cfm.

Chapter 1: How to Find Your Calling

"Air Conditioning." http://exhibits.lib.usf.edu/exhibits/show/discovering-florida/technology/air-conditioning.

Birnbach, Lisa. *The Official Preppy Handbook.* New York: Workman Publishing, 1980.

Galbraith, John Kenneth. *The Great Crash 1929.* Boston: Mariner Books, 1954.

Rosen, Rebecca. "Keepin' It Cool: How the Air Conditioner Made Modern America." *Atlantic*, July 14, 2011.

Teproff, Carli. "Miami's No. 1. Its prize? The Biggest Gap Between Rich and Poor." *Miami Herald,* October 05, 2016.

Chapter 3: How to Turn Forty

Popova, Maria. "Seneca on True and False Friendship." Brainpickings.org.

Chapter 4: How to Raise Children

Donnellan and Lucas. "Age Differences in the Big Five Across the Life Span."

Chapter 5: How to Hear

Dunson, David B., Bernardo Colombo, and Donna D. Baird. "Changes with Age in the Level and Duration of Fertility in the Menstrual Cycle." *Human Reproduction* 17, no. 5 (May 1, 2002): 1399–1403.

Lachman, Margie E. "Development in Midlife." *Annual Review of Psychology* 55 (2004): 305–31.

Mathews, T. J., and Brady E. Hamilton. "Mean Age of Mothers Is on the Rise: United States, 2000–2014." *NCHS Data Brief,* no. 232 (January 2016).

Oster, Emily. *Expecting Better.* New York: Penguin Books, 2014.

Rothman, K. J., L. A. Wise, H .T. Sørensen, A. H. Riis, E. M. Mikkelsen, and E. E. Hatch. "Volitional Determinants and Age-related Decline in Fecundability: A General Population Prospective Cohort Study in Denmark." *Fertility and Sterility* 99, no. 7 (2013): 1958–64.

Shweder, Richard A. *Welcome to Middle Age! (And Other Cultural Fictions).* Chicago: University of Chicago Press, 1998.

Twenge, Jean. "How Late Can You Wait to Have a Baby?" *Atlantic*, July/August 2013.

U.S. Department of Health and Human Services. "Births: Final Data for 2015." *National Vital Statistics Reports* 66, no. 1 (January 5, 2017).

Chapter 6: How to Have Sex

Cain, Virginia S., Catherine B. Johannes, Nancy E. Avis, Beth Mohr, Miriam Schocken, Joan Skurnick, and Marcia Ory. "Sexual Functioning and Practices in a Multi-Ethnic Study of Midlife Women: Baseline Results from SWAN." *Journal of Sex Research* 40, no. 3 (August 2003): 266–76.

Carpenter, Laura M., Constance A. Nathanson, and Young J. Kim. "Sex After 40?: Gender, Ageism, and Sexual Partnering in Midlife." *Journal of Aging Studies* 20 (2006): 93–106.

Carpenter, Laura M., and John DeLamater. *Sex for Life: From Virginity to Viagra, How Sexuality Changes Throughout Our Lives.* New York: New York University Press, 2012.

Druckerman, Pamela. "French Women Don't Get Fat and Do Get Lucky." *Washington Post*, February 10, 2008.

Lemoine-Darthois, Régine, and Elisabeth Weissman. *Un âge nommé désir: Féminité et maturité.* Paris: Albin Michel, 2006.

Lindau, Stacy Tessler, L. Philip Schumm, Edward Laumann, Wendy Levinson, Colm A. O'Muircheartaigh, and Linda J. Waite. "A Study of Sexuality and Health Among Older Adults in the United States." *New England Journal of Medicine* 357, no. 8 (August 23, 2007): 762–74.

Mercer, Catherine H., Clare Tanton, Philip Prah, Bob Erens, Pam Sonnenberg, Soazig Clifton, Wendy Macdowall, Ruth Lewis, Nigel Field, Jessica Datta, Andrew J. Copas, Andrew Phelps, Kaye Wellings, and Anne M. Johnson. "Changes in Sexual Attitudes and Lifestyles in Britain Through the Life Course and over Time: Findings from the National Survey of Sexual Attitudes and Lifestyles (Natsal)." *Lancet* 382 (2013): 1781–86.

Sontag, Susan. "The Double Standard of Aging." *Saturday Review of the Society*, September 23, 1972.

Thomas, Holly N., Chung-Chou H. Chang, Stacey Dillon, and Rachel Hess. "Sexual Activity in Midlife Women: Importance of Sex Matters." *JAMA Internal Medicine* 174, no. 4 (April 2014): 631–33.

Ussher, Jane M., Janette Perz, and Chloe Parton. "Sex and the Menopausal Woman: A Critical Review and Analysis." *Feminism and Psychology* 24, no. 4 (2015): 449–68.

Wilson, Robert A. *Feminine Forever.* New York: M. Evans and Company, Inc., 1966.

Chapter 9: How to Be an Expert

Interview with David O. Russell.

Chapter 10: How to Have a Midlife Crisis

Barruyer, Cendrine. *"40 ans pourquoi la crise?"* Psychologies.com.

Blanchflower, David G., and Andrew Oswald. "Is Well-being U-Shaped over the Life Cycle?" NBER Working Paper No. 12935 (February 2007).

Agenda for scientific meeting of British Psycho-Analytical Society on June 5, 1957, and minutes of meeting. Provided by Joanne Halford, archivist, Institute of Psychoanalysis.

Donnellan and Lucas. "Age Differences in the Big Five Across the Life Span."

Erikson, Erik H., and Joan M. Erikson. *The Life Cycle Completed.* Extended Version. New York: W. W. Norton & Company, 1997.

Finch, David. "Live Long and Prosper? Demographic Trends and Their Implications for Living Standards." Intergenerational Commission Report, January 2017.

Fried, Barbara. *The Middle-Age Crisis.* New York: Harper & Row, 1967.

"An Intellectual Odyssey: From Alchemy to Science: A Dialogue Between Elliott Jaques and Douglas Kirsner." Elliott Jaques Trust, 2017.

Jaques, Elliott. "Death and the Mid-life Crisis." *International Journal of Psycho-Analysis* 46 (October 1965): 502–14.

Karlamangla et al., "Evidence for Cognitive Aging in Midlife Women."

King, Pearl. "Memories of Dr. Elliott Jaques." *International Journal of Applied Psychoanalytic Studies* 2, no. 4 (2005): 327–31.

Kirsner, Douglas. "The Intellectual Odyssey of Elliott Jaques: From Alchemy to Science." www .psychoanalysis-and-therapy.com/human_nature/free-associations/kirsnerjaques.html.

Lachman. "Development in Midlife."

———. "Mind the Gap in the Middle."

Lachman et al. "Midlife as a Pivotal Period in the Life Course."

Lawrence, Barbara S. "The Myth of the Midlife Crisis." *Sloan Management Review* 21, no. 4 (Summer 1980): 35.

Lavietes, Stuart. "Elliott Jaques, 86, Scientist Who Coined 'Midlife Crisis.'" *New York Times*, March 17, 2003.

"Life Expectancy for Men and Women: 1850 to 2000." *Life Expectancy Graphs*. http://mapping history.uoregon.edu/english/US/US39-01.html.

Mortality.org

Muson, Howard. "Society." *New York Times*, December 31, 1972.

Nickle, Blair Warman, and Robert C. Maddox. "Fortysomething: Helping Employees Through the Midlife Crisis." *Training and Development Journal* 42 (December 1988).

Pitkin, Walter B. *Life Begins at Forty*. New York: McGraw-Hill Book Company, Inc., 1932.

Schmeck, Harold M., Jr. "Mid-life Viewed as a Crisis Period." *New York Times*, November 19, 1972.

Schopenhauer, Arthur. *Essays of Arthur Schopenhauer: Selected and Translated by T. Bailey Saunders.* New York: A. L. Burt, 1902. https://archive.org/stream/essaysofarthurs00scho/essaysofarthurs 00scho_djvu.txt.

Setiya, Kieran. "The Midlife Crisis." *Philosopher's Imprint* 14, no. 31 (November 2014).

Sheehy, Gail. Commencement speech at University of Vermont, 2016. www.youtube.com/watch ?v=5ISkqQ3oAI0.

———. *Passages: Predictable Crises of Adult Life*. New York: Ballantine Books, 1974.

U.S. Department of Labor. "Age Discrimination." www.dol.gov/general/topic/discrimination /agedisc.

Wethington, Elaine. "Expecting Stress: Americans and the 'Midlife Crisis.'" *Motivation and Emotion* 24, no. 2 (2000).

Chapter 11: How to Be Jung

Boynton, Robert S. "In the Jung Archives." *New York Times*, January 11, 2004.

"Carl Gustav Jung: Falling from Favour." *Economist*, March 11, 2004.

Corbett, Sara. "The Holy Grail of the Unconscious." *New York Times Magazine*, September 16, 2009.

Goyer, Amy. "The MetLife Study of Gen X: The MTV Generation Moves into Mid-Life," April 2013.

Jung, Carl G. *Modern Man in Search of a Soul*. New York: Harcourt, Inc., 1933.

McGuire, William, ed. *The Freud/Jung Letters: The Correspondence Between Sigmund Freud and C. G. Jung*. Princeton, NJ: Princeton University Press, 1974.

Perry, Christopher. "The Shadow." Society of Analytical Philosophy. www.thesap.org.uk/resources /articles-on-jungian-psychology-2/about-analysis-and-therapy/the-shadow/.

Schmidt, Martin. "Individuation." Society of Analytical Philosophy. www.thesap.org.uk/resources /articles-on-jungian-psychology-2/about-analysis-and-therapy/individuation/.

Shamdasani, Sonu. "About Jung." Philemon Foundation. http://philemonfoundation.org/about -philemon/about-jung/.

Staude, John-Raphael. *The Adult Development of C. G. Jung*. Boston: Routledge & Kegan Paul Ltd., 1981.

Stein, Murray. "Midway on Our Life's Journey . . . : On Psychological Transformation at Midlife." www.murraystein.com/midway.shtml.

Trilling, Lionel. "The Freud/Jung Letters." *New York Times*, April 21, 1974.

"Who Is Philemon?" Philemon Foundation. http://philemonfoundation.org/about-philemon/who -is-philemon.

BIBLIOGRAPHY

Chapter 12: How to Get Dressed

Alfano, Jennifer. "Dressing Your Age." *Harper's Bazaar*, April 25, 2013.

Berest, Anne, Audrey Diwan, Caroline de Maigret, and Sophie Mas. *How to Be Parisian Wherever You Are*. New York: Ebury Press, 2014.

Buisson, Simon. *"Quand Simone Veil enlevait son chignon pour la seule fois en public."* RTL, July 1, 2017.

De la Fressange, Ines, with Sophie Gachet. *Parisian Chic: A Style Guide by Ines de la Fressange*. Paris: Flammarion, 2010.

De Maigret, Caroline. "Style Gurus." *Madame Figaro*, January 24, 2015.

Engeln, Renee. "The Problem with 'Fat Talk.' " *New York Times*, March 13, 2005.

Miller, Daniel. *Stuff*. Cambridge, UK: Polity Press, 2010.

———. *A Theory of Shopping*. Cambridge, UK: Polity Press, 1998.

Salk, Rachel H., and Renee Engeln-Maddox. "If You're Fat, Then I'm Humongous!: Frequency, Content, and Impact of Fat Talk Among College Women." *Psychology of Women Quarterly* 35, no. 1 (March 2, 2011): 18–28

Schwartz, Barry. *The Paradox of Choice: Why More Is Less*. New York: Harper Perennial, 2004.

Tett, Gillian. "Power with Grace." *FT Magazine*, December 10/11, 2011.

Thomas, Isabelle, and Frédérique Veysset. *Paris Street Style*. New York: Abrams Image, 2013.

Chapter 13: How to Age Gracefully

Barrett, Anne E., and Cheryl Robbins. "The Multiple Sources of Women's Aging Anxiety and Their Relationship with Psychological Distress." *Journal of Aging and Health* 20, no. 1 (February 2008).

Chayet, Stéphanie. *"La vie est belle! Rencontre Charlotte Gainsbourg."* *Elle*, September 30, 2016.

Clarke, Laura Hurd. "Older Women's Bodies and the Self: The Construction of Identity in Later Life." *Canadian Review of Sociology/Revue canadienne de sociologie* 38 (2001): 441–64.

Diski, Jenny. "However I Smell." *London Review of Books*, May 8, 2014.

Gullette, Margaret Morganroth. *Declining to Decline: Cultural Combat and the Politics of the Midlife*. Charlottesville: University Press of Virginia, 1997.

Kuper, Hannah, and Sir Michael Marmot. "Intimations of Mortality: Perceived Age of Leaving Middle Age as a Predictor of Future Health Outcomes Within the Whitehall II Study." *Age and Aging* 32 (2003): 178–84.

Levy, Becca R., Alan B. Zonderman, Martin D. Slade, and Luigi Ferrucci. "Age Stereotypes Held Earlier in Life Predict Cardiovascular Events in Later Life." *Psychological Science* 20, no. 3 (2009): 296–98.

Popova, Maria. "Ursula K. Le Guin on Aging and What Beauty Really Means." Brainpickings .org. www.brainpickings.org/2014/10/21/ursula-le-guin-dogs-cats-dancers-beauty/.

Shweder, Richard A. *Welcome to Middle Age! (And Other Cultural Fictions)*. Chicago: University of Chicago Press, 1998.

Chapter 14: How to Learn the Rules

Babylonian Talmud: Tractate Yebamoth, Folio 54a. www.come-and-hear.com/yebamoth/yebamoth _54.html#54a_2.

Klimek, Klaudia. "Dress British, Think Yiddish: Newest Exhibition of the Vienna Jewish Museum." *Jewish Journal*, April 29, 2012.

"Peanut Butter Bracha." Mi Yodeya. https://judaism.stackexchange.com/questions/10218/peanut -butter-bracha.

"Popcorn, Potato Chips, Corn Chips and Pringles: What Bracha?" Matzav.com, January 5, 2010.

Chapter 15: How to Be Wise

Agarwal, Sumit, John C. Driscoll, Xavier Gabaix, and David Laibson. "The Age of Reason: Financial Decisions over the Life-Cycle with Implications for Regulation." *Brookings Papers on Economic Activity*, October 19, 2009.

Ardelt, Monika. "Being Wise at Any Age." In *Positive Psychology: Exploring the Best in People. Volume 1: Discovering Human Strengths,* ed. S. Lopez. Westport, CT: Praeger, 2008, 81–108.

———. "Wisdom as Expert Knowledge System: A Critical Review of a Contemporary Operationalization of an Ancient Concept." *Human Development* 47 (2004): 257–85.

Baltes, Paul B., and Ursula M. Staudinger. "Wisdom: A Metaheuristic (Pragmatic) to Orchestrate Mind and Virtue Toward Excellence." American Psychologist 55, no. 1 (January 2000): 122–36.

Bergsma, Ad, and Monika Ardelt. "Self-Reported Wisdom and Happiness: An Empirical Investigation." *Journal of Happiness Studies* 13 (2012): 481–99.

Carey, Benedict. "Older Really Can Mean Wiser." *New York Times*, March 16, 2015.

Goldberg, Elkhonon. *The Wisdom Paradox: How Your Mind Can Grow Stronger as Your Brain Grows Older.* London: Free Press, 2005.

Grossmann, Igor, Jinkyung Na, Michael E. W. Varnum, Denise C. Park, Shinobu Kitayama, and Richard E. Nisbett. "Reasoning About Social Conflicts Improves into Old Age." *Proceedings of the National Academy of Sciences of the United States of America* 107, no. 16, 7246–250.

Grossmann, Igor, Jinkyung Na, Michael E. W. Varnum, Shinobu Kitayama, Richard E. Nisbett. "A Route to Well-being: Intelligence Versus Wise Reasoning." *Journal of Experimental Psychology: General* 142, no. 3 (August 2013): 944–53.

Grossmann, Igor, Mayumi Karasawa, Satoko Izumi, Jinkyung Na, Michael E. W. Varnum, Shinobu Kitayama, and Richard E. Nisbett. "Aging and Wisdom: Culture Matters." *Psychological Science* 23, no. 10 (2012): 1059–66.

Hall, Stephen S. "The Older-and-Wiser Hypothesis." *New York Times Magazine,* May 6, 2007.

———. *Wisdom: From Philosophy to Neuroscience.* New York: Alfred A. Knopf, 2010.

Hartshorne, Joshua K., and Laura T. Germine. "When Does Cognitive Functioning Peak? The Asynchronous Rise and Fall of Different Cognitive Abilities Across the Life Span." *Psychological Science* 26, no. 4 (2015): 433–43.

Korkki, Phyllis. "The Science of Older and Wiser." *New York Times*, March 12, 2014.

Qvortrup, Matthew. *Angela Merkel: Europe's Most Influential Leader.* London: Gerald Duckworth & Co, 2017.

Sternberg, Robert J. *Wisdom: Its Nature, Origins, and Development.* Cambridge, UK: Cambridge University Press, 1990.

Chapter 16: How to Give Advice

Kalman, Maira. Commencement speech at Rhode Island School of Design, June 2013. https://vimeo.com/67575089.

Popova, Maria. "Wendell Berry on Solitude and Why Pride and Despair Are the Two Great Enemies of Creative Work." www.brainpickings.org/2014/12/17/wendell-berry-pride-despair-solitude/.

Shandling, Garry. *Comedians in Cars Getting Coffee.* http://comediansincarsgettingcoffee.com/garry-shandling-its-great-that-garry-shandling-is-still-alive.

Chapter 18: How to Figure Out What's Happening

Ekman, Paul, Richard J. Davidson, Matthieu Ricard, and B. Alan Wallace. "Buddhist and Psychological Perspectives in Emotions and Well-Being." *Current Directions in Psychological Science* 14, no. 2 (2005).

Epley, Nicholas. *Mindwise.* New York: Vintage Books, 2015.

Hartshorne and Germine. "When Does Cognitive Functioning Peak?"

Kidd, David Comer, and Emanuele Castano. "Reading Literary Fiction Improves Theory of Mind." *Science*, October 3, 2013.

Jones, Daniel P., and Karen Peart. "Class Helping Future Doctors Learn the Art of Observation," *Yale News*, April 10, 2009.

"Make Sure You're Not Totally Clueless in Korea." Seoulistic.com, April 8, 2013.

Moskowitz, Eva S. *In Therapy We Trust*. Baltimore: Johns Hopkins University Press, 2001.

Weir, William. "Yale Medical Students Hone Observational Skills at Museum." *Hartford Courant*, April 10, 2011.

Chapter 19: How to Think in French

Baudry, Pascal. *French and Americans: The Other Shore*. Translated by Jean-Louis Morhange. Pascal Baudry, 2005.

Carroll, Raymonde. *Cultural Misunderstandings: The French-American Experience*. Translated by Carol Volk. Chicago: University of Chicago Press, 1988.

Cranston, Maurice. *The Noble Savage: Jean-Jacques Rousseau, 1754–1762*. Chicago: University of Chicago Press, 1991.

Galantucci, Bruno, and Gareth Roberts. "Do We Notice When Communication Goes Awry? An Investigation of People's Sensitivity to Coherence in Spontaneous Conversation." *PLOS One 9*, no. 7 (July 2014).

Imada, Toshie, Stephanie M. Carlson, and Shoji Itakura. "East-West Cultural Differences in Context-Sensitivity Are Evident in Early Childhood." *Developmental Science* 16, no. 2 (March 2013): 198–208.

Kitayama, Shinobu, Hazel Rose Markus, Hisaya Matsumoto, and Vinai Norasakkunkit. "Individual and Collective Processes in the Construction of the Self: Self-Enhancement in the United States and Self-Criticism in Japan." *Journal of Personality and Social Psychology* 72, no. 6 (1997): 1245–67.

Masuda, Takahiko, and Richard E. Nisbett. "Attending Holistically versus Analytically: Comparing the Context Sensitivity of Japanese and Americans." *Journal of Personality and Social Psychology* 81, no. 5 (2001): 922–34.

Markus, H. R., and S. Kitayama. "Culture and the Self: Implications for Cognition, Emotion, and Motivation." *Psychological Review* 98, no. 2 (1991): 224–53.

Nisbett, Richard E., Kaiping Peng, Incheol Choi, and Ara Norenzayan. "Culture and Systems of Thought: Holistic Versus Analytic Cognition." *Psychological Review* 108, no. 2 (2000): 291–310.

Chapter 20: How to Make Friends

Barlow, Julie, and Jean-Benoît Nadeau. *The Bonjour Effect*. New York: St. Martin's Press, 2016.

Carroll. *Cultural Misunderstandings*.

Donnellan, M. Brent, and Richard E. Lucas. "Age Differences in the Big Five Across the Life Span: Evidence from Two National Samples." *Psychology and Aging* 3 (September 23, 2008): 558–66.

Chapter 21: How to Say No

Bovenberg, Lans. "The Life-Course Perspective and Social Policies: An Overview of the Issues." OECD, May 31, 2007. www.oecd.org/els/soc/38708491.pdf.

Brim, Orville Gilbert, Carol D. Ryff, and Ronald C. Kessler. *How Healthy Are We? A National Study of Well-Being at Midlife*. Chicago: University of Chicago Press, 2004.

Harford, Tim. "The Power of Saying 'No'" *FT Magazine*, January 17/18, 2015.

Kolbert, Elizabeth. "No Time: How Did We Get So Busy?" *New Yorker*, May 26, 2014.

Kuper, Simon. "Stuck in the Rush-Hour of Life." *Financial Times*, October 1, 2010.

Lachman. "Mind the Gap in the Middle."

Schulte, Brigid. *Overwhelmed*. London, Bloomsbury, 2014.

"Women of the Hour with Lena Dunham: Zadie Smith," podcast episode 4.

Chapter 22: How to Control Your Family

Druckerman, Pamela. "Curling Parents and Little Emperors." *Harper's Magazine*, August 2015.

———. "We Are the World (Cup)." *New York Times*, June 6, 2014.

Ekiel, Erika Brown. "Bringing Up Bébé? No Thanks. I'd Rather Raise a Billionaire." Forbes
    .com, March 7, 2012.

Chapter 23: How to Be Afraid
Kuper, Simon. "Paris Witness: Simon Kuper in the Stade de France." *Financial Times*,
    November 14, 2015.

Chapter 24: How to Know Where You're From
Bemporad, Elissa. "Minsk." www.yivoencyclopedia.org/printarticle.aspx?id=886.
Korkki, Phyllis. The Science of Older and Wiser. *New York Times*, March 12, 2014.
Staudinger, Ursula M. "The Study of Wisdom." www.ursulastaudinger.com/research-3/the-study
    -of-wisdom/
United States Holocaust Memorial Museum. Holocaust Encyclopedia, Minsk. www.ushmm.org
    /wlc/en/article.php?ModuleId=10005187#seealso.
Yad Vashem. "Minsk: Historical Background." www.yadvashem.org/righteous/stories/minsk-his
    torical-background.html.
———. "Online Guide of Murder Sites of Jews in the Former USSR." www.yadvashem.org/yv/en
    /about/institute/killing_sites_catalog_details_full.asp?region=Minsk.
Yahad in Unum. Transcripts of testimonies on Minsk.

Chapter 25: How to Stay Married
Bloch, Lian, Claudia M. Haase, and Robert W. Levenson. "Emotional Regulation Predicts Marital
    Satisfaction: More Than a Wives' Tale." *Emotion* 14, no. 1 (February 2014): 130–44.
Carroll. *Cultural Misunderstandings.*
Finkel, Eli J. "The All-or-Nothing Marriage." *New York Times*, February 14, 2014.
Finkel, Eli J., Elaine O. Cheung, Lydia F. Emery, Kathleen L. Carswell, and Grace M. Larson.
    "The Suffocation Model: Why Marriage in America Is Becoming an All-or-Nothing Institu-
    tion." *Current Directions in Psychological Science* 24, no. 3 (2015): 238–44.
Greenspan, Dorie. "The Evening-in-Paris Dinner." *New York Times Magazine*, October 25, 2017.
Hefez, Serge, with Danièle Laufer. *La danse du Couple*. Paris: Pluriel, 2016.

Conclusion: How to Be a Femme Libre
André, Christophe. *Imparfaits, libres et heureux*. Paris: Poches Odile Jacob, 2006.
Beauvoir, Simone de. *The Second Sex*. Paris: Gallimard, 1949.
Fabre, Clarisse. *"La nouvelle gloire de Virginie Efira."* Le Monde, May 12, 2016.
Jeanne-Victoire. *La Femme Libre, "Appel aux Femmes,"* August 15, 1832. http://gallica.bnf.fr
    /ark:/12148/bpt6k85525j/f4.image.
Loustalot, Ghislain. *"Claire Chazal: Une envie de douceur."* Paris Match, September 18–24, 2014.

Pamela Druckerman is the author of the No. 1 *Sunday Times* bestseller *French Children Don't Throw Food* (published in the US as *Bringing Up Bébé*), which has been translated into twenty-seven languages. She's a Contributing Opinion Writer at *The New York Times* and an Emmy Award-winning documentary producer. She lives in Paris with her English husband and their children.

Also by Pamela Druckerman

FRENCH CHILDREN DON'T THROW FOOD

*The book everyone is talking about: how the French manage to raise
well-behaved children, and have a life!*

Who hasn't noticed how well-behaved French children are, compared
to our own?
* How come French babies sleep through the night?
* Why do French children happily eat what is put in front of them?
* How can French mothers chat to their friends while their children
  play quietly?
* Why are French mothers more likely to be seen in skinny jeans
  than tracksuit bottoms?

'I couldn't put it down' Chris Evans

FRENCH PARENTS DON'T GIVE IN

**Parenting advice from *French Children Don't Throw Food*,
now distilled into 100 short and easy tips.**

In response to the enthusiastic reception of her bestselling parenting
memoir *French Children Don't Throw Food*, Pamela Druckerman now
offers a practical handbook that distils her findings into one hundred
short and straightforward tips to bring up your child *à la française*.

Includes advice about pregnancy, feeding (including meal plans and
recipes from Paris crèches), sleeping, manners, and more.

'Her book should be dispensed on prescription' *Spectator*

CHEZ NOUS

5

handwritten notes in left margin:
Don't intrude.
oblique
compell
i compell

Chez Nous

A Domestic Comedy
in Two Acts

by
PETER NICHOLS

handwritten notes:
Scene Two. 16.
"   4 – 32 (Diana
11   4 – 37 (Diana

Faber and Faber
London

First published in 1974
by Faber and Faber Limited
3 Queen Square London WC1
Printed in Great Britain by
Latimer Trend & Company Ltd Plymouth
All rights reserved

ISBN 0 571 10602 1 (Paper Covers Edition)
ISBN 0 571 10583 1 (Cased Edition)

All rights whatsoever in this play are strictly reserved and applications for permission to perform it, etc., must be made in advance, before rehearsals begin, to Margaret Ramsay Ltd., 14a Goodwin's Court, St. Martin's Lane, London WC2

CHARACTERS

Dick, a paediatrician
Liz, his wife
Phil, an architect
Diana, his wife
A French farm-labourer
Burt, a journalist
Zoe, his wife

The action takes place in France

The play was first presented by Memorial Enterprises at the Globe Theatre, Shaftesbury Avenue on 6 February 1974. The cast was as follows:

Dick	DENHOLM ELLIOTT
Phil	ALBERT FINNEY
Diana	GERALDINE McEWAN
Liz	PAT HEYWOOD
Gunga Din	DENIS CAREY
Zoe	BETH PORTER
Burt	GLENN BECK
Director	ROBERT CHETWYN
Production Designer	MICHAEL ANNALS
Lighting by	MICK HUGHES

The setting represents three walls and part of the roof of an old barn. It has been renovated and turned into a sophisticated 'play-space'. The original rough-stone walls remain and the beams, still unfinished, but now hung with banners painted by children. Modern light fittings, black or chromium, project from the walls or hang from the roof.

On the audience's left, occupying much of the wall, are the main doors, large enough to admit a loaded hay-cart.

Nothing interrupts the facing wall except a staircase of stained but unpainted wood. This leads from right centre to a granary doorway in the right wall. There is a landing before the door itself and a balustrade enclosing it. Hanging on to the balustrade, from the roof-beams, is a steel trapeze with nylon ropes.

Below this attic door is another, on ground level. The floor is fitted with brown terracotta tiles.

Up left corner, an old ox-cart which has been brightly but crudely painted, probably by children. Other relics hang on the walls or stand free: a wooden yoke, ironwork from ploughs and harrows, great broken pots with bullrushes standing in them, a wooden pallet for an oven.

Steel or wooden furniture stands about, all easily movable, very bright and modern. Under the stairs, three up-to-date children's bikes of slightly different sizes.

ACT ONE

SCENE ONE

Main doors are closed at start but light comes from windows in fourth wall to show us the set in detail.

Almost at once the double doors are pulled outwards, staying like that and cutting off any real view of the outside. More light floods in, bright sunlight.

DICK and PHIL come in, carrying suitcases. They are the same age, forty, but PHIL looks younger. They wear casual clothes but DICK manages to make them look slightly formal. PHIL speaks with a regional accent.

They look about at the barn, putting the cases down to do so. Or PHIL looks and DICK awaits his reaction.

DICK: Voila!

PHIL: Ah, oui.

DICK: Chic, n'est ce pas?

PHIL: Chouette alors! Vous avez fait une grange de grand-standing.

DICK: C'est ça.

PHIL: Tout cela c'est de nouveau, n'est ce pas?

DICK: Plus ça change, plus c'est la même chose.

PHIL (*like housewife in interview*): Oh, definitely.

(*LIZ and DIANA follow on, carrying small bags, baskets and odd articles of clothing. They are two years younger than their husbands. LIZ looks older and leaves her grey hair undyed. She is more practical than DIANA and less elegant. She has a regional accent too but is more inclined to conceal it than PHIL is. She often speaks as though addressing a meeting. DIANA is languid and a bit actressy, changeable, self-indulgent. She looks*

ἄζοyος

νωθρός

9

around, as PHIL *did.*)

DIANA: Oh, Yes!

LIZ: D'you like it?

DIANA: Oh, yes!

DICK: Oh, good. I'm glad you like it. *We* do.

DIANA: When you think what it was like when we first saw it, Phil!

PHIL: All dust and bird-shit.

DICK: We've breathed on it a bit.

DIANA: Yes, but without spoiling the original rural atmosphere. You've done it beautifully.

DICK: Not actually *us*. Now we're in the money we can afford the local artisans.

DIANA: Oh, I didn't mean you'd actually *done it*.

DICK: They come in their Citroën vans and black berets and shake hands all——

LIZ (*interrupting*): What we wanted was a place where the kids can do what they like. A kind of—aaah—sophisticated play-space.

DIANA: Yes.

LIZ: An—aah—adventure playground where they can—aah— sleep if they're tired of bedrooms——

DICK: Only in the summer, of course——

LIZ: Oh, yes, it's too cold in winter.

DIANA: Cold? Really? Is it ever cold?

DICK: At Christmas——

LIZ (*almost at same time*): We had snow at Christmas. And on the same day sat in the orchard having tea with our shirts off.

DICK: It's being so far inland, you see, we——

LIZ: What we've got is a really—ahm—a truly—ahm— continental climate.

(*Pause.* DICK *stands silenced, looking at the ground. The others look elsewhere.*)

Cold at night and hot by day.

(PHIL *breaks away, looks about.*)

PHIL: Very good, the children's art-work.

DICK: We let them mess about in here but they're strictly not allowed to bring their junk into the main house.

(*Pause.* PHIL *looks at cart.*)

PHIL: Great, their decoration of the ox-cart. And what's this?

DICK: That's a pallet for removing bread from an oven.

LIZ: You haven't seen my bread-oven.

PHIL: I haven't had that pleasure, no.

   (*The women laugh.*)

DIANA: We did catch a glimpse of it last summer.

PHIL: *You* may have done.

   (DIANA *laughs*)

DIANA: You remember, it was stuffed up with old kindling and
   charcoal.

   (PHIL *winces. The women laugh again.*)

LIZ: Anyway I cleared it out and got a through-draught going.
   Lit a faggot in the middle to heat the inside. And now I
   bake all our bread that way.

   (DIANA *and* PHIL *have been steadily chuckling at all this.*
   DICK *stares at floor. If there is an expression on his face, it is
   an obviously false smile.* LIZ *is intimidated by his attitude.*)

DIANA: If you've got a bread-oven, keep it in use.

PHIL: That's what she always says.

DIANA: That's what I always say.

PHIL: So this is for pushing in and out.

   (DICK *turns his smile towards* PHIL. *Pause.*)

DICK: Exactly. (*Moves to it and shows him.*) I'm afraid it's got
   the worm rather badly.

   (DIANA *bursts again.* PHIL *tries not to chuckle.* LIZ *looks
   nervous.*)

   But a few coats of Rentokil.

PHIL: Works wonders.

   (DICK *smiles even more falsely.*)

   And these stairs are new, of course——

DICK: Yes, and that's my study. It was you suggested
   making a room of that loft. Don't you remember? We were
   only renting the place when you came last——

PHIL: Yes——

DICK: But we talked about buying one of these farms if we ever
   came into money and you said you'd turn the citerne into a
   bathing pool, get rid of the mosquitoes, put in the stairs and

II

tile the floor. . . .

LIZ: Yes, and it was your idea to leave the rough wood of the old stalls over there——

(*They all look towards the Audience.*)

—keep some of the original features, you said, so no one would ever forget what it used to be like.

DICK: We profited from your advice and never paid a fee.

PHIL: Be my guest, I can't remember.

DIANA: Which is why everyone gets rich but us.

DICK: Actually we did discuss asking you to come out and supervise the artisans but——

(*As soon as* DICK *started speaking, a little* FRENCHMAN *came from door, right, carrying a battered tin kettle. He wears a tartan cap, with ear-flaps, a grey shirt, black trousers and plaid-patterned carpet slippers. He is obviously startled to find them there. He begins talking at once in a falsetto gabble, incessant and unintelligible. He comes forward as* DICK *turns to him. They shake hands.* DICK *talks over his gabble, though the man sometimes pauses and might be listening.*)

M'sieur, bonjour . . . ça va? . . . Ça va. M'sieur, vous êtes passé par cette pièce? . . . ah, oui, mais—pendant quelques jours ce monsieur et sa femme——

(*This reminds the* MAN *of his social duty and he goes to the women and shakes hands with them, talking and nodding. They put in their pleasantries.*)

. . . alors . . . ils vont y dormir——

(*The* MAN *goes up to* PHIL *and shakes his hand.*)

PHIL: Monsieur.

(*The* MAN *looks at* PHIL *and stops talking. We hear* DICK *clearly at last.*)

DICK: Alors—si vous pourriez passer par l'autre chemin—à l'autre côté de la grange—ou——

(*The* MAN *nods and begins gabbling again, making his good-byes and backing away towards the doors, left. They watch him go in silence.*)

LIZ: D'you think he understood?

DICK: He doesn't listen.

LIZ: He's very deaf.

12

DICK: I asked him not to come through that room for a few days while you're here.

PHIL: Yes I got that.

DIANA: I didn't.

LIZ: He's an itinerant vine-labourer. When he's in these parts he lives in a hut by the road made of plastic sacks, old fertilizer sacks.

DIANA: I remember him from last year, yes.

DICK: Took one look at your face and backed——

LIZ (*cutting in*): We call him Gunga Din. Because he seems to have an ancient right-of-way through this property to fetch water from the source in our field. He used to work here when it was a farm.

DICK: If he tries coming through your room again, do tell him he's. . .

LIZ: Well, he must be told. He keeps popping up in the most embarrassing situations. Like when we're having a cuddle. Or I'm feeding little Sam in the kitchen.

DIANA: Oh, Dick, he's lovely! Don't you love him?

DICK: I don't know that I *love* him. He's certainly a curious little chap. His tartan cap and his battered tin kettle.

DIANA: Not him. Your son. Your new baby.

(*They laugh.*)

DICK (*smiling falsely again*): Oh, him. Now you're talking. He's lovely.

DIANA: There was nothing about him in the papers. Everything else about you but not that. So I was amazed when your letter came saying you had a new baby.

LIZ: The whole point—ahm—in coming down here was to keep it a secret.

DICK: We didn't want our family exploited for publicity. You know, they'd make capital out of the baby to run down the book.

DIANA: Well, of course, that occurred to me as soon as I got your news.

DICK: You can see it. 'Teenage-sex-champion's wife has son at thirty-eight.'

PHIL: Oh, I got it all wrong. I thought you said it was a tax

13

<u>dodge.</u>

LIZ: That too, yes. As soon as we got that outraged reaction from all the—ahm—professional moralists, of course the first edition sold out. Ahm——

DICK: They got out a reprint as soon as they could, by which time we could see that, as they say over there, we had a tax problem.

PHIL (*American*): Every beautiful human being should have such a problem.

DICK *(together)*: So we decided to——
LIZ: Our accountant said if we wanted——
(They break off. DICK *falsely smiles and indicates that she go on.)*

LIZ: Our accountant said we shouldn't keep any of the money unless we spent a year abroad so—ahm—ahh—straight away we got in touch with the owners and said if the farm was still for sale, we'd like it.

DIANA: How have the children settled in?

LIZ: Oh, terribly well. We're closer to them than ever and, as you know, we've always been a close family.

DICK: We worried about disturbing their education at first but apart from Jane, they're under ten, so I finally decided that—um——

LIZ: You said—ahh—that—ahm—well—acquiring French at their age was—ahm—more useful than yet another school project on the Crystal Palace.

DIANA: I should think so.

LIZ: With the result they all gabble away like mad in froggy lingo.

DICK (*to* PHIL): Ben and Sarah go to the village school up the road and Jane's at the local lycée.

LIZ: You'll be able to hear. They're coming home the day after tomorrow for Jane's birthday.

PHIL: We may not be staying that long.

LIZ: Whyever not?

PHIL: You know me. Not a country boy. The beaches are beckoning.

DIANA: We'll stay, don't worry. Where are they now?

14

LIZ: On the coast with friends.

DIANA: Of course I want to see them, but it's nice to have a day or so completely to ourselves.

LIZ: Yes, smashing! It never occurred to me you wouldn't be bringing Emma.

DIANA: She's with mother.

LIZ: How *is* your mother? (*And to* DICK.) Oh, come on, let's put the cases in their room, then make us a drink and I'll serve the lunch.

(*Picks up luggage and so does* DIANA.)

DIANA: Oh, she's much the same. She says the country's become a second-rate power. You can always tell, she says, when a nation's in decline: it starts producing elaborate postage stamps.

(*They move towards door, right.*)

LIZ: She's right, too, isn't she? All those tiny little Turners and Constables. . . .

(*They exit into room.*)

PHIL: I enjoyed the book, by the way. Very much.

DICK: Oh, thank you, very kind.

PHIL: It didn't seem all that shocking.

DICK: No. Nor to me. That was unscrupulous promotion.

PHIL: Yeah, like that dust-jacket. That must have sold a few copies. The naked nymphet with the school satchel over her crotch.

(DICK *turns to back wall and finds a life-size blow-up, with its front to the wall. He turns it and we see that it's the photograph* PHIL *described. No book title, though, to conceal the* adolescent *girl wearing only a satchel. She's facing the camera and the straps go round her breasts to the bag itself, which she holds in front of her.*)

PHIL: That's the one. That sold a few copies all right. And calling the book *The Nubile Baby*.

DICK: Well, as you know, that was *not* my title.

PHIL: I didn't. What *was* your title?

DICK: *Authoritarian Assumptions in Secondary Education.*

PHIL (*doubtfully*): Well. . . .

DICK (*coming down*): That *is* what the book's about.

15

PHIL: You can see the publisher's point.

DICK: Only too well. Shall we get a drink?

(*Takes case to room, right.* PHIL *picks up his and makes to follow.*)

PHIL (*going*): Still the same pompous prick!

(*Lights to black.*)

SCENE TWO

Lights same as Scene One. LIZ *comes from main doors, left, pushing a white baby-carriage, with its hood raised.* LIZ *wears a skirt and bolero, with slip-on sandals. She has a good, but not a deep, sun-tan.*

LIZ: No, you've had enough sun. It's too hot for you in the afternoon. You have a little snooze in the shade. (*She puts the pram, with hood downstage, somewhere left of centre, out of the patch of bright sunlight falling through the doorway.*) Yes, yes, you must have forty winks and no arguing.

(DIANA *comes from room, right, wearing a loose shirt over a bikini, with quite elaborate sandals, dark glasses, a scarf enclosing her hair, and carrying a basket with other apparatus. Her skin is pale.*)

It's no use flashing those great big smiles at me. No, no, I say it's no use at all. No use at all.

(*She does this playfully, tickling the baby, then* DIANA *goes to main doors and stands in the sun for a moment, frowning into it, shielding her eyes, then comes back into cool.*)

DIANA: I wish they'd bring back pale skin. For women with my complexion this is purgatory. I wish we could wear veils like the Edwardians.

LIZ: Wasn't that to hide their syphilis?

DIANA: I don't know. It was very elegant.

LIZ: Put the oil on first, then sit in the open doorway. We can hear people coming before they see us.

DIANA: And retreat into the shade——

LIZ: And we can move back if it gets too hot.

(DIANA *looks into pram and smiles, while* LIZ *gets two folding*

16

chairs and opens them near but not in the sun.)

DIANA: You didn't worry at all about having the baby abroad?
(*She puts down her basket on a chair. During the scene, she anoints her face and limbs with bottled oils.* LIZ *only puts on a little but helps* DIANA *with the difficult places.* DIANA *removes her shirt where necessary.*)

LIZ (*shrugs*): Dick knows a good deal of obstetrics. And by then we could afford to take on a proper nurse for the other kids. I can't bring myself to call her a nanny. To my class of person, nanny means grandma. Anyway, whatever you call her, she's splendid. She makes it all possible, this lovely life we've got here. And, as you see, I trust her completely to take them away to the seaside for a week without a second thought.

DIANA: You look very well on it.

LIZ: We *should* look well. Everything's turned out so well for us. The book and the baby and this lovely old farm. I always felt—aah—you know, so—ahm—trapped in London. You can't be self-sufficient there. If they dropped the Bomb, for instance. But here—no diesel fumes, no noise, no crowds . . . only fresh well-water, peaches and apples in the orchard . . . cherries and walnuts . . . local wine, wood fires . . . honestly—ahm—sometimes during the last year, with Dick working on his new book up there and the children sauntering home from school with pockets full of pine-cones . . . and I've perhaps been bottling the fallen fruit or scrubbing the flags and honestly I've felt like Tolstoy's wife.

DIANA: And it's such a help that the water's pumped by electricity and having a deep-freeze and a beater. . . .

LIZ (*missing the irony*): And a mixer, yes, and the fridge, oh, yes.

DIANA: Look at that beautiful lizard!

LIZ: Hullo, Percy, what are you after, eh?
(*Pause. They both return to their oiling.*)
And, I mean, it's not even as though we're exploiting the locals or living in a fascist society. The agriculture's gone co-operative and this bit isn't worth cultivating. So there isn't a man under fifty in the whole commune. But I think

if enough people buy up the old farms and get the locals to work on them, we might stop the drift to the cities. You remember the village—ahm—not a bistro, not a shop of any kind. The church will be a ruin in ten years.

DIANA: You don't find you miss people?

LIZ: People come to *us*.

DIANA: Really?

LIZ: You're here. And tomorrow two Americans will be interviewing Dick.

DIANA: Amazing they come this far.

LIZ: Oh, there's a steady stream. Journalists, students, television people. We put a lot of them off but you feel a sort-of—ahm—obligation to help promote the book. Especially now it's coming out in America.

DIANA: You seem to have fallen on your feet.

LIZ: Oh, but, Diana, he's the *greatest* blessing. (*She goes quietly to pram and looks in. Smiles.*) Fast asleep. Are you going to try for another child before it's too late? It's marvellous at our age, really.

DIANA: I can't, dear. My tubes were tied up years ago.

LIZ (*remembering*): After the Caesarean. After Emma, yes——

DIANA: Doctor Donald said I'd better not risk another, my pelvis simply wasn't made for it. Philip was no help at all.

LIZ: He wanted a child of his own, I suppose——

DIANA: Exactly——

LIZ: Not being Emma's father——

DIANA: Quite——

LIZ: Men worry about all that——

DIANA: But I couldn't go against Doctor Donald, could I? I was left very knocked-about down below. I've never undressed in front of him since. His body's still quite firm and he stands in front of the glass drawing in his stomach and slapping his behind——

LIZ: He's very boyish——

DIANA: But I'm not going to have him lie there criticizing my poor crepey skin. Or asking me to take part in acrobatics.

LIZ: I get that too.

DIANA: And what d'you say?

18

LIZ: I laugh at him.

DIANA: I said; 'Quite enough bones slip out of place as it is.' Doctor Donald would have a fit if he saw the positions Phil suggests.

LIZ (*laughing*): He bought a book mail order. It was the best laugh I've had for years.

DIANA: It's not that we don't enjoy ourselves.

LIZ: Oh, so do we.

DIANA: We've got a terrific sex-life——

LIZ: Ours is smashing——

DIANA:—as far as I'm concerned.

LIZ: They always complain, whatever you do. Dick kept on moaning about how seldom we had it, so I started keeping a record. I had this little engagement diary and I started putting M for morning, A for afternoon and N for night, with a cross for when I had the curse. And after three months I collated the figures and I went to him and showed him and I said, 'Now just you look at that!' We were well above the national average published in the *Guardian*.

DIANA: Absolutely. Phil says I get rid of my libido on the cat. It was all because he heard Emma and me talking to each other about the cat one day. And Emma said she thought he was the most mysterious cat she'd ever seen and she was sure he'd been a handsome prince and he'd been turned into a cat by some wicked witch. And one day the right person would come along and kiss the cat and break the spell.

LIZ: How sweet!

DIANA: And Phil said, 'Yes and he'll wake up as a prince and discover his balls have been cut off.'

LIZ: Phil's always had a marvellous sense of humour.

DIANA: He thinks the cat aggravates our asthma. That's another continual cry.

LIZ: He could be right.

DIANA: I think he *is* right. I sometimes watch Emma playing with the animal and I say, 'Now, Emma, just you leave the cat alone because if you go on breathing close to his fur, you'll find yourself gasping for air, you'll be stifling, and the more you try to get your breath, the more you'll panic

. . . and then you'll be lying there wheezing away—as we both of us do on a bad day—and I can't do a thing for you except fetch your atomiser. . . .'

LIZ: But is it wise to talk to her like that? Don't you excite her more?

DIANA: Wise! There's never been much wisdom in my life, dear.

LIZ: Oh, now, Di——

DIANA: Look at the facts. Look at my love-life. Emma's father was no good to me, himself, our daughter or his wife. And for the sake of that worthless man I sent poor Clive to his death.

LIZ: Who?

DIANA: You remember, he was killed in action soon after I told him he had no chance. People said it was virtually suicide. I don't know. I only know some kind of demon's pursuing me through life. And, like my asthma, seems to have been inherited by poor Emma. (*She undoes her top and begins oiling her pale breasts.*) And what good have I been to Phil? Or he to me, for that matter?

LIZ: Oh, come on, Di, you've given each other——

(*The little* FRENCHMAN *has come from the room, right, and wandered across, obviously taking his usual short-cut to the water. He carries in one hand his battered tin kettle, in the other, by its feet, a live fowl. He almost collides with the pram, looks up and sees them and is startled. They have heard him now and turn, as embarrassed as he is. They cover their bodies. He begins gabbling at once in his falsetto French, looking at the ground.*)

LIZ (*putting a brave front on it*): Monsieur. Vous êtes passé encore par cette pièce?

(*He now decides there is no retreat and comes forward to them.* LIZ *smiles nervously. He puts down his kettle and shakes hands with* DIANA, *then* LIZ, *talking all the time. He then picks up the kettle again, then holds out the live fowl to* LIZ. *He seems to expect her to take it, so she does.*)

For me? Oh, merci, merci bien. God, it's alive! C'est vivant.

DIANA: Is it a gift?

20

LIZ: He often brings a peace-offering—strawberries, walnuts, whatever's in season. Mais, m'sieur, merci beaucoup, très gentil. Mais—ahm, ahh, erm, est-ce que c'est possible à tuer cette poulet? Monsieur!
(At her loud tone he stops speaking.)
Est-ce que possible à tuer? Parce que je suis—ahh—je ne suis pas une femme de campagne. Je crois que je ne puis pas—vous comprenez?
(He makes elaborate signs of understanding, then of breaking the bird's neck, then gabbles on again, with a little laugh. Takes fowl from her and goes off through main doorway.)
Merci bien, monsieur . . . oui, bon à manger. . . .

DIANA: Is he a Peeping Tom?

LIZ: Perhaps he didn't understand Dick telling him not to take that short-cut. All his life he's been coming through here, from the road through the cattle-sheds. That used to be his room at one time.
(They are ready for the sun now and prepare to leave.)
Just in case he comes back with the dead fowl, let's go into the orchard.

DIANA: I think so.
(LIZ tidies the chairs, DIANA puts her oils, etc. in the basket and goes to the pram. She looks at baby.)

DIANA: Phil wants a son. He was so jealous when we got your letter. 'Another boy,' he said, 'they've got another boy.' For days he went round talking about adopting one.

LIZ: Why don't you?

DIANA: I said all right, if that's what he wanted, though it seemed too late in the day. But he never went through with it. He wants the boy to be his.

LIZ: Well, you're sterilized, it's out of the question. He might as well face facts.

DIANA: Exactly. I'm no damn use to him at all.
(She wanders towards the main door, picking up a folding chair, then moving off. LIZ watches, then:)

LIZ: The tragedy queen. I've seen it all before. I saw it first at school. Clytemnestra, was it, or Antigone? One of those. And ever since we've had this carry-on. . . . *(Looks into pram.*) You can't win with her. Whatever you say, she goes one worse. Doesn't she, love? Yes, you know, don't you? Yes, you do.

(*She wheels off the pram after* DIANA, *talking to the baby.*)
(*As she passes through the doors, lights quickly go to black.*)
(*Few seconds' pause.*)
(*Long flash of lightning.*)
(*Two seconds' silence then sudden crack of thunder, very loud.*)
(*More lightning flashes, almost at once, then more bursts of thunder.*)

SCENE THREE

During one of the lulls, DICK *comes in at main doors, then* PHIL. DICK *switches on lights, artfully disposed spots and strips concealed behind beams. They wear same clothes, but* PHIL *has bottle of wine and a glass. He has obviously drunk some already.*

PHIL *gets badminton racket and hits shuttlecock up and down. Then at* DICK, *who fails to catch it with his hand.* DICK *picks up racket and hits it back to* PHIL *and they play. But* PHIL *makes* DICK *run and in the end* DICK *lets the bird fall. He puts the racket and bird away, climbs stairs to study.*

PHIL: I help?
DICK: Thank you very much.
(PHIL *puts down bottle and follows him. A louder burst of thunder and the lights flicker and go out for a moment.* LIZ *and* DIANA *enter laughing, by main door. They have changed into trouser-suits. They each have a glass.*)
DIANA: Rentacloud!
LIZ: I knew this would happen. We've had sunshine for weeks but the moment you arrive——
DIANA: D'you remember our night at the Post Office Tower?
LIZ: The restaurant turning round and rain beating against the glass. Ahm—London quite invisible.
DIANA: And they were so *proud* of it!
LIZ (*pouring drinks for both*): The Isle of Wight!

22

DIANA (*laughing*): The Isle of Wight! Sou'westers in the sun
　　lounge!
　　(PHIL *and* DICK *come from study, bringing apparatus.*)
PHIL (*portentously*): The storm-clouds were gathering over
　　Europe.
DIANA: It's the Isle of Wight all over again!
PHIL: The Isle of Wight! Sou'westers in the sun lounge!
LIZ: And the notice on the glass doors, ahm—d'you remember
　　that?—ahh—'High winds, danger of breakage, please use
　　other entrance.'
　　(*The men bring down the apparatus and during this dialogue
　　they fit up a slide projector and a screen on the facing wall.
　　There is a wall-plug by the door, right.*)
DICK: Who was it suggested we hire ourselves out to countries
　　with a water shortage?
DIANA: That was Phil.
DICK: He said, 'If they paid us to meet in the Sahara——'
LIZ: That was me, as a matter of fact, ahm——
DICK: '—it would be much cheaper than planting all those
　　trees.'
LIZ: Or building dams, yes, that was me.
　　(*The women move chairs into position to watch the screen.*)
PHIL: While you're standing there taking the credit for my
　　jokes, perhaps you could pour me a glass.
　　(*She does, laughing.*)
LIZ: Lie back and I'll drink it for you.
　　(PHIL *is upstage arranging the screen, the other three down,*
　　DICK *fitting up projector.*)
　　It wasn't always rainy when we met. In the early years it
　　was always sunshine.
DICK: That's not how I remember it.
LIZ (*to* DIANA): He never remembers sunshine.
DICK: D'you mean the years before I went in the army?
LIZ: When we were at school, yes, and you and Di were in love
　　and I used to be gooseberry.
DIANA: Oh, yes, before Phil, yes. The rain didn't start till Phil.
LIZ: Hullo, Hullo——
PHIL (*coming down, drinking*): This is the local wine, you say?

23

DICK: The Mayor's, yes, the Mayor of the village. He sells us wine and eggs.

LIZ: At one franc a litre, it's less than Coca Cola.

PHIL: Nice and fruity too. I usually drink draught Guinness but when in Rome. . . .

DIANA: He's developing a beer-belly too.

(DICK *has finished the preparations and switches on projector, throwing a white light on the screen. A lightning flash outside and all lights go off for two seconds. Groans from everyone. Thunder. Lights go on again. Cheers.*)

DICK: Right.

(*Goes to door, right, switches off lights. Only screen and projector lit. Women and* PHIL *have found seats.* DICK *stands at projector.*)

This is a selection, a short-list, a top ten of last year's snaps. If you want more, I've got them, but the quality of the photography will steadily deteriorate the wider we cast our net. Not all of these are of visual interest and the first dozen or so tend to be mainly personal, but all, I think, reach a certain—— (*Breaks off.*) —anyway——

(*Shows first picture—attractive colour print of farmhouse in southern or central France, with sand-rendered walls, white woodwork and decorated eaves. Mutters of approval and recognition continue, as well as the real dialogue.*)

(*Second picture: a boy of ten, a girl of eight, against a stone wall, wearing only trunks.*)

DIANA: That's nice.

LIZ: Ben and Sarah.

DIANA: Was that when we were here?

DICK: You were here—when?—July?

DIANA: Yes.

DICK: That *was* in July, I think. They're not all July in this batch. They're scattered through the year, but perhaps ninety per cent would be July.

(*Third picture:* SARAH *and another girl of eight, posing with bicycles.*)

LIZ: Yes, there's Emma. So it must have been while you were here.

DIANA: They got on terribly well together. She's always asking when are we going to Sarah's again?

LIZ: Then why didn't you bring her this time?

DIANA: Phil said he wanted a holiday without her.

PHIL: Don't blame it on me. *I* was happy to bring her. *She* wanted to stay with your mother because she——

DIANA: I didn't think it polite to mention that.

PHIL: —because she gets anything she asks for there.

DIANA: This again?

PHIL: You going to tell me she doesn't get spoilt?

DIANA: She loves her granny, that's all. We're terribly close, all three of us.

PHIL: I'll give you that. Ever since your Mam threw your Dad out——

DIANA: Threw him out? He left——

PHIL: —you've been a right bloody trio.

DIANA: He left her all alone with a growing child——

PHIL: Alone? What about the ever-present Doctor Donald?

DIANA: Ee bai goom.

PHIL: A little touch of Dettol in the night.

DIANA: Ee, thah knows, oor Phil's got a cruel tongue on him. (*Pause.*)

LIZ: Tuppence they fight.

(*Laughter. Fourth picture: same three children together, dressed as princesses and a knight.*)

DIANA: Oh, sweet! Doesn't Ben get all resentful being here with a lot of girls?

DICK (*pouffe voice*): Thanks very much I'm sure.

LIZ: No, he did at first, you must admit, love. You tended to spend so much time *writing* about children, there wasn't much left when you could actually be *with* them. Aashm. Even before, when you were at the hospital half the time and often on call. But—erhm, ahh—after Ben started going to the village school he settled down.

DICK: He *was* a bit alone at this time, though. So many girls. If *you* could have brought a boy or one of——

LIZ: Poor Ben, the centre of attention at bath-time. The only one with a willie.

25

(*Fifth picture:* LIZ *and a* GIRL, *posing under a hanging vine or fruit-tree, wearing attractive sun-suits.* LIZ's *hair is dyed dark brown and she looks years younger.* JANE, *her daughter, is a mature fourteen with a cool demeanour.*) συ+ηιφιφοεὲ

DIANA: You could be sisters!

LIZ: Oh, come on.

DICK: That may be because Jane looks old for fourteen rather than that you look young for thirty-eight.

LIZ: Thank you.

DICK: I'm sorry, that's awful. No. In fact, you *do* look fantastically young but——

LIZ: Too late now.

PHIL: It's partly your hair, of course. Why have you stopped dyeing it?

LIZ: Imagine the bother here! Awful hairdressers in the local town or doing it myself. One surely only does it at home because everyone else does.

DIANA: Quite.

PHIL: I had a shock when I saw you, though. You realize how old most women would look without cosmetics.

LIZ: But they'd all look the same, it would cancel out.

(*Sixth picture:* PHIL *lying in hammock between two trees, wearing shorts. Laughter.*)

DIANA: Social realism now.

(*Flash of lightning. Picture flickers and goes out briefly but recovers. Thunder.*)

(*Seventh picture:* DIANA *in hammock.*)

PHIL: Soon got kicked out of that.

DIANA: You'd been there hours. I asked you to take our picture.

DICK: Ah, that's it. You took it, yes. Only it's got a bit of the camera case at the bottom there. See?

PHIL: Oh, yeah. See that, Di? Bit of the camera case?

DICK: The blur at the bottom.

(*Eighth picture: men playing boules in village square.*)

PHIL: That's better. D'you take this, Dick?

DICK: Yes.

PHIL: You can tell.

(*Silence. As no one says anything, he goes on to the ninth; a*

26

fortified village church.)

Très solide, uh?

LIZ: The village church.

PHIL: Très solide, très folklorique, n'est ce pas?

(*Tenth:* DICK *in swimming trunks at lake or sea.*)

Très solide aussi. Formidable.

LIZ: One of the days we persuaded him to come for a swim.

DICK: That was yours, wasn't it, love? Rather nice.

(*Eleventh: similar scene but* PHIL *and* JANE *in swimming clothes, both reaching for a ball. Reactions indistinct and casual.*)

(*Twelfth:* JANE, *same clothes, lying in long grass.*)

DIANA: How could she lie in the grass like that with all those insects and vipers about? I used to look at her bare legs sometimes and think to myself: That girl's asking for it.

DICK: Who took this? I didn't.

LIZ: Not me.

DIANA: No.

PHIL: I might have, I can't remember.

(*Thirteenth:* BEN *at wheel of Citroën, smiling, wearing warmer clothes.*)

DICK: I think this was in the winter, this one. Ben reversing up and down the yard.

(*Fourteenth:* LIZ *with grey hair, wearing bikini.*)

DIANA: Must be later, yes, your hair's grey.

LIZ: This was spring, yes. You see what we were saying about cold nights and warm days, even in January we could wear those clothes.

(*Fifteenth: rather soon, the little* FRENCHMAN, *with a hoe, formally facing camera.* PHIL *and* DICK *at once start imitating his falsetto gabble.*)

Oh, did I tell you, love, he came through their bedroom again today, quite unexpectedly?

DICK: Oh, no——

LIZ: Yes, just as we were oiling our bosoms.

DICK: I'll speak to him again.

DIANA: Dick, let's see that last picture again. I didn't really see.

(*Fourteenth again:* LIZ *in bikini.*)

27

This can't have been in spring, can't possibly, Liz, you're not pregnant.

DICK: No, this is much earlier, before Christmas, it was pretty chilly in November, then we got these warm afternoons. No, showing it after Ben in the car, I thought it was the same group but obviously——

DIANA: Not November surely, your hair's completely grey. You were in England in October. We met in town, d'you remember? By chance. Your hair was dark-brown then. It couldn't have gone completely grey in a few weeks.

DICK: I expect that was her wig. When you met in town. Must have been.

(*They don't reply.* DICK *puts on picture of little* MAN *again, then next, which is* JANE *on a bike. Lightning flash, thunder crack close by. But* LIZ *has crossed to the wall right and switches on the lights. They all look at her.*)

LIZ: This is stupid. Don't you think so, love?

DICK: Now steady on, don't get excited——

LIZ: I'm not, but Di and Phil are supposed to be our friends, they should share our secrets.

(*Pause. The picture of* JANE *remains on the screen, dimmed by the other lights.*)

I wasn't pregnant in that picture because I'm not Sam's mother. I'm his grandmother.

DICK: Oh, dear.

LIZ: It was Jane who was pregnant, not me. We'd hardly got back to England last year when she told us.

(*They are moving about, she and* DICK. DIANA *and* PHIL *stay seated, listening.*)

Well, of course we thought it must have happened at her comprehensive school. Which I think is a natural assumption.

DICK: And which she initially claimed to be the case.

LIZ: She was frightened and confused, poor love——

(*He turns off the projector.*)

DICK: I'm not blaming her——

LIZ: I know you're not, but we mustn't give the impression she wasn't honest with us. She only lied because she was

28

confused and partly also—ahm——

DICK: Trying to cover up for Monique.

PHIL: Monique?

LIZ: That au-pair girl we had last year, you remember, she was helpful with the language but not much else.

DICK: Well, I could date the beginning of pregnancy and of course she had to admit it had happened in July——

LIZ: While we were staying on the farm.

DICK: Which seemed mysterious——

LIZ: But she at once made a clean breast of the whole business. D'you remember one night she went to town with Monique? I was afraid of her French car-driving.

DICK: The least of our worries.

LIZ: We couldn't know they were going to meet these local boys. They'd picked them up earlier that day while they were supposed to be fetching the family ice-creams. And this night they met in a bar and afterwards went for a country drive and Sam was started in the back of our car.

DIANA: How frightening for you!

DICK: Well, of course, it's easy to look back, now that the worst is over, and pretend to ourselves it wasn't a shock, but if we're honest, we'd have to admit——

LIZ: We had a good cry. But what for me helped to heal the shock and pain was Jane's trust in us. God bless her, as soon as she saw there was no covering up for Monique, she told us everything and said she'd do whatever we thought was best.

PHIL: Did you try to find Monique?

DICK: We knew her address in France——

LIZ: But whatever for? We were dealing here with the promise of a new life.

(LIZ *and* DICK *come together and he puts his arm round her shoulder.*)

And we all agreed that life mustn't start in a cloud of punishment and blame.

DIANA: Didn't you think about an operation?

DICK: Briefly, yes.

LIZ: Oh, Diana, here was I, my children growing up, suddenly

29

presented with a brand-new baby. Ahm, a grandmother at thirty-eight and every chance of living to be a great and even a great-great-grandmother. Ahm. How could we talk about operations?

DICK: Not that it was all that simple. This was in September. *The Nubile Baby* had just come out.

PHIL: I was thinking, yes——

DICK: You see, Phil?

PHIL: Yes. βρωμια

DICK: The <u>filth</u> they'd spread across the papers? The way they'd <u>persecute</u> Jane?

LIZ: And the other children. Not to mention Dick himself.

DICK: And, though in some ways the event seemed to be a stunning specific instance of the book's general proposition——

LIZ: We none the less felt—and I mean I think we were <u>unanimous</u> pretty much from the start—ahm—we felt we οἱ ἀγυιᾶς couldn't submit Jane to all that professional and public hostility.

DICK: So, as soon as it was clear the book was a best-seller, I bought the farm and got a year's leave from the hospital and off we went.

(*Lightning and a great burst of thunder, close. The lights falter, go out and resume.*)

We'd better get back to the house. These lights may go if the storm gets closer. (*He takes down screen, dismantles projector.*)

DIANA (*standing*): Whose child is he, officially?

LIZ: Oh, Jane's. The local people know, of course. We kept her away from school towards the end but anyone who saw her here would know.

DIANA: The little man?

LIZ: Gunga Din, exactly. But nobody cares and except for the children we live like hermits, don't we, love?

(DICK *nods, busy packing. He goes upstairs with apparatus.*)

But I think the most thrilling aspect of the whole affair is— ahm—the fact that—ahm—Sam's arrival has brought us even closer together as a family. Of course I know that in suffering people find new and deeper relationships, but this was no catastrophe, this was a blessing, yet even so—ahm——

(*Lightning. Lights falter.*)

I think Dick will bear me out here——

(*Thunder overhead. Lights go.*)

PHIL: Jesus, *what a storm!*

(DICK *appears from bedroom shining torch.*)

LIZ (*continuing*): We all feel as though we've been through the fire together and, though it hasn't always been——

DICK: I'm coming! Hang on.

PHIL: Somebody got the wine? I've found it. Take your glasses.

(DICK *now leads them off towards the main doors as more flashes are followed by more crashes.*)

LIZ: Certainly hasn't always been a picnic, none the less—aah— we've found our way through to a deeper family harmony based on absolute trust . . . ahm—in the birth of little Sam we've been, so to speak, regenerated. . . .

(*As she goes off with* DIANA, *led by* DICK, PHIL *follows. He sings above the thunder.*)

PHIL (*singing*):

Singing in the rain
Just singing in the rain——

(*In a flash of light we see him dancing.*)

What a wonderful feeling
I'm happy again. . . .

SCENE FOUR

Storm dies away in darkness.

Morning light comes up, as in Scene One.

The little FRENCHMAN *opens the door of* DICK's *study, above right, and comes on to the landing. He is silent and stands uncertainly for a moment, looking back into the room. Then he starts to come downstairs. As usual, he carries the old tin kettle. Reaching the floor, he makes towards the main doors as* DICK *comes from his room.*

31

DICK: Alors, m'sieur!

(*The* MAN *stops, turns and waits, while* DICK *follows him down.* DICK *approaches him. Beneath his courtesy he seems distracted, anxious.*)

Vous devez vous trompez, je suis certain . . . mais——

(*The* MAN *begins denying this, shyly, not looking at* DICK *directly.*)

Oui, oui, je l'ai compris, mais——

(*The* MAN *goes on talking and* DICK *talks over him.*)

Il ne faut pas parler de cette affaire à personne. Merci. Au revoir, m'sieur.

(*Offers his hand and they shake. The little* MAN *holds up his kettle and asks if he may fill it at the spring.*)

Je vous en prie! Mais—rappelez—cette pièce est occupée. . . .

(*He points at the bedroom and the little* MAN *nods and says he won't go through there any more. Then he turns and goes by the main doors. As he goes out of sight we hear* LIZ *and* PHIL *greeting him and short, correct replies from him.* DICK *is obviously alarmed by the sound and looks at his watch, glances up at his room as a possible refuge, makes towards the stairs but before he can climb them,* LIZ, PHIL *and* DIANA *come in. The women are in skirts and* PHIL *in shorts and a loose shirt.* DIANA *also wears a hat and dark-glasses, which she takes off on entering the semi-darkness of the barn.*)

LIZ: Hullo, love, how are you?

DICK: Hullo.

(*She goes straight to him and embraces him. She kisses him on the mouth and makes relishing sounds.* DIANA *sits in a convenient chair, fanning herself with the hat.*)

LIZ: Did Gunga Din disturb you?

DICK: What?

LIZ: We saw him going, he'd been through here, did you talk to him?

DICK: Yes. Yes. He came through the room again and I heard him and came down and told him not to and then——

LIZ: You shouldn't have broken off from your work.

DICK: My work was going badly anyway.

LIZ: Oh, poor love.

PHIL: I told you, you should have come with us.

DICK: And I explained that my publisher has commissioned a second book and I'm obliged to try and deliver the——

DIANA: He only asked you to come to stop you working. Stop you writing another best-seller.

PHIL: No, but on a day like this Dick surely deserves a walk in the woods.

LIZ: I wish you'd come, love, we never met another soul——

DICK: Well, I'm glad you had a nice time. As I said, my morning wasn't nice at all.

LIZ: Poor Dick! I shall make you an extra-special lunch with all your favourite things—ahm—beetroot soup, quiche . . . I got some quiches in the market——

PHIL: Shall we tell him what we really did?

LIZ: Ahm—peaches and brugnons——

PHIL: Shall we, Di?

DIANA: Why ask me?

PHIL: When we got to the pool beyond the clay-pits——

LIZ (*quickly*): We had a swim.

DICK: Oh, good.

PHIL: Yes, but in the——

LIZ: In the nude. We had no costumes.

DICK: Oh, yes. All of you?

DIANA: Not me.

PHIL: Being a nature-lover, she's afraid of the water-snakes. I told her water-snakes don't bite and there we stood, all hot and dizzy after the walk——

LIZ: It was sweltering, love——

PHIL: Discussing the pros and cons and suddenly it seemed to be getting all too tight-arsed so I dropped my knickers and so did Liz and in we went.

LIZ: It was all very innocent, love.
(*Pause.*)

DICK: We're not innocent, love. Nothing we do is innocent.

PHIL: This was. A simple spontaneous climax to a——

DICK: You said you stood there discussing it.

DIANA: It was a scream from where I stood.

C   33

PHIL: On the bank.

DIANA: D'you remember those awful films with groups of naked people waving at departing Land-Rovers. . . ? (*She laughs.*)

PHIL: Well, of course you've developed a kink about stripping off.

DIANA: Girls in G-strings swabbing the decks of yachts.

LIZ: It was all very middle-aged and middle-class and funny, I suppose, but—ahm—we—ahh—we felt we had to tell you because—ahm—otherwise it would have become something nasty and secretive.

(*Pause.*)

DICK: Why should I ever have found out?

(*Pause.*)

LIZ: Oh, love, I'd have had to tell you sooner or later. (*Then to the others:*) We haven't any secrets from each other. Perhaps that's boring and unsophisticated, but that's the way we are.

DICK: You should have sensed it would be better later. Not this morning, when I've been stuck here, struggling to express some idea that may eventually provide the money to pay for the scenery in which you can go off exposing yourselves in the wood——

PHIL: Oh, come on, Dick, you're building up a fantasy—we were hot, we wanted a swim, we didn't have any trunks—by Christ, Diana sat there watching us!

LIZ: I wished you'd come, darling, there was nothing in it.

DICK: You may not be the best judge of that.

(*She looks at him. He is moving about in an agitated way.*)

I've been told something that I can't possibly ignore, much as I'd like to. If I don't face you with the accusation at the outset, I might get into some kind of paranoid sweat because the implications are——

LIZ: Accusation?

DICK: Well——

LIZ: Who's accusing who?

DICK: No, that's not right, no one's accusing anyone. When I heard Gunga Din coming through that room, startling the baby, making him cry out, I came down and told him not

34

to go through any——

LIZ: Did he wake up? You didn't tell me.

(*She goes towards door but he stops her.*)

DICK: I got him off again. He's all right. Listen to me, please! He said of course he wouldn't and he was sorry he'd woken Sam and wasn't he a fine specimen, which of course we agreed on, then he asked where his father was.

LIZ: Nosey bugger.

DICK: That's what I thought.

LIZ: I hope you told him where to go.

DICK: But after all he's only a funny old peasant——

LIZ: We'll have to stop him coming through altogether——

DICK (*continuing and forcing her to silence*): And happens to have come to do the vines in March and saw Jane pregnant. So I said, 'We don't know who the father is, some young man in town.'

LIZ: I should have said——

DICK: Which seemed to confuse him. No, he said, the man in that room.

LIZ: What man? Who does he mean?

DIANA: Phil?

PHIL: Me?

DICK: Yesterday, when you arrived, d'you remember he seemed to look a bit funny when he saw your face?

LIZ: Of course!

PHIL: Yes. I was puzzled by that.

DIANA: So he thinks you're the father?

LIZ: No wonder he looked a bit funny. (*She laughs.*)

DIANA: I'd have looked a bit funny. (*She laughs too.*)

PHIL: What gave him the idea?

DICK: Well, according to him——

LIZ: He must be cracked.

DIANA: Wouldn't you be cracked if you lived in a polythene cabin?

LIZ: A misconception of that kind illustrates—ahm—how wide a culture gap can exist even between Europeans.

DICK: According to him, one day last year he was fetching water from his source in the field and wandered on a little further

35

to pick some ceps and——

DIANA: Pick some what?

DICK: Ceps. Fungi. ~~φανταίωα~~

DIANA: Like chanterelles?

DICK: Not exactly but——

LIZ: Oh, no, chanterelles are small and frilly. Ceps are large and fleshy with brown domes and yellow stalks.

DICK: Anyway——

LIZ: You can feed a family with one good cep.

DICK: He was picking these mushrooms——

LIZ: But you'd need a bowlful of chanterelles.

DICK: —and going deeper into the woods to——

LIZ: The locals call them girolles, of course.

DICK (*shouts*): For Chrissake! What's it matter?

(*They all look at him, surprised. He does his false smile at* LIZ.)

Sorry. Sorry. But please let me finish. He was going deeper into the woods to find these repulsive bloody mushrooms—and then he says he came across Phil and Jane in a clearing with no clothes on. Now obviously he's mistaken but you asked what gave him the idea you were Sam's father, so I'm telling you.

(*They look at* PHIL.)

PHIL: That's funny. I didn't notice him. Well, well.

DICK: You were in the woods with Jane?

PHIL: Yes.

DIANA: With no clothes on?

PHIL: Sunbathing, yes. She said she always sunbathed in the nude down here.

LIZ: We all do.

PHIL: Right. I could see that by her tan. I mean, there weren't any white strips. (*He scratches one eye.*)

LIZ: Why didn't you mention it? You wanted to mention our bathe at once. As soon as we met Dick.

PHIL: Didn't Jane mention it?

LIZ: No.

PHIL (*shrugs*): There you are then. Why should I?

DICK (*false smile*): Now steady. Let's take it steady, darling——

36

LIZ: I am steady. I'm not made unsteady by—ahh—people sunbathing, any more than by people taking off their clothes and swimming in a pool. Aaah——

DICK: All right. If that's all. (*To* PHIL.) You were sunbathing?

PHIL: You were all in town or at the lake, I can't remember exactly——

DICK: Yes, all right, yes——

PHIL: And Jane came to me in the hammock. I was playing cassettes and drinking wine. She brought a couple of peaches and asked if I'd seen the cress-bed.

DIANA: The what?

PHIL: The watercress-bed.

DIANA: I've heard some names for it.

LIZ: Near the old man's source.

PHIL: Right. Which is why he saw us. Though I didn't see *him*.

DICK: Well, actually, what he says is that you weren't only sunbathing. He could be mistaken, of course, I'm sure he is, but he says you were lying on her.
(*Pause.*)

LIZ: Lying on Jane?

DICK: Yes.

LIZ: You mean on top of her?

DICK: How else can you lie on someone?
(*They all look at* PHIL. *He looks at floor, then sighs and shrugs.*)

PHIL: I'm sorry.
(DIANA *stands.*)

DIANA: What?

PHIL: I don't know what to say.

DIANA: Are you telling us it's true?

LIZ: You slept with Jane?

PHIL: There wasn't much sleeping. As you know, she's a lively girl and the whole incident——

DICK (*moving threateningly*): Do I understand you to be making a joke? Do I? Are you? Are you making a joke——

PHIL (*backing away*): No, I was only——

DICK: —out of raping my fourteen-year-old daughter?

LIZ: Thirteen. She was thirteen then.

37

DICK: D'you know that's a criminal offence? Do you? Do you know the age of consent is sixteen?

PHIL: This wasn't rape! I never assaulted her. What d'you take me for?

DIANA: A dirty old man.

PHIL: I don't feel old. I'm more at home with kids. As you know, love.

DIANA: Don't call me 'love'.

PHIL: Don't even feel grown-up.

DICK: Time you did.

PHIL: What?

DICK: Grew up.

PHIL: True.

DICK: High time.

DIANA: The greedy spoilt eldest boy who's never been denied anything. Whose mother gave him not only his own butter ration but his sister's too. Who never learnt to resist.

PHIL: Di——

DIANA: You must be three times her age. So Sunday papers! Plastic macs and gym-slips and bicycle saddles, the whole tatty apparatus of——

PHIL: No, no, there was nothing disgusting. I tell you, Di, it was innocent and beautiful.

DIANA: Oh, Jesus Christ.
(She goes quickly to the bedroom, right, and slams the door behind her. PHIL doesn't follow. Hear door bolted.)

LIZ (*to Audience*): How could she lie so carefully? For a whole year? A girl of that age? And when she most needed help. What have I done wrong?

DICK (*to Audience*): I've spent the last nine months down here! Covering up for him! My grandson is his son! (*Then turns and speaks to LIZ, pointing at PHIL.*) You're his son's grandmother!
(She looks at him, moves up a few steps.)

LIZ: No other response? What matters to me is Jane herself and the way she deceived us so cleverly. It's not natural for a girl of that age. She's suddenly a stranger.

DICK: Don't you feel resentful? Cheated?

38

LIZ: You never feel anything else.

DICK: I know that but I'm asking about you.

LIZ: I'm going to get some lunch. Is anyone hungry? We'll all think better with a lining to our stomachs. (*She goes out by main doors.*)

DICK (*to Audience*): They could carve that on her grave. (*Without looking at* PHIL *again, he follows* LIZ. PHIL *tries to open bedroom door, then knocks. No answer.*)

PHIL: Di! (*Pause.*) Diana! There's a lot more to say. There's a lot I couldn't say to them. Let me in, please. This isn't something you can shout through a door. (*Pause. No answer.*) Honestly, I never guessed about the baby. Jane hasn't been in touch. Mind you, I was nervous when you said, 'Let's stop at the farm for a day or so.' But then Liz answered that all the kids would be away so. . . . (*Shrugs.*) How could I visualize all this? (*Silence. He makes an angry gesture at the door, nearly moves away, then remembers and says.*) Lunch is nearly up. Why not come and have some lunch?

(*No answer. This time he moves half-way across the barn towards main doors. The bedroom door is suddenly opened and the white pram is pushed out.* PHIL *turns to catch it as it rolls. The bedroom door is shut again and bolted.* PHIL *looks into pram and we hear sounds of baby preparing to cry.*)

You want some, do you? Want some lunch? (*Makes a face and recoils slightly.*) Need changing too. Shall I change you? Daddy change him? Right. Daddy change. (*Pushes pram towards main door and off.*)

END OF ACT ONE

39

ACT TWO

SCENE ONE

Afternoon. Bright sunlight.

Door of bedroom, right, at first shut, is soon opened and DICK *and* DIANA *enter pushing an old wooden wheelbarrow containing clogs, books and journals, bottles and a papiermâché corset, which stands erect like a sculptured trunk. They put the barrow centre.*

DIANA: Fantastic a house like that should be allowed to fall apart. Why haven't the English bought it?

DICK: Too far gone, perhaps.

DIANA: At home it would be snapped up. Filled with paper lampshades and stripped pine dressers. . . .

DICK: We found so much interesting stuff in the beginning, I felt sure there was nothing left by now, we've been looting there so often.

(DIANA *puts down clogs and steps into them. She hobbles about.*)

DIANA: Yes. Well. Perhaps they'll do for decoration. (*Takes them off, picks them up.*) Good soak in Rentokil.

(DICK *looks at them as she returns them to basket.*)

DICK: I'll put them on the fire.

DIANA: Oh, no. . . .

DICK: The Mayor of our commune told me that the two most vital innovations here were running water and—*what,* d'you think?——

DIANA: Electricity?

DICK: Rubber boots. These sabots accumulated clay till you could hardly walk, they stuck in the ground. Then the poor buggers had to bang them together before they could go on. With boots, the soil slides off.

40

DIANA: I'll take them home. Home? After this morning?
(DICK *looks at her, then they turn to other loot.*)
DICK: This written inscription, look!
DIANA (*looking at prayer-book*): Isn't that Latin? I can't read Latin.
DICK: No, but the date. Look at the date. 1789.
DIANA: Oh, yes.
DICK: Imagine her, whoever she was, the woman who owned this missal——
DIANA: Gunga Din's great-great-grandma?
DICK: Possibly. And here she was in 1789, with all that fuss going on in Paris, walking to the village church, prayer-book in hand, nodding at the neighbours—as bovine as her animals——
(*Drops book.* DIANA *takes up corset.*)
DIANA: D'you see her wearing this?
(*She puts it around her trunk.* DICK *helps to push it tight. He drums on it noisily.*)
DICK: Très solide.
(*He takes it off, puts it in basket. He seems restless, but she's interested in the objects. Dog barks some way off.* DIANA's *taken up a crumbling journal.*)
DIANA: 1909. Three cows sold . . . one cow bought . . . one bull bought . . . one wagon of earth . . . six calves sold . . . chàr à boeuf. . . .
(*Suddenly the screaming whistle of a jet aircraft, diving low directly overhead.* DIANA *clutches* DICK's *arm. The noise is gone as suddenly as it came but it leaves dogs barking and birds singing.*)
DICK: That happens occasionally. Jet-fighters from Cognac.
DIANA: Where can you escape? Is there anywhere left? When I see a hundred people have died in a jet-crash, I think what a tatty way to go. Smack into a mountain listening to Burt Bacharach.
DICK: I like the planes going over. I like the cars that pass. Anything that moves fast and gets somewhere. Anything for a change. I hate this junk we find in the old house. I hate the old house.

(*He kicks the basket of junk. He seems exhilarated by this confession.*) Oh, Christ! This fucking place! A geriatric ward with trees! Everyone under sixty's gone to work in Paris and Bordeaux. Their factory jobs pay them enough to buy Simca saloons in which to drive down here and visit the old folk. Shoot some birds, if they can find any. Then back to town as quick as mustard, thanking God they got away. All very well for English people to buy these dumps, tart them up and carry on about clear well-water drawn up by their electric pumps. Or the fruity local wine that's cheaper than Coke. Or how they feel like Tolstoy's wife. They weren't here in November.

DIANA: I suppose that's not such fun.

DICK: When the rain comes down and the whole place dies? You'd love it.

DIANA: No. You're right. We enjoy it because it's all a change.

DICK: Any place I live in future there won't be anything old. I want everything to be new this week and next week change it all. What's the point of having money otherwise?

DIANA: Now you're going to extremes.

DICK: We're *at* extremes! This situation's extreme! Which is why I welcome it with open arms. We can't pretend we don't know. We can't go on as we did before.

DIANA: Well, all right, yes, but it's not that easy to——

DICK: Even Phil won't let it pass. And he's always had a tiresome attachment to the past. Even he's asking for a a change.

DIANA: Is that how you see him? Attached to the past?

DICK: Yes, with his trad jazz and Utopian Socialism and Radiant Cities.

DIANA: He thinks that's modern and all that happened since is tatty profiteering. Where there's muck there's brass.

DICK: In the army in Malaya he and I used to spend hours swatting mosquitoes, planning the new society. It was old hat even then.

DIANA: It always seemed to me like the Co-op, only sexy.

DICK: We thought it could happen. And we of course would be the prime movers. Him with his plate-glass, me with the

42

National Health.

DIANA: You grew up and he didn't.

DICK: Well, I lost that kind of simple faith.

DIANA: He's an innocent. With most men, this Jane business would seem lavatorial but somehow with him——

DICK: And he does see its true importance: that it puts us in a new light. He and Jane are forcing us to change. We should thank them for that.

(DIANA *looks over the junk again, putting it in the barrow.*)

DIANA: I don't care that much for old things. Second-hand things. Just that all our friends at home spend half their lives collecting——

DICK: This situation puts us beyond doing what our friends do. (*Wheels barrow upstage.*) That's why I'm so glad the old man saw them at it by the spring and——

(*Breaks off as* LIZ *enters by main doors carrying a shopping-basket full of corked but empty wine-bottles.*)

LIZ: I thought you might be here. He wants to talk to us.

DICK: What about?

LIZ: I don't know. There's plenty to talk about.

DIANA: I shan't listen. (*Makes towards bedroom.*)

LIZ: Well, love, you'll have to sooner or later. These Yanks are coming some time today and we ought to have sorted out our—ahm—our—erm—intended procedure before they—aaah—before they arrive.

DICK: Intended——?

LIZ: Aaahm——

DICK: Procedure?

LIZ: Then again, tomorrow afternoon all the children are coming home——

DICK (*persevering*): What is there to proceed with?

LIZ: And we've got to know where we stand before we talk to Jane.

DICK: Talk to Jane?

LIZ: Well, obviously. We must talk it over surely?

(PHIL *comes on carrying a large glass bottle in a wickerwork container.*)

PHIL: You sure Sam's all right in the orchard? The sun won't be

43

too hot for him?

LIZ: Through the trees? No.

PHIL: I left the hood up.

(*And during the following dialogue,* LIZ *and* PHIL *pour red wine from the bonbonne into the bottles. To begin with, it is so heavy that* PHIL *has to support it between his thighs.* LIZ *uses a funnel to get the wine in.* DIANA *sits watching.* DICK *stands.*) Well. I've been thinking. I dare say we've all been thinking. You don't want my apologies.

LIZ: No, we've had them.

PHIL: Right.

LIZ: Over lunch.

DICK: Diana hasn't. She wasn't there.

DIANA: Hasn't this gone a bit beyond apologies? A thirteen-year-old girl?

PHIL: A very precocious thirteen, nearly fourteen——

DIANA: This isn't like the others, Philip. I mean the secretary, the jazz-band vocalist, the student-nurse——

PHIL: Come on, love, this is——

DIANA: Don't call me 'love'.

PHIL: I say this is all beside the point——

DIANA: I suffered those in silence——

PHIL: Not exactly.

DIANA: What?

PHIL: Not exactly silence.

DIANA: Because I was grateful to you. For marrying me when I was pregnant by another man. Well, I think this puts me well in the black.

PHIL: I wasn't going to mention that, but all right, I'm not Emma's father and after she was born you got sterilized.

DIANA: You agreed.

PHIL: Yeah, sure. By Christ the whole birth was touch-and-go, I thought you were going to die. I'd have given anything to keep you. (*Concentrates on pouring wine. Pause.*) So after that you had your tubes tied up.

DIANA: I said we could adopt a boy.

(PHIL *shakes his head.*)

PHIL: The point is now I've got a son. Like you've got a

44

daughter.

DIANA: Emma's father wasn't a thirteen-year-old boy.

PHIL: No. He was a second-hand car salesman. Let's not bicker, Di, that's a dead end. Out there in the orchard is a baby who's given a lot of trouble to his—Liz and Dick. Just as their family's growing up and away and they've every right to expect a bit of time to themselves, spread their wings, see the world, they find themselves with a few more years of stinky-poohs.

LIZ: You needn't think that's any——

PHIL: Droopy-drawers.

LIZ: —hardship because both of——

PHIL: Please, can I finish? I want a son. Di can't have one. You've got three children of your own. And one of mine. The answer's obvious. We'll adopt Sam.

DIANA: We'll what?

PHIL: Is this one full yet?

LIZ: A bit more.

DIANA: Don't you think the very fact that it's happened is bad enough without having a constant reminder in the house all day——

LIZ: Whoa!

(PHIL *stops pouring*.)

PHIL: Emma's been a constant reminder to me since we married. What about some sexual equality?

DIANA: A reminder to me that you seduced a child.

PHIL: She's not a child.

DIANA: Thirteen?

PHIL: You've read his book. They're ready at thirteen, some earlier. Your daughter was a constant reminder to me that you'd slept with half the men in town.

DIANA (*moving towards bedroom*): Bloody hell!

LIZ: That's what they used to say, love. You slept with half the men in town and I slept with the other half.

DICK: I wonder whether this is strictly to the point.

LIZ: Difficult to see myself as the same girl now.

DICK: You're not.

LIZ: Still, I'm not sorry. If I hadn't made myself so available,

45

you might never have <u>plucked up the courage.</u> You never
had with anyone else, had you, love? Not even Diana.

DICK: Oh, terrific! Tell everyone, go on! D'you think any man
of forty wants the world to know he's only had one girl?

PHIL: We knew already. You told me in our billet in Singapore.
I told you about my Chinese bit and asked if you'd care to
meet her friend——

DICK: I was scared stiff——

PHIL: —but you said you were saving yourself for Di. And
stood her photo on your bedside locker in a bathing suit.

DIANA: We'd sworn undying love before he went away.

LIZ: What's wrong with undying love? It happens.

DIANA: At fifteen? I was fifteen!

PHIL: But you did keep yourself——

LIZ: Just about——

PHIL: —for eighteen months.

DIANA: In those days girls of sixteen didn't jump into bed with
every Tom, Dick and——

PHIL: You jumped with me soon enough.

DIANA: I fell for the suntan.

PHIL: And quickly got the taste. Went off me and tried it with
the butcher, the baker, the candlestick-maker——
(DIANA *goes off to bedroom.*)

LIZ: You were always there to catch her on the rebound.

DICK (*to* PHIL): Remember why you went to her in the first place?

PHIL: Yes, to deliver the silk you'd bought her.

DICK: And she wrote thanking me and said she'd fallen for the
postman.

PHIL: A mess-pot.

LIZ: I was lucky, wasn't I? If Phil hadn't been <u>demobbed</u> first,
you'd have probably gone back to Di. But I'd always
fancied you and so when I saw you sad and shy at a party,
I took you off to a bedroom and showed you there was
nothing to it. I was your first.

DICK: Yes.

PHIL: You're naturally monogamous.

DICK: How can anything be natural that needs such constant
attention? Such <u>pruning</u> and watering?

46

(DIANA *returns with cigarettes and lighter, quickly takes in new situation, smokes during following.*)

LIZ: What about that goose? The—aahm—the greylag goose? Aren't they supposed to be faithful to their mates for fifty years? Surely that's natural?

DICK: Natural to the greylag goose. Not us. We can be anything. Promiscuous, polygamous, polyandrous, carnivorous, homosexual——

LIZ: You're a one-woman man and I'm a one-man woman.

DICK: You can be smug about our monogamy because you've had so much of the other. You're all the same, all three of you!

PHIL: We played the field when we were young. What's the difference now?
(*Resumes decanting.*)

DICK (*emphatically*): I missed my chance and I can never be young again. One of an army of sad middle-aged men forever pining for a youth that passed while we weren't looking.

DIANA: Not only men.

PHIL: You've nothing to complain of.

DIANA: You think not?

LIZ: Diana, really! Half the men in——

DIANA: That! Most of that was a mess. (*To* DICK.) Surely you mean more than *that*.

LIZ: What?

DIANA: Love, surely? Being in *love*.

LIZ (*to* DICK): Love? You? Romantic love?

DICK (*hurt by her tone*): Yes, all that! Careless rapture.

LIZ: You were too ambitious. You were going to be a specialist. Even before you'd settled on paediatrics, you—aahm—you——

DICK: I wanted to practise medicine and——

LIZ: You—aahm—you talked of nothing but being a consultant.

DICK: —had to find the field where I could be most effective——

LIZ (*interrupting, to Audience*): Even as a student walking the wards——

DICK (*giving up*): Oh, shit——

LIZ: —he had a powerful sense of direction. Aaahm—he—
aah——
(*The others, in their different ways, turn their eyes away.*
DICK *stares at the ground.*)
I don't mean to say he was mercenary or materialistic, he
was in many ways as much an idealist as Phil. Which was
arguably their only common factor.

PHIL: That's what brought us together in the——

LIZ: Aaah! However. Aaahm. What he had that Philip, ahm,
that Philip lacked was a strong sense of his own importance
to the world and the fact that he would one day be an
influential and—erm—distinguished figure. Aaah.
(*Pause.* DICK *speaks to Audience more quietly.*)

DICK: And of course in the early years I was always at the
hospital or on call in the night, we hardly saw each other.
She went on teaching for the first year but only part-time
after Jane was born. We treasured all the hours we could
snatch to be together. Even someone's flaws can be
attractive then. Even their warts. (*To* LIZ.) I was aware of
your schoolmistressy manner, of course——

LIZ (*smiling*): My what, love?

DICK (*louder, silencing her*): After all, you'd coped with thirty-five
teenage roughs and somehow managed to prevent them
burning down the school. But this bossiness was never a
serious problem till we came down here to look after
Philip's son. When at last we were with each other morning,
noon and night. (*And again to Audience:*) I'd noticed at
home, of course, at dinner-parties, how her voice went
ranting on, repeating the same half-formed opinions, and
everyone very sorry for her, staring at the tablecloth hoping
she'd stop. And when she didn't I'd try to interrupt but no,
that's as bad as some yob calling out in class . . . so she
aahs and ahms until she's thought what to say next and
everyone waits till she's finally talked herself to a standstill.
You must have noticed.
(*Pause.*)

PHIL: We're all embarrassing at times. We all get kicked under
tables.

48

LIZ: If we're going to mention each other's shortcomings, you're a far cry from Mister Universe. What about your moccasins? (*To Audience.*) He pads about the place like some filthy old panda. Flip, flop, flip, flop——

DICK: How about that portable litter-bin you call a handbag?

PHIL: Christ, the squalor of handbags! Bus-tickets and toffee-papers stuck to combs . . . and shopping-lists with 'List' written at the top.

DICK: Handbags are a symbol of their bondage.

DIANA: What about you? Your ears? (*To* LIZ.) He puts his finger into his ear and wiggles it about till you can hear the wax move.

(PHIL *gets a bottle and drinks from it during scene.*)

LIZ: Yet we're still expected to be glamorous!

DICK: Glamorous? You don't even bother to dye your hair!

LIZ: I dye my hair in *London*. Ahm. But your wind doesn't stop wherever we are. I'll bet you never fart in front of the nurses.

DICK: You've never objected to my wind before.

LIZ: I shouldn't *need* to. (*To Audience.*) Should I? During meals he does it.

PHIL: She objects to *mine*. She never stops.

DIANA (*to Audience*): Not so much to the wind as the way he stands there afterwards enjoying it.

DICK: Now steady. These trivial physical differences might—all things being equal—might be part of our affection for each other.

PHIL: Right. I know couples have farting *contests*.

DIANA: I'm sure you do.

DICK: I'm trying to explain what I've learnt down here. For years we were happy—my career, her house, our family——

LIZ: *My* house?

DICK: But it's gradual, like growing old. How could we tell each other we were bored?

LIZ: I wasn't.

DICK: I sent for an illustrated book of sex techniques. You glanced at it, roared with laughter and never opened it again.

D   49

LIZ: Well, honestly, picture books! That's not the way to excite a woman.

DICK: What then? Love play? If I try that, she says, 'Stop messing about, get on with it.'

LIZ: No. I mean winning ways, airs and graces.

PHIL: Wining and dining?

LIZ: Absolutely. Dick's hopeless. He parks the car a mile from the restaurant and I have to walk in the rain. Then he wants me to explain the menu——

DICK: I don't care that much for food.

LIZ: I don't care for sexual acrobatics.

DIANA: Food's not the point.

LIZ: Of course not.

DIANA: It's being taken out, looked after, confidently escorted . . . low lights, ice-cold drinks, flowers, brazen glances from elegant men——

PHIL: *I* take you out.

DIANA: To some noisy basement stinking of beer.

PHIL: She means the jazz-club.

DIANA: Where you eventually join in with the band——

PHIL: *Sit in*——

DIANA: Plonking away on a banjo leaving me to dance with a succession of clumsy Egyptians.

PHIL: I thought you enjoyed the jazz-club.

DIANA: When we were young. It's years since I told you I enjoyed the jazz-club.

PHIL: What *do* you want then?

DIANA: Something better.

PHIL: More expensive. I can't afford it.

LIZ: Dick could.

DIANA: Not more expensive. More suitable. We're middle-aged.

PHIL: So are the other people in the jazz-club.

DIANA: The jazz-club *suits* them. I want something better.

PHIL: It suits me.

LIZ: She's always wanted something better. Even at school.

DIANA: That's all I learnt at school: to long for something better.

LIZ: You had a lovely time at school. We both did.

DIANA: How can you say that?

50

LIZ: You sat there so cool and smug, surrounded by a bevy of hangers-on, dopey girls, not worthy of you, And I found myself forced to show I was a cut above them. But—aahm —however much one shone, she still preferred Shirley Doncaster and Glenda—aahm——

PHIL: Taylor.

LIZ: Glenda Taylor. How do you know?

PHIL: She still sees them.

DIANA: Glenda never married.

PHIL: Meaning you didn't either till you bloody well had to.

DIANA: At school Glenda and I were always waiting for some fabulous episode.

PHIL: Glenda's still waiting.

DIANA: So am I. For life to begin. Like Emma Bovary or Anna Karenina. I'm as lonely as the women in Jean Rhys. Somewhere the right people in the right place are moving across some hotel lobby. Scott Fitzgerald people——

PHIL: You wouldn't last five minutes. You're more at home in Dulwich.

DIANA: Motorway-protests and parent-teacher meetings.

PHIL: There you are!

DIANA: I could scream sometimes. I sleep so much, that's my escape. Once he's at the office and Emma's at school, I often go back to bed and sleep till it's time to meet her. And when he's away, I go to bed at nine and sleep eleven hours at night as well.

PHIL: Some day her prince will come.

DIANA: That's right. And I mean to be ready.

LIZ: How can you be ready if you're fast asleep?

DICK: Psychiatrists regard excessive sleep as a distress signal.

PHIL: I think while she's been snoring away upstairs, the big thing's happened and you haven't even noticed.

DIANA: What?

PHIL: The birth of Sam.

DIANA: Where's the romantic element in that? It's pure *News of the World*.

PHIL: You haven't even heard my side.

DIANA: I don't want to.

51

PHIL: You're not being fair——

DIANA: Any more than I want to hear the point of view of the lurkers you sometimes see outside Emma's primary school. With their raincoats and ankle-length trousers.

PHIL: Jane was nearly fourteen! And a precocious fourteen, you must admit. Liz?

LIZ: Precocious enough to deceive us for a whole year.

PHIL: But physically too! She could pass for eighteen.

DIANA: As her parents, I'm surprised you can listen to this. *I* can't.

PHIL: All right. But once these Americans come, we may not have a chance to speak, so let me say again: what could be more reasonable than adoption?
(*They have now moved back into the scene and ignore the Audience.*)
Look, from the outside world's point of view, we want a son, you've had one late, we're friends. No one need ever know.

DIANA: But *I* shall know.

PHIL: I know about Emma. I live with *that*.
(DIANA *moves upstage and nobody speaks for some time.*)

DIANA: Thanks for protecting Emma. I'm sorry we didn't have a boy, that's hard on you, but in a few years' time now she'll be independent. And then, when the whatever-it-is comes that's going to wake me up, I don't want another toddler to cope with. I want to be ready.

PHIL: For the handsome prince cutting through the overgrown garden. That neutered cat of yours perhaps? You'd make a good pair.

DIANA: Thank you.
(PHIL *turns away and drinks from bottle.*)

LIZ: Excuse me interrupting, but aren't you leaving someone out? How's Jane going to feel?

DICK: Judging by her past behaviour——

LIZ: Aahm! I mean, what do any of our feelings matter until we've asked her?
(DICK *hides irritation by going to flask and continuing decanting.*)

52

PHIL: There are safeguards. No adoption's final for ages. I believe the mother can reclaim the child up to—how much? six months afterwards. That right?

LIZ: Talking away as though she doesn't count. Sam's *her* son, after all. She'd never part with him.

DICK: What makes you say that?

LIZ: Aaahm.

DICK: Don't aahm me. You're not teaching now. What makes you say she wouldn't part with him? She doesn't care, she never has.

LIZ: What d'you know about her? Or any of them, come to that? You're so busy writing about children in general you never notice them in particular.

DICK: Apparently neither of us knows a lot about Jane.

LIZ: Sam's part of our family.

PHIL: And ours.

DIANA: Over my dead body.

DICK: I find his solution quite acceptable, in the circumstances.

LIZ: You would! And I don't! Why did we reorganise our whole way of life, move to a foreign place, go through all this pantomime when we could far more easily have fixed an operation? Well, I'm not parting with him, so get that straight.

(*Turns and goes, by main doors.* DICK *continues decanting wine.* DIANA *goes to help him.*)

PHIL: He's my son.

DIANA: How d'you know? He's certainly *Jane's*.

DICK: We saw him born.

DIANA: But the fact that you and she—how shall I put it?— 'made love' doesn't necessarily mean you're the father. I'm sorry, Dick, but——

DICK: No, no——

DIANA: She did go into town with the French girl. Perhaps her story's true as well. About the back of the car.

PHIL: Come on, what d'you take her for?

DIANA: Well, she made love with you—Uncle Phil. Where d'you expect her to draw the line?

53

PHIL: I'm the father.

(*They look at him.*)

I know.

DICK: No man ever knows for sure.

PHIL: I know.

(*Drinks again, finds bottle empty, goes to basket and puts in empty bottle, takes out full one, uncorks it and drinks.* DIANA *looks up from holding funnel for* DICK.)

DIANA: Please don't get drunk.

PHIL: That's all right as long as it's Scott Fitzgerald. Yes?

(*She attends to the wine.* PHIL *wanders off, left. She looks after him.* DICK *takes the flask now and* DIANA *the funnel. They continue decanting.*)

DIANA: Whoa.

(*He stops. She corks the bottle and puts it in basket. They begin another.*)

DICK: See what I mean now? What I said about change? Nothing's going to be the same. We're speaking the truth to one another for the first time.

DIANA: I don't know about truth. Whether someone wears slippers or says 'aah'.

DICK: Even that much is a beginning. Perhaps by degrees I may learn to tell her that she's splendid in many ways, wonderfully capable, make some man a marvellous husband, but—she reached her high-point years ago. And I feel mine hasn't come yet.

DIANA: You heard me try to tell *him* that.

DICK: Yes.

DIANA: You hear what he said: I wouldn't last five minutes. He's always laughed at my feeling that life so far's been a kind of sleep.

DICK: So's she.

DIANA: Well, since I married him. Before that, I was awake all right.

DICK: Yes.

DIANA: And if I dare to mention the man who killed himself for me, you should hear the peals of laughter then!

DICK: Killed himself?

54

DIANA: Oh, we quarrelled. We were always quarrelling. But then I went with another man on the rebound and Clive was so shattered he joined the army. Within a year he was reported killed on active service.

DICK: The Middle East?

DIANA: Catterick. Officially he drove his jeep into a wall. What they couldn't know was he'd been willing his death all along. It's since then life's been a kind of sleep.

DICK: Intensity, that's what they can't understand. You and I feel life's not simply a lot of feeding and sleeping and waking and reproducing the species.

DIANA: That's Phil's dream city—where everyone has enough to eat and there's no war, no conflict. An open-air jazz-club. I say to him, there must be conflict, not this interminable comradeship.

DICK: That's why Liz doesn't really mind that he rogered our daughter. To them that's all the wonder of life. The old, the young, the middle-aged, we're all the same, all happy, as long as we get three square meals a day and regular cuddles. But I've been well behaved and helpful too long. I want to be exceptional! If I told her that, she'd fetch me a bowl of soup to line my stomach.

DIANA: Of course I've always *felt* exceptional. But I've made all the wrong decisions.

DICK: Choosing Phil when he brought my silk. That was the worst.

DIANA: Don't remind me. But if you felt like this, why didn't you go before?

DICK: Cowardice. I buried myself in work. I was afraid of being alone after so much family life.

DIANA: Men are lucky, you can go it alone, but women have to wait till—whoa!

(*He stops pouring. Puts down flask, goes to look out of barn door. She corks bottle and puts it in basket, stands, moves away. He goes to her.*)

DICK: Till what?

DIANA: What?

DICK: Women have to wait till—what?

55

DIANA: Till they're rescued, I suppose.

DICK: Diana, there are two of us now. The same two as before. You've been waiting for a writer, didn't you say? I've written a best-seller, will that do? I'm well-off. What's to stop us?

(*He touches her arm and she faces him.*)

DIANA: D'you mean leave them?

DICK: We must.

DIANA: How could we?

DICK: My in-tray's full of invitations to international culture-fests, to crack my jaw about modern youth. Ha-ha. We'll take the furthest off.

DIANA: What, go from here, now?

DICK: It'll be like that hotel lobby you mentioned.

DIANA: How about my daughter?

DICK: She's with your mother.

DIANA: Yes.

DICK: You said they get on well.

DIANA: I could let them know. They won't be sorry, they never cared that much for him.

DICK: We'll go first, think later. Further south, for a start, till we've sorted out——

DIANA: The Riviera, yes.

DICK: Or Languedoc or Spain!

DIANA: Is this really happening at last?

DICK (*moves about*): After so long believing myself to be a husband and father, I suddenly realize I've been untrue to my nature. I'm the kind of man who leaves home!

DIANA: I hate family life. The kind of family *they* want. Suffocation!

DICK: Yes.

DIANA: Boredom!

DICK: Even children bore me.

DIANA: Oh, no, I love Emma.

DICK: I *love* mine, but they're boring! Come on, commit the ultimate modern blasphemy—say it with me. Children are boring.

DIANA: From you it's good. A paediatrician. (*He embraces and*

56

kisses her. Then looks at her.)

DICK: Wakey, wakey, Princess.

DIANA: That's Emma's favourite story. The dogs opened their
eyes and started barking, the kitchen-boy caught the
spider——

(*Sounds of car-horn, off.* DICK *goes to see.*)

DICK: The Americans' taxi.

DIANA: Oh, no!

DICK: They're only here this afternoon.

DIANA: I want to go now.

DICK: Tomorrow. I've worked it out. Listen.

DIANA: Worked it out?

DICK: Jane's birthday party. We'll have to take three cars to
meet the kids at the station and fetch her guests on the way
back——

(*Hear* LIZ, *off, greeting* BURT *and* ZOE.)

You come with me in the slow one, the Deux Chevaux,
we'll let them lose us on the way, we'll drive to Bordeaux
Airport.

DIANA: We'll have to spend another night with them!

LIZ (*off*): Dick! Where are you, love?

DICK: Hullo! Coming! (*To* DIANA.) Pack a case in the morning,
my love.

DIANA: I can't spend a night with *him*!

DICK: Think of some excuse to keep him out.

(*Squeezes her hand and goes, main doors, taking wine.* DIANA
thinks for a moment. Hears DICK's *greeting.*)

DIANA: Asthma! My asthma's coming on. I can feel it. Where
did I leave my puffer? (*Turns and goes off to bedroom, shuts
and bolts the door.*)

(*Lights to black.*)

SCENE TWO

Lights come up, but cooler. Early evening.

The door in the study, upstairs, is opened and ZOE *comes on to the
landing. Early thirties, wears* homespun *clothes which emphasize her
stocky, masculine figure. Her hair is done in a bun but locks are always*

57

breaking free to fall over her face, and she makes vain attempts to tuck them away. No shoes, no make-up. Hanging from her neck are cameras and exposure meters. Leaves door open and the voices of DICK *and* BURT *are heard. She looks at barn, goes to stairs, notices blow-up of the cover-girl. She carries it down the stairs and props it against the stone wall. Uses register, adjusts her camera, takes a couple of pictures.* DICK *comes from study with* BURT, *her likeness in many ways, wearing white shorts. A shirt, sandals and spectacles with library frames, which he often wipes.*

BURT: . . . hopefully sell the movie rights and buy myself a place like this, further south where it's even hotter, sling my hammock . . . plant a field with marijuana . . . Shangri-la! Tahiti before the tourists!

ZOE: Dick, how about coming down on the swing? Make a nifty picture.

DICK (*false smile*): Wouldn't that look a bit childish?

ZOE: Aren't you a child specialist?

DICK: I'm not a child.

(DICK *comes downstairs.* BURT *unties trapeze.*)

BURT: Please, teacher, may I do a wee?

ZOE: You may. (*He swings down.*)

BURT: Whee!

(ZOE *laughs, whoopees and takes picture. He comes to rest but remains sitting on bar.*)

ZOE: All right now, Dick, what have we done so far? The other house, the orchard, down by the pond, outside the barn, your study——

DICK: The bread-oven——

ZOE: Right. A few in here will wrap it up.

BURT: I'm almost through as well.

ZOE: Stay right there, Dick, terrific, between me and that blow-up. Beautiful.

DICK: Blow-up? (*Turns to see picture, moves away.*) Oh, no.

ZOE: But that's your cover picture.

DICK: My publisher's, not mine.

BURT: She's beautiful, though, don't you think? Before I'd even heard of you, I bought the book because of those tits on the

58

bookstall.

ZOE: He almost came in the street.

BURT: I really did. And let me tell you I stood in line with some pretty strange people to get it, too. All the Humbert Humberts in New York City.

DICK: Sorry. I'm not posing with that.

ZOE: All right. On the cart.

(DICK *walks up the shaft on to the cart.*)

Hands on the side, look towards the light. Now to me with your eyes. Oh, nifty. Very nifty. (*She works, sometimes giving instructions quietly to* DICK.)

BURT: Isn't that an ox-cart? On the way from the airport we saw some natives ploughing with an ox-team. Can you imagine such medieval agriculture in the age of the Apollo programme?

ZOE: What d'you want? Poisoned lakes? No birds, no bugs. Only chemical crap?

BURT: Come on, Zoe, you know me.

ZOE: After six years of marriage, believe me.

BURT: I love the country. I was telling Dick, a place——

ZOE: You'd die in the country, Burt, you'd be so bored. Really fantastic, fine.

(*Takes down camera,* DICK *leaves cart.*)

BURT: Bored?

ZOE: I know, I'm a country *girl*.

BURT (*to* DICK): Wisconsin.

DICK: Really?

ZOE: You know Wisconsin?

DICK: No.

ZOE: Wisconsin in the spring? Beautiful. And best of all are those goddam local cherries. No hope, I simply can't resist them. First day of the season I buy a whole one-pound bag and (*using her hands to demonstrate*) I just—gobble and gulp and—swallow—those goddam cherries, spitting out the stones and stuffing more in my mouth, they're so red and shiny.

BURT (*getting off trapeze, shouting*): And she ought not to do that! Because of her goddam stomach! She *can't keep them*

59

in!

ZOE (*laughing, then shouting*): Pretty soon my pants are full, it's
running down my legs at the back. I make for home at the
double——

BURT: I hear this crazy drumming at the door, I open up and
she staggers in, with half the dogs in town licking at her
legs. I kick them away, you lousy brutes, get outa here——
(*Both act the scene.*)

ZOE: I put all my clothes in the machine——

BURT: I wash down her legs, it's awful——

ZOE: I take a bath, Oh Jesus. But next spring, first day of the
cherry season, there I am again, with a whole one-pound
bag, stuffing them in my mouth, spitting——

BURT: Christ!
(*They recover.* DICK *stands smiling.*)

DICK: When anyone mentions spring I shall always think of you.
And your cherries. (*Does false smile.*)

BURT (*Noël Coward voice*): You and your cherries.

ZOE: Sit on the swing now and I'll do some faces.
(BURT *moves about*, DICK *sits on swing.* ZOE *clicks, moving
round.*)

BURT: You once said something that seems to me to encapsulate
your entire thinking on the conventionally structured home.
You said, 'The Family is like the car. Out of date but we
go on using it.' Remember?

DICK: No. I said that?

BURT: I have it amongst your quotes.

DICK: After being stuck in a traffic-jam most likely. One says a
good few silly things to journalists, present company
excepted. And the silly things you forget to say, they make
up for you.

BURT: All right, but you believe the Family is obsolescent as a
viable structure? Which in any case won't be too fresh a
concept to our level of readership.

DICK: The Family as we've known it. The human pair-bonding
that makes possible our artificially extended childhood.

BURT: Right. What zoologists call neoteny.

DICK: Yes.

60

BURT: Prolonged retention of larval characteristics. And this, you say, is the basis of all our educational systems?

DICK: After all, we've got so much to learn, so many tricks, so many techniques, that we stretch the learning stage to the twenties, sometimes the thirties.

ZOE: I got friends of fifty still living on Guggenheim.

DICK: The Victorians invented childhood. Before that kids were just young people. But the new factories needed semi-literate clerks and skilled workers by the million. And popular education's never looked back.

BURT: But your thinking is not to burn down the schoolhouses. Rather that kids should quit school at puberty and spend their teens in sexual and social experimentation and, if they choose, bearing children.

DICK: I hope you won't exaggerate the sexual aspect. But after all we are physiologically ready at puberty and authoritarian attitudes frustrate the impulse, postpone conception and produce all the effects we know so well: boredom and violence, terrified teachers facing gangs of energetic kids, imprisoned in schools but longing to be out working, living——

BURT: Screwing——

ZOE: Turn this way. Beautiful. Gorgeous.

(DICK *obediently swings to face away from main doors and she takes him from upstage.* PHIL *wanders in, at main doors, carrying a half-empty bottle, stands listening.* BURT *sees him but not the other two.*)

DICK: And later on another lot of twisted middle-aged men and women, forever wondering what they missed. Knowing they only had one youth and somehow missed it. Time passing like the wind, death coming as sure as night. And a pornographic industry to tickle their chronic itch.

BURT: Hullo.

PHIL: Pretend you can't see me. On my way to the bedroom. Sorry. (*Makes across to door, right.*)

DICK: Diana's asleep.

PHIL: Oh. (*Stops at door, listens, knocks quietly.*) Hullo, love? (*He listens.*)

BURT: All right, as soon as a boy and girl have the equipment, they should get busy fucking. Fine as far——

DICK: Liz is in the house, cooking dinner. We'll join you soon, we've nearly finished here.

(PHIL *turns from door, takes swig at bottle, moves a bit unsteadily towards the left but stops at the blow-up.*)

ZOE: Where've you been all afternoon?

PHIL: Walking.

BURT: Dick, d'you read me?

DICK: What?

PHIL: Taking in the scene.

BURT: All the kids are screwing at twelve, there are contraceptive automats in every school corridor——

DICK: They wouldn't be at school, would they, if my proposals were——

BURT: Right. So they're out in the world, on the pill or having babies and no contract, secular or spiritual, will imply any partnership is permanent.

DICK (*unhappily*): More or less.

PHIL: You got enough film to take my picture, Zoe?

ZOE: Be my guest.

PHIL: Against this blow-up?

ZOE (*shouting*): We got another Humbert here.

BURT: Get in line, Mister.

(PHIL *and* ZOE *continue arranging pictures, which she takes during next dialogue.* PHIL *stands in front, behind and at the side of the blow-up.*)

Dick, there's something bothers me: a very marked disparity between your precepts and your practice. What I mean, there you are in the book advocating the immediate demolition of the Family, free fucks for all at twelve, state nurseries, most child-bearing finished by twenty-five and it's a rare man that knows his own father. Then we arrive here to find you have three children at school, you've been married fifteen years and your forty-year-old wife——

DICK: Thirty-eight——

BURT: Pardon me, your thirty-eight-year-old wife is drooling over her newborn baby. In short, about as cosy a domestic

62

set-up as you'd find outside the cereal commercials.

ZOE: How old d'you think she is? That model?

PHIL: I wouldn't know.

BURT: You must admit, that's <u>intriguing</u>, though. An angle that will appeal to our level of readership. Jesus, it appeals to *me*!

ZOE: Sixteen at least.

PHIL: I wouldn't know.

ZOE: She's too <u>nubile</u> for twelve or thirteen.

DICK: Nubile doesn't mean large-breasted.

ZOE: No?

DICK: It means marriageable.

ZOE (*Noël Coward voice*): Terribly sorry. All finished now, thanks. (PHIL *replaces blow-up at back wall.* ZOE *takes no more pictures but unloads film.* DICK *has left swing and is moving about.*)

BURT: You wouldn't object to that angle for the piece? Here's what he says: The Family bla-bla-bla, here's how he lives——

DICK: Phil, why don't you go and help Liz with dinner? She's obviously got a lot to do——

PHIL: I'm interested in this point he's making.

ZOE: Can *I* give her a hand?

PHIL: The gulf between fact and fiction. That right?

BURT: I'm thinking of the ordinary Joe with hairy <u>armpits.</u> Hasn't he a right to expect his gurus to practise what they preach?

DICK: I advocate a new society but I live in the one we've got. Engels was a capitalist.

PHIL: I know this one. The Socialist millionaires, the limousine Liberals,
(LIZ *comes from main doors, wiping hands on teacloth.*)
the middle-class conservationists writing to *The Times* about motor traffic as long as they don't have to give up their own Jags and Volvos——

LIZ: I thought you were interviewing *Dick*.

BURT: I'm trying.

DICK: Phil's coming to help with dinner.

63

LIZ: Lovely, you can pour some drinks for——

PHIL: No, listen, our friend here from Disneyland——

ZOE: I can help, I'm all through——

PHIL: —has asked Dick why he lives such a quiet life when he's got such sexy ideas.

BURT: Is that what I said?

PHIL: Didn't I get it right? Here's Dick's book saying we should all be free-and-easy where we find our horizontal refreshment and in real life——

LIZ: Now why don't you pour us all a drink, then have——

DICK: You keep going on about sex but in fact the real subject is education——

PHIL: What *I* missed—shall I tell you?——

LIZ: No, love.

PHIL: What I missed was any mention of innocence, first love, romance——

BURT: Right. That kind of subjective phenomena——

PHIL: Which is why only oldies read those books. Written by oldies for oldies. But young people know what they've forgotten.

LIZ: '*They've* forgotten'? Aren't you an oldie too?

DICK: That's not how he sees himself.

PHIL: Well, am I really? I never felt at home in my generation, once they all learnt to be powerful and successful members of various establishments.

LIZ: You mean you still play banjo in a college jazz-band, still march and demonstrate and call on other people to wake up. Pass a joint and abuse the fuzz. Aaahm. You—erm— you can do that only by sheltering behind your business partner. He does all the dirty work, ahm, fixing contracts for you to design a supermarket——

PHIL: He gets all the money too.

LIZ: —or a multi-storey carpark—which incidentally's a very far cry from those ideal cities you built in the old days.

(BURT *and* ZOE *are very embarrassed by this exchange.*)

PHIL: You remember those?

LIZ: They were only cardboard, of course.

PHIL: They're still set out in the cellar. Our generation never wanted them built. The powers-that-be.

LIZ: You think the new generation will?

PHIL: No. Our lot have shat on architecture. Handed over to the brutes. Brutalism is the measure of all things. Or tatty glitter. You'd admire me if I'd put up a Hilton. Or one of your new hospitals that *looks* like a Hilton.

LIZ: We'd admire you if you'd taken a few risks. The risk of failing. Or growing up.

DICK: Becoming like the rest of——

LIZ: Aaaahm, yes, exactly, becoming like the rest of us. Boring, grey, responsible, sitting on committees, facing facts.

PHIL: Facts, what facts? The facts in that book of his? A smoke-screen to hide the real facts. Inequality——

LIZ: Why d'you think Diana's got sleeping sickness? She knows you're never going anywhere.
(*Pause.* PHIL *looks at her.*)

DICK: Liz, come on, love, you and Phil go——

LIZ: Yes, right. Sorry. Sorry, Phil. Better out than in.
(*Smiles, moves towards main doors but* PHIL *won't follow.*)

PHIL: Never going anywhere, no, I suppose not. Then again I've got nothing to lose either.

LIZ: Come on.

PHIL (*to* BURT): You've absolutely put your finger on what's wrong with his book. Like someone said—it was you, Liz— he's so busy looking at children in general he never sees them in particular.

DICK: I see them a good deal as a matter of fact. Mostly illiterate, unsophisticated, underprivileged, often seriously ill——

PHIL: You ought to stay till tomorrow, meet their kids, can't you?

BURT: We'd love to but our schedule's pretty——

PHIL: Their daughter's birthday-party. She's fifteen. You got a family, Burt?

BURT: Up to the present time we don't have any but——

PHIL: You want kids, do you?

ZOE: Actually we have a fertility problem.

BURT: Hopefully we'll adopt.

PHIL: My wife's got a daughter, by a previous marriage. And I

E   65

want a son. You see. I want a son.

(*He pauses, suddenly overcome. They watch.*)

LIZ: Dinner's burning.

(PHIL *finds his voice to stop her.*)

PHIL: Have you thought about that question, Liz? That question I asked about Sam?

LIZ: I must go. You and I can talk privately, love, it's a private matter.

PHIL: A family matter.

BURT: Time we got the show on the road.

ZOE: Yes. We can eat in a restaurant.

LIZ: Oh, but I've done you a Périgordine speciality——

PHIL: You've seen the baby, have you? Her new baby.

BURT: Honestly, Phil, we've stayed too long already——

PHIL: What d'you think of him? Wouldn't you be proud of a boy like that? Burt?

BURT: Sure.

PHIL: Sure you would. He's a beautiful human being, yes? And according to Dick's book, he should go to whoever wants him, whoever deserves him. But when someone comes along and stakes a claim, he and Liz close ranks.

DICK: Who's closed ranks? You can have him.

LIZ: I'll run you to a village——

ZOE (*to* PHIL): Why should you have him?

DICK: He seems to be the father.

BURT: Yeah, well, this is none of our business.

DICK: Not more in line with my preaching?

ZOE: A family matter.

DICK: Family! Our families are breaking up. Our two families. Coalescing. That's in line with the book, surely?

LIZ (*ushering them out*): You can eat fairly well in a village the far side of——

DICK: I see what you're thinking. She's Sam's mother? No, it's better than that.

LIZ: Dick, honestly, I——

DICK: D'you know who is? Our teenage daughter. How will that go down with your level of readership?

(LIZ *shrugs, giving up. They hesitate near main doors.*)

66

BURT: I'm out of my depth.

PHIL: I'd never have said it.

DICK: You're out of *your* depth? What about me? I've spent my life in the shallow end and now, suddenly, at forty, I can't touch the bottom. Which is a marvellous sensation for a decent law-abiding man.

ZOE (*to* LIZ, *quietly*): D'you mean Phil made love to your daughter?

DICK: Yes. Made love, yes! How's that going to look across a double-page spread?

BURT: You'll never know. Not from us, anyway.

DICK: Mmm?

BURT: What do you take us for? Muckrakers?

DICK: Think of the angle, though.

ZOE: Burt, remind me to tell you I love you. (*To* LIZ.) We shan't breathe a word.

DICK: Why?

ZOE: Why? We respect family life, that's why.

DICK: You too?

BURT: Family life may not be perfect but, like they say about democracy, what else do we have?

PHIL: Right. Most people want to watch their children grow, every day of their lives, through every phase, not just in visiting hours. What's for us in state nurseries?

DICK: D'you know what the permissive society won't permit? A dislike of children. Even being indifferent to children. They are the one class of person we must all love. But what if we don't.

(LIZ *turns and goes.* ZOE *follows but* DICK *catches* BURT *by the arm.*)

I spent my youth paralysed with shyness and my manhood in a mist of drying nappies——

BURT: Start thinking lucky. You're one of the world's over-privileged. I'm blown out of my mind by your whole set-up. . . . (*He goes and is off by this time.*)

DICK (*almost simultaneously*): Decent law-abiding people every-where I look.

(*They both go.* PHIL *stands near main doors looking off. He*

E*   67

holds the bottle up to the light to see how much is left, but does not drink again.)

(DIANA comes from bedroom, right, quietly. Her hair has been let down and she is wearing only a sheet, tied above the bust like a sarong. Sees PHIL and advances. Near the swing, she speaks, quietly.)

DIANA: Bonjour, matelot.

(He moves across to her, offers the bottle. She swigs. Returns bottle to him, sits on swing, turning round and round, twisting the ropes.)

Are they going?

PHIL: I don't know.

DIANA: I've been listening. I woke up when you knocked.

PHIL: You heard all that we——?

(She nods. Smiles.)

What you still haven't heard is *my* side. I had to spare her parents' feelings as much as possible . . . let them believe the best of Jane . . . but ever since it came out, I've been trying to talk to you . . . have you been avoiding me? I'd only thought of Jane as one of the children till that morning when you'd all gone to town. Very athletic. Healthy appetite. Used to sit down to children's tea, then again to grown-ups' supper. Well, you'd all gone and I was in the hammock.

(She takes her feet off the floor and spins on the swing.)

She came in shirt and shorts and offered to show me the watercress-bed. Hot morning, like today, with thunder coming and I'd started early on the wine. After the cress, she showed me the chanterelles, then told me she often went down there to take the sun. I took my shirt off and we lay there listening to the grasshoppers . . . squinting at the dragonflies . . .

(DIANA is still now, not looking at him, but listening.)

She took some wine and I got the bottle back and she tried to grab it and we wrestled a bit. Then I let her get me down, she rolled over me with her long hair falling on my face. But what I chiefly remember is the smile she had, as though I'd said she could stay up late or have second

puddings. She wanted a *treat*. I'm not a womanizer, you
know that, but I do respond to—physical situations.

DIANA: Like Southampton.

PHIL: What?

DIANA: It's obvious when you're going to play with the band in
Southampton. You always sing in the bath. You may not
sing for weeks, then suddenly, like last week, I hear you
singing. It's the thought of horizontal refreshment. The
prospect of Southampton.

PHIL: Only when you're freezing me out. Such as recently.
Think. In the last few weeks, how many cracks have I had
at the title? How many turns on Shooter's Hill?
(*He pushes her knees so that she swings away and back to him.*)
And last July, down here, the same. You were always asleep
before I undressed. Lying there, turned away, your skin
glistening with insect repellent.
(*She has hands on ropes of swing and is leaning back. He leans
over her, his face close to her hair.*)
Not wearing any at the moment, are you?
(*He puts the bottle on the floor. She swings and falls back to
him. He takes the sheet where it is knotted and pulls it open.
She stands quickly and moved slightly downstage, wrapping
the sheet around her again. PHIL takes her hands and firmly
opens them, so that she is holding out the sheet. They stand at
arms' length for a moment, PHIL looking at her. Then he moves
closer and embraces her behind the sheet. She envelops them
both. He goes down on his knees to kiss her body. DIANA stands,
covering herself with the sheet, but loosely, as with a robe.
PHIL stands. She goes to bedroom and PHIL gets the bottle and
follows. Sound of a bolt being pushed into place behind door.*)
(*Go to black.*)

SCENE THREE

A dull midday light with no shadows. Cloudy.

LIZ *comes from main doors carrying tray set with crockery, cutlery
and cloths. She is wearing an excellent wig and looks years younger,*

dressed in whatever costume makes the best of her figure. Places tray on chair then goes to bedside door and switches on lights. Thunder, some way off. PHIL *and* DICK *enter by main doors carrying a long table with folding legs.*

LIZ: About there.

PHIL: D'you hear that thunder?

LIZ: Yes.

PHIL: Hard by.

LIZ: Which is why we must get the food over here before we go for the kids. Then we shan't be running about in the rain with trays of jelly.

PHIL: Shame! I was looking forward to a fête-champêtre in the orchard. Dappled light through the cherry-trees. Straw hats.

DICK: Small cigars.

PHIL: Samovars.

LIZ: Fetch those benches from the cowshed, love. They're in those mangers by the bread-oven. They'll need brushing down. We've got to seat fourteen.

(Men have set up table down left centre.)

PHIL: Fourteen?

LIZ *(counting on fingers)*: Us four. Jane, Sarah, Ben. Margaret. That's eight.

PHIL: Margaret?

DICK: Our mother's help.

LIZ: And six French kids from the villages.

PHIL: Fourteen.

(DICK has gone off and PHIL follows.)

I hope they all turn up——

LIZ: Yes. *(Thinks.)* Why?

(But he is gone. LIZ *takes cloth from tray and begins unfolding it.* DIANA *comes from her room, refreshed and dressed.)*

DIANA: Talk about Rentacloud!

LIZ: Hullo, love. Had a nice lie-in?

DIANA: Smashing. Too many drinkie-poohs last night, I'm afraid.

LIZ: Phil *said* they gave you a decent meal. I always enjoy her food. Specially the moules.

70

DIANA: I had no appetite.

LIZ: Then it's a good job you didn't stay for my Périgordine supper.

DIANA: Ah.

LIZ: I'd laid for you but suddenly we saw your car turning into the road. Dick went to see if you were in your room but came back saying you'd gone with Phil.

DIANA: We wanted to sneak away. We couldn't face the Yanks again.

LIZ: Didn't matter. They ate like horses, I'll say that for them. Peasant soup I gave them, pâté, crudités, melon, écrivisses, guinea-fowl——

(*They were unfolding the cloth together and spreading it on the long table. A white cloth, the only bright thing on a dull stage.*)

DIANA: Nice. We looked for you when we——

LIZ: Aaahm. White and green beans, goat and cow cheese, peach flan—aahm—then, after coffee, and cognac, Dick ran them to their hotel while I cleared away. His face had been like Rentacloud all night. He seemed to be trying to show that he didn't want anything to do with Sam. Trying to keep up the mood of our quarrel.

DIANA: We looked for you when we came back last night but you seemed to have gone to bed.

LIZ: Well, that was it. I thought to myself: the time has come for a few feminine wiles. So I put on a flowing nightgown that's always made him randy—with nothing underneath, and rummaged through the trunk for that book on sex techniques. I had an idea it hadn't been thrown out. Well, I was always afraid of the dustman seeing it.

DIANA: And not quite right for Oxfam.

LIZ: No.

DIANA: You've put your wig on too.

LIZ: Oh, this morning, yes.

DIANA: How many places?

LIZ: Fourteen.

(*They lay places with cutlery and crockery.*)

I shan't embarrass you with the sordid details but let's say

71

one or two of the old tricks came back out of the dim and
distant past and—aahm—well, I let him keep the light on
and rolled my eyes a bit and made noises—anyway—aaahm
—the point is, I don't think now he'll be supporting Phil's
demand to adopt the baby.

(DIANA *has stopped laying the table.*)

DIANA: I see.

LIZ: Which will surely be a weight off your mind.

DIANA: Yes. But yesterday Dick didn't seem at all prepared——

LIZ: That was yesterday!

DIANA: He didn't seem to care about Sam one way or another.

LIZ: That was bravado. Pique. Men are so concerned about who
performed the actual insemination, aren't they? As though
it mattered.

DIANA: I'm glad you've made it up. Because Dick yesterday
certainly seemed very upset——

LIZ: That was only a tiff, my love. We've been fighting for
sixteen years. And what about you and Phil?

DIANA: I wore a sheet.

LIZ: Oh, I've done that before now. Yes.

DIANA: We had a marvellous afternoon.

LIZ: It's best in the afternoon. Before the kids get home from
school.

DIANA: And again this morning.

(*Thunder, closer.*)

LIZ: I'm so glad we're all back together again for Jane's party.
With no disagreements over Sam. I know you didn't want
him, understandably——

DIANA: That part's not so simple, dear.

(*And as* LIZ *stops laying.*)
I pointed out to him the weakness of his case. What claim
has he got, after all? The most he can expect is any crumb
you like to throw him. He understands that, of course, but
that's no consolation. He even talked about paternity pleas
but it wasn't serious. However I think we could fob him off
with a promise from you.

LIZ: Promise? Of what?

DIANA: Couldn't you offer to let him come and see the baby now

72

and then? Whenever he wants? And you could say that later on, when he's grown a bit, they could go to football or the zoo. In fact, he'll probably go off the whole business after a year or two. Promises don't cost anything. You don't want him making scenes like that with the Americans.

LIZ: I wouldn't mind. And perhaps while he's a baby, you could have him at your place now and then.

(Pause. DIANA looks away.)

If I'm going to make concessions, you must—aahm—reciprocate. I'm doing it to keep your husband sweet.

DIANA: Not only. It's in your interest too.

LIZ: But you'll have to make an effort.

DIANA: It needn't be too often. You don't want to part with the child and I don't want to have him.

LIZ: Just enough to satisfy his pride.

DIANA: And Dick's contented?

LIZ: Oh, yes. He's quite fond of the children in fact——

DIANA: But generally——?

LIZ: We're going to back to London, of course. He'll be happy there. He misses all those boozy male lunches. We've maybe got a bit *too* close. But you can't keep a quarrel going in a double bed. Here they come. Shall I make Phil the offer?

DIANA: If you like. Only don't give away too much——

(Breaks off as the men return bringing two wooden benches. PHIL puts his down and kisses DIANA.)

LIZ: Oh, that's super! Now if you can rustle up some chairs, one of you, and the other help me bring the food.

PHIL: Food? That sounds like me.

LIZ *(taking his arm and leading him off)*: Right. You didn't say what madam gave you after the confit d'oie.

PHIL: After the confit d'oie . . . comme dessert—soufflé au grand marnier . . .

(DICK and DIANA alone. She goes on laying places. He arranges benches, goes upstage as if to get a chair, watches PHIL and LIZ go. Then comes to her. They both start speaking at once.)

DICK: Whatever made you go out with him last night? I thought he'd gone off alone till I went and knocked on your door and discovered you'd gone too——

73

DIANA: Oh, Dick, I'm so glad you've decided to stay with Liz, I couldn't think how I was going to face you after saying I'd go away with you——
(*Both stop. Thunder.*)

DICK: Sorry. Never mind. We may only have a minute. Are you ready?

DIANA: Ready?

DICK: Have you packed a case? If not, don't worry. We'll let them go first and say we'll follow in the little car and you can pack one after they've gone. The further we let them get ahead the better.

DIANA: You still want to go? Oh, dear.

DICK: What?

DIANA: Liz seems to think that last night you and she—during the night—you——

DICK: Oh, that! She's hopeless at that, honestly. She's not got the least idea.

DIANA: How d'*you* know?

DICK: What? Well, of course I'm no authority, but—surely it can be better than that! She's more interested in confit d'oie or whatever it is.

DIANA: You shouldn't be *that* disloyal. It's unattractive.

DICK: I'm very fond of her, I love her dearly in many ways. Only I just can't stand her!
(*She goes to get a chair for the table. He follows and gets another.*)
Was he too much of a pest? I was afraid, when I saw you'd gone out together——

DIANA: Listen, Dick.
(*Her tone makes him stop and look at her. She stands behind the chair she's brought.*)
When you asked me yesterday, I was too confused to think. Not to mention excited. At my age, a famous author! As you know, that's been my dream for years, many years. Perhaps too many. And your enthusiasm carried me along, I meant to go, I locked myself in the bedroom and told myself I had asthma. Even began to believe it. Started wheezing and had to use my puffer.

DICK: Are you better now?

DIANA: It stopped.

DICK: Good.

DIANA: Yes, it stopped when I began to think out the implications. Then you and the journalists tramped about upstairs and talked your heads off——

DICK: That's advertising——

DIANA: —and then Phil came and knocked and of course I didn't answer. I was going away with you and couldn't bear the thought of sharing a room with him when I knew next day I'd be leaving.

DICK: Yes. *I* felt very miserable last night deceiving Liz but——

DIANA: Well, as you all talked and Phil interrupted and Liz came in and they had a set-to, everything came clear to me. We need them. We must hang on to them. They're lifegivers and we're in love with death.

DICK: What?

DIANA: You and I.

DICK: Starting in a new direction at our age doesn't sound like death. Slowly decomposing, that's being in love with——

DIANA: You're Cancer, aren't you? Like me.

DICK: Leo, for what that's worth——

DIANA: An early Leo. That's nearly Cancer. Liz and Phil are Aquarians.

DICK: That's hopeless crap, you know it is——

DIANA: Isn't your favourite season autumn? That's when I come alive.

DICK: Because your asthma's calmer then, you can breathe——

DIANA: We're too alike, Dick! We need their vitality! Together we'd be in a madhouse in six months.

DICK: You're right, you've been waiting for this too long. And now the moment's here, you're backing away out of cowardice. But you mustn't be afraid, Diana.

DIANA: I've had to face that too, yes. I am a coward.

DICK: Don't give way to it. You've spent the best years of your life regretting what might-have-been. Don't waste the rest.

DIANA: I'm not a free agent. When she's got a child a woman must know where she's going, she must be sure of her legal

75

rights——

DICK: Look, here's the note I've written Liz explaining—— (*Shows her an envelope.*)

DIANA: If I went away with you, I'd give up any claim on Phil. And then—if you got tired of me——

DICK: Oh, come on—— (*Puts away envelope.*)

DIANA: Or I of you. We easily could. Two Cancers together.

DICK: Tired of you?
(*Attempts to embrace her but she resists.*)

DIANA: Where would I be? At thirty-eight? With a child?

DICK: All last night in bed with her, d'you know what I kept remembering? Your mother's carpet. The carpet in your mother's flat where I used to come on the way from school, yes?

DIANA (*struggling*): You'd get sick of me and my asthma——

DICK: I'm a doctor! I can help!

DIANA: Emma too. When she came to join us. Both of us puffing away.

DICK: We used to put cushions on the floor in front of the gas-fire. We nearly drove each other mad.

DIANA (*beginning to laugh*): Wheezing across the hotel lobbies of the world!

DICK: Then your mother would come from work at six and sometimes we'd go out—you with burning ears and me with an ache between the legs.

DIANA: Dick, stop it——

DICK: I fainted with frustration once, remember? Actually passed out. In a cinema. Staggering up the aisle——

DIANA: You're making me laugh——

DICK: Till some usherette shone the torch in my face—don't laugh!

DIANA: I can't help it! You keep pointing out the funny side.

DICK: You're laughing out of fear——

DIANA: That when my Famous Writer came along, he turned out to be Dick of the gas-fire, twenty-five years older——
(DICK *attempts to kiss her again. A moment's struggle and the little* FRENCHMAN *comes from the bedroom door and is moving across before he sees them, then starts talking at once.* DICK

76

turns, leaving DIANA. *The* MAN *has his kettle and a plastic bag.*)

DICK: M'sieur—ça va? Nous preparons un gouter d'enfants. Oui, l'anniversaire de ma fille . . .

(*The* MAN *shakes hands with both, embarrassed, moving on towards the main doors.*)

DIANA: What an impression he must be forming of English family life!

(LIZ *enters by main doors, carrying loaded trays.*)

LIZ: M'sieur, bonjour! Vous voudrez tirer de l'eau à la source? C'est entendu.

(*Puts tray on table, which* DIANA *goes on laying.* FRENCHMAN *comes to shake hands with* LIZ, *then offers the bag explaining that it's a present for her.*)

Pour moi? Un cadeau? Encore un cadeau? Mais—aahm—vous avez donné un poulet déjà. (*Shows an egg from the bag.*) Très gentil. He's trying to make up for interfering.

DIANA: Take more than a bag of eggs.

LIZ: Merci bien. He didn't know what he was doing. He *was* here first. He was brought up here. (*She is taking eggs from bag and putting them into pudding bowl on table.*) He knew this barn when it was full of beasts. Ca y est. Merci bien, m'sieur.

(*Returns him empty bag. He shows kettle, speaks.*)

Je vous en prie. Il ne faut pas demander.

(*He nods and thanks her, shakes hands with all of them. Wishing them au revoir and a good party, he makes for main doors and almost collides with the white pram, being pushed on by* PHIL. *They look at each other. The* MAN *stops talking and goes past and off.*)

PHIL: Our roving reporter.

(*Puts pram centre. Thunder, closer. The hood is up and on the carriage is a square board and on this a birthday cake with fifteen candles.* LIZ *goes to pram.*)

Though he'd be best under cover.

LIZ: I'm in the Land of Nod, he says. Let's hope the thunder doesn't wake him.

(PHIL *holds up the cake.*)

77

PHIL: Aaah!

LIZ AND

DIANA: Aaah! (*Put it on table, prominently.*)

LIZ: And see what I've brought! (*Four glasses of opaque Anis, which she gives him.*)

PHIL: We shall need a few Pernods to get through this.
(*Takes a glass to* DICK, *who remains apart.*)
We'll finish here, then drive to Mussidan, have another drinkie-pooh, then a leisurely lunch. (*Kisses* DICK, *moves back to others at table.*)

PHIL (*to* DIANA): We haven't got her——

LIZ: Aaahm—down to the gare in time for their train, get over the moment of your meeting——

PHIL: We ought to have bought——

LIZ: Then home through the villages picking up their French guests on the way.

PHIL: We should have bought her a present.

LIZ: Time before lunch.

DIANA: Yes. A box of Leggo? A Dutch cap?
(*Pause.*)

PHIL: An Action Man?
(*They smile, slightly embarrassed.*)
Cheers.

LIZ AND

DIANA: Cheers, le vôtre, etc.
(*They drink. Thunder. Lights flicker.*)

DICK: We'll have to take all three cars. The Deux Chevaux as well.

LIZ: Shall we?

DICK: Fourteen people. And the baby.

LIZ: We'll all be driving separately. What a shame!

DICK: Diana's a passenger. She can come with me.

LIZ: What for?

DICK: So that I can put my hand on her knee.

PHIL: Be my guest. Very sexy cars, Deux Chevaux. Bobbing up and down. I've had erections just driving behind them.

DIANA: I'll go with Phil.

LIZ: And I'll take Sam.

78

PHIL: Listen. We were in the kitchen putting the candles on and your wife made a proposition.

DIANA: Hullo, hullo——

PHIL: She's suggested I can take Sam out whenever I like.

LIZ: Whenever you like?

PHIL: And also Diana wouldn't mind him staying with us from time to time. Now that's an advance on the stalemate we had before—me wanting adoption and Liz saying no. And surely Dick, raising the boy entirely as yours wouldn't be half so easy now you know. You'd see the old genetic rubber stamp clarifying year by year, my features pushing through——

LIZ: Oh, this again? What's it matter who the father is?

PHIL: It matters to him and me.

LIZ: Because you're so competitive. I wish you clever chaps would appreciate another man's work as we do another woman's baby. Just be glad of its existence. But men naturally crave success, the fruits of competition, which is why we're going home, eh, love?

(She smiles across, holds out her hand as though hoping DICK *will come and take it, but quickly sees he won't and moves to him, stands with arm round his waist.)*

We'll be back in London, you'll be trotted out at parties, young girls rolling their eyes at you because you're the author of *The Nubile Baby*.

DICK: Is that how you see my aspirations?

LIZ: What?

DICK: Rolling eyes?

LIZ: Well, fame, celebrity. All the fun you've missed down here.

PHIL: But, is it going to work? Sam spending half the time with you and half with us?

DIANA: Half?

PHIL: He's going to be like a shuttlecock.

DIANA: That surely isn't quite what Liz suggested . . .

PHIL: We've somehow got to arrange our lives around him.

LIZ: Now, Phil, I was only making one or two concessions——

PHIL: I know you were. And that's all wrong. We must take an imaginative leap, think of our two families merging,

79

coalescing . . . after all, we're relations now.

LIZ: Can I first of all explain my feelings?

PHIL: Did you sell your house in London?

LIZ: Yes.

PHIL: You'll be looking for another? Right?

DIANA: You'll keep this on as well?

LIZ: Oh, yes, this is our lifeline.

DIANA: Where you can be self-sufficient?

LIZ: Oh, yes.

PHIL: Listen. You know what I'm thinking, Di?

DIANA: What?

PHIL (*to* LIZ *and* DICK): The Camberwell scheme. Our partnership's done this scheme, this group of houses in the garden of an old rectory. Six dwellings. A real community, with the original landscape kept all around, shared by the residents. Now why don't you take two of those and let us have a mortgage on one? With all your royalties, money's no object, surely? Bank of fun, it must be.

LIZ: I don't think Dick's that mad on community living, are you, love?

PHIL: Or simply let us rent one? Good investment . . .

LIZ: Very smashing idea in some ways, but do let's cross that bridge when we get there. All we can say now is we accept some degree of sharing. Our immediate problem is meeting Jane at the station.

DIANA: We'll hang about in the car.

LIZ: We'll warn her on the platform, let her know you're here.

PHIL: It could be a shock if mine was the first face she saw.

LIZ: She needs a shock, that daughter of mine.

DIANA: Phil's very considerate. You don't like hurting people, do you?

PHIL: Not if it can be avoided.

DIANA: Or unless it interferes . . .

(*Thunder and lights go black.* PHIL *takes matches from tray and lights candles on cake.*)

PHIL: Aaah.

LIZ
DIANA $\Big\}$: Aaah!

80

DICK: Alors. If you want to shop before lunch, we'd better be going. I shan't keep up with you in the Deux Chevaux. We'll meet at the restaurant.

LIZ: Can't we manage them in two cars?

DICK: Fourteen people. No point in trying.

LIZ: I'll hang back for you.

DICK: No, you show them shops.

DIANA: We can find the shops.

(PHIL *has taken an egg from the table and is holding it.*)

PHIL: Have you ever tried to break an egg by squeezing it between forefinger and thumb?

LIZ: Really? Is it a joke?

PHIL: No. Hold it lengthwise and press as hard as you like. Go on.

LIZ: I can feel it giving slightly.

PHIL: Very resilient.

LIZ: Amazing.

DIANA: Press hard, go on.

PHIL: That's the principle of the earthquake-proof hotels. Give but don't crack.

DIANA (*takes egg from* LIZ *and squeezes*): I've seen a party of strong men tie themselves in knots . . . and in the end there was the egg as safe as houses . . .

(*Dick takes and squeezes the egg and it breaks*)

DICK: Shit!

DIANA: Christ!

LIZ: Dear oh dear.

(*He catches much of the eggshell and drops it on plate.* LIZ *gives him napkin to wipe hands.*)

DIANA: I've never known that happen.

PHIL: You must have cheated.

DICK: Cheated?

PHIL: Dug your finger-nails into the shell. It couldn't have broken otherwise.

(*He tries it with another egg but it doesn't break.* DIANA *moves to main doors.* LIZ *has finished wiping up mess of egg.*)

DIANA: Seems to be passing.

PHIL: Right, let's get the show on the road. D'you girls want to change your knickers or anything?

(LIZ *is at table covering food with white napkins.* PHIL *crosses to pram.*)

I'll bring the baby. Where's the carricot, Liz?

LIZ: In the big car.

PHIL: We'll be starting all that again. The carricot and the carricot transporter and the rubber sheets and safety pins. And clearing all the lower shelves of books. Remember what Emma did to my political literature? *The British Road to Socialism*? Torn to shreds. Hallo, hallo, has a lickle seep? And is he going to see the choo-choo?

(DIANA *goes into bedroom.* DICK *takes out envelope, looks at letter.*)

LIZ: Dick, you come with me in the big car. We'll squeeze them in, they're mostly children.

DICK: Sorry, I must rewrite this letter.

LIZ: Won't it wait?

DICK: No, it should have gone off long ago.

PHIL: Daddy show him the gee-gees on the way.

LIZ: Three-four-five-six——

PHIL: All the bow-bows.

LIZ: Eleven-twelve-thirteen-fourteen.

PHIL: We'd have to start designing all the fittings and fixtures for children of all ages.

(PHIL *takes out baby from pram.*)

LIZ: Shall I take him?

PHIL: I can manage. Di?

(DIANA *comes from bedroom wearing raincoat.*)

DIANA: Getting my puffer.

PHIL: Do you think you're going to need that?

DIANA: You never know.

LIZ (*kisses* DICK): 'Bye, love. Usual place?

PHIL: Bientôt, tout a l'heure, au revoir.

(*All three exit.*)

DICK: Yes. Au revoir. 'Bye 'bye.

(*Returns eagerly to table, takes out letter to* LIZ, *then pen. Turns letter over and writes on the back.*)

Dear Liz? Dearest Liz? 'Liz.'

(*Writes.*)

82

No.

(*Crosses out. Writes again.*)

My. Dear. Liz. Not 'My'.

(*Crosses out. Throws down pen and paper. Absently picks up an egg from plate.*)

My love—after so many years together how can I——?

How can I begin to——?

(*Holds egg over plate but it will not break. Squeezes harder. Egg still whole. Again and again he tries, standing, straining at the egg.*)

Oh, no! Break, break, you bastard, break!

(*As he struggles* THE CURTAIN FALLS.)